CHRISTIANITY AND POLITICS

Christianity and Politics

by Rev. James V. Schall, S.J.

ST. PAUL EDITIONS

NIHIL OBSTAT:
    Rev. Richard V. Lawlor

IMPRIMATUR:
    +Humberto Cardinal Medeiros
    Archbishop of Boston

IMPRIMI POTEST:
    Josephus P. Whelan, S.J.
    Praepositus Provinciae Marylandiae

ISBN 0-8198-1406-7 cloth
      0-8198-1407-5 paper

Printed in the U.S.A. by the Daughters of St. Paul
50 St. Paul's Ave., Boston, Ma. 02130

The Daughters of St. Paul are an international congregation of
religious women serving the Church with the communications
media.

CONTENTS

Introduction: **The Lost Art of Christian Political Theory** 1

Chapter I: **On the Non-Existence of Christian Political Philosophy** 16
An Objection to Christianity — The Evolution of Christian Thought on Politics — Any Agenda for Christians? — Public and Private Salvation

Chapter II: **On the Teaching of Ancient and Medieval Political Theory** 42
Testament for the Future — Curriculum Proposal for Political Thought — Elementary Guide

Chapter III: **The Effect of Christian Thought on Politics** 65
Man, the Political Animal — The Multiplicity of Ethical Choices — Politics and the Expansion of the Human Potential — The Question of Evil in Politics — The Problem of Finitude — The Common Mission of Man

Chapter IV: **Atheism and Politics** 94
The Christian Possibility of Unbelief — The Atheist Project — The Christian Reaction — The Atheist World — The Ecological Version — Faith as Its Own Guide

Chapter V: **On Taking Possession of the Whole Universe** 118
A Received Existence — Space and Christianity — Cosmology and Social Thought —

The Purpose of the Rest of the Cosmos —
The Reach of Our Knowledge — A Chris-
tian View About the Possession of the
Universe

Chapter VI: **Revolutionary Spirituality** 149
Exterior and Interior Spirituality —
Ascetics and Political Promises — Culture
and Class Struggle — Incorporating Clas-
sical Mystical Writers to Revolutionary
Spirituality — Pluralism and Praxis — A
Normal Christian Spirituality

Chapter VII: **Christianity and the "Cures"
of Poverty** 178
New Analyses of Poverty — Tradition and
Progress — Scope and Sources — The
Christian Context

Chapter VIII: **On the Christian Statement
of the Natural Law** 213
Questions for Political Theory — Standards
— Rational and Religious — Current
Trends

Chapter IX: **Political Philosophy and
Catholicism** 243
Faith and Reason Reconsidered — Per-
tinence of Pure Philosophy — Disciplinary
and Intellectual Integrity — Signs of
Change

Chapter X: **America in Recent Catholic
Social Theory** 267
Anti-American Christian Social Thought —
The Problem of Capitalism in Avoiding
Ideology — The Purely Human Solution —
Finding a Christian Solution

Chapter XI: **On Remaking Man and the World** 295

    Optimists and Pessimists — A Rereading of
    Thomas à Kempis — What Is To Be Con-
    templated? — The Religious Question

Conclusion: **Christianity and Politics** 315
Bibliography 327

No earthly pleasures, no kingdom of this world can benefit me in any way. I prefer death in Christ Jesus to power over the farthest limits of the Earth. He who died in place of us is the one object of my quest. He who rose for our sakes is my one desire.

—St. Ignatius of Antioch, Bishop and Martyr,
Letter to the Romans. 107 AD.

The Catholic Church, that imperishable handiwork of our all-merciful God, has for her immediate and natural purpose the saving of souls and securing our happiness in heaven. Yet, in regard to things temporal, she is the source of benefits as manifold and great as if the chief end of her existence were to ensure the prospering of our earthly life.

—Leo XIII, Pope, Immortale Dei,
All Souls' Day. 1885

We are all in some way aware that in this passing world it is not possible to realize the full measure of justice.... Justice is, in a certain way, greater than man, than the dimensions of his earthly life. Every man lives and dies with a certain sense of insatiability for justice, because the world is not capable of satisfying fully a being created in the image of God.

—John Paul II, Pope, General Audience, Rome.
November 8, 1978.

Introduction: The Lost Art of Christian Political Theory

When a significant part of the Christian intellectual world seems in practice to deny that there even might be such a thing as a unique, "Christian" approach to politics, or else, if there be one, that it is only with difficulty distinguishable from marxism or ecology, it may seem rash to refocus attention precisely upon Christianity *and* Politics. In doing this, I have no intention of bringing back the old idea of Constantine, or of the Holy Roman Empire, of the Two Swords, or of the newer ideas of Christian Democracy, Solidarism, or even the question of Religious Liberty as argued in Vatican II.

Rather what I am concerned about is the failure of current trends of politically oriented theology, which, as Dale Vree has argued, flow largely from Christian "heresy," not Christian orthodoxy.[1] This failure consists in an inability to account for the realities of politics and economics, while, at the same time, avoiding the absolutist traditions and totalitarian overtones that often arise from the efforts of Christians to establish justice or peace in the world.[2] Furthermore, from the other side, I am concerned with the degree of ignorance that secular and academic political thought has shown for the real values of Christian tradition in public life.[3]

Consequently, I wish to restate the "orthodox" view, if we might still put it that way. This will mean a lessening of the importance of politics, which has been so over-valued in many circles, religious and civil, in recent years.[4] On the other hand, if religion has become too political, it can likewise be argued that politics, as a consequence, has become too "secular." In a reassessment of the place of religion, *The Economist* of London stated well what I propose to treat anew in the following chapters:

> In 1980, most people over the age of 25 who think of themselves as members of the intellectual class—especially most politicians and journalists—have grown up to assume that life is externally about the efficient or compassionate management of rapid technological change and internally about the rational explaining away of private unhappiness....
>
> The counterattackers say the internal part of life certainly cannot be managed successfully, and the external part probably cannot, unless the human condition is re-examined in a wider context. The transcendental, they argue, has to be rediscovered, the balance between material and

spiritual restored: this will be the proper study of mankind in the late twentieth and coming twenty-first centuries.

If this is true, the lesson for the old, big churches is plain. *It is pointless for them to try to recover their lost popularity by switching from theology to politics—partly because most politicians do politics better than most parsons, but mainly because politics is not going to be the top-priority item on the coming agenda.*[5]

Thus, the failure of politics can often be perceived at those precise limits wherein politics has become a mobilization, all-embracing ideology seeking a complete reform of our earthly enterprises. The temptation to use religion as a cohesive force for purely political purposes is very great here.[6] The result is that religion is conceived as having no overall place of its own. And yet, the fact that it does may be, as *The Economist* suggested, the paradoxical political reality of our coming era.

Douglas Jerrold gave what is still one of the best intellectual statements of what is at issue in orthodox Christian political thought:

Christian civilization is not just one among many; it is...the only civilization built on the rights of the human personality, rights which derive from the belief in the immortality of the soul of man.

So wholly is our thought, our tradition, and our language Christian, that we tend to take for granted what in fact is a revolutionary conception. The doctrine of man's fall and redemption, of the equality of all men before God, of the ability and the obligation to win salvation, and consequently of the sanctity, dignity, and responsibility of the individual personality—these doctrines changed the face of the world. They gave a wholly new direction to human activity and necessitated a revolution in politics and morals.

The contemporary enemies of our civilization are aware of these fundamental truths; they have realized all too clearly that it is Christian belief, and the institutions and the political philosophy which derive from this belief, which stand forever as an obstacle to the realization of the tyrant's dream, the assertion of the absolute right of the State to command the actions and thoughts and to dispose of the lives of its citizens.[7]

I do not wish to deny that if Christian doctrine is interpreted in a way other than that of the tradition, some other political structure will follow. This is indeed what does happen. What I propose is rather that the traditional affirmations are the more fertile and correct ones, if we want to keep a sensible politics which will not promise to men and women something that no politics can deliver.

For some time, of course, the neglect of much serious attention to the religious context of our political situation has been understandable in the light of Christianity's own confusions.[8] However, such things as Watergate, the poverty of the Third World, May 1968, Jonestown in Guyana, Islamic mullahs, and even ecology have forced a re-entrance of some kind of moral judgment into the very heart of politics. Such headlines as "Moral Standards Take a Beating in Britain: Public Dishonesty, Inflation Erode Traditional Law and Order," are not uncommon.[9] The Hastings Center reports a growing interest in ethics courses in universities as a result of such problems.[10]

The understanding of the religious origins of contemporary problems, then, has been too long neglected. There is a kind of "counter-faith" which holds that we can explain ourselves without faith. Perhaps the major shift towards a more realistic appreciation of religion is due to a widespread suspicion that the dire conditions of much of mankind are themselves rooted in spiritual forces. This suspicion is aided by a belated but growing admission that the very ideology which has defined religion as the "opium" of the people is itself by all odds the largest practitioner of human persecution. Alexander Solzhenitsyn has spoken with more than irony:

> ...Communism has always been most ruthless of all in its treatment of Christians and advocates of national rebirth.... The authorities make no attempt to hide the fact that they are crushing the Christian faith with the full force of their machinery of terror. And at this moment, when

religious circles in the U.S.S.R. are being
persecuted with such unmitigated ferocity—how
fine and edifying it is to hear Russian Orthodoxy
reviled by the Western press![11]

Moreover, the Enlightenment tradition of unlimited progress through science and technology is
now itself being denied or at least strongly ques-
tioned.[12] Thus, both poverty and riches, rights
and crimes are political issues with religious
overtones, as Scripture itself always suspected.

What I wish to repropose in the issues of this
book, then, is a new approach to political
thought and practice. But when I say "new," I do
not intend, in the fashion of the 19th Century
French philosopher Henri de Saint-Simon and
his long progeny, to make of Christianity
something it was not intended to be. Saint-
Simon, indeed, is quite pertinent even yet, for he
wanted to make Christianity into a mobilization
organism to help the poor. He wanted to make it,
in other words, into a this-worldly enterprise.[13]
Historically, of course, because of the doctrine of
the Incarnation, Christianity has been characterized, and rightly, as a worldly religion. Indeed, it was the only religion originating largely
among the poor and the oppressed, the one
whose earthly performance is itself an intrinsic
part of the world as well as an essential part of
belief. Men are supposed to "see" how believers
"love one another," how they "turn the other
cheek," how they "offer a cup of water."

But Christianity is also proposed as a judgment on the world. Essentially, it deals with the *First* Commandment, the love of God, and the Second only in its light. Thus, Christians are forbidden to define happiness or virtue in exclusively this-worldly terms. When they do, they are disloyal precisely to the world itself as well as to their faith. Probably, if there is any constant temptation in the history of Christianity, from reaction to Christ's rejection of Jewish Zealotism on to current debates about the relation of marxism to the Kingdom of God, it is the pressure to make religion a formula for refashioning the political and economic structures of the world. One of the major political-theological tasks, in any era, not excluding our own, is clearly to understand what exact form this ultimately "heretical" idea takes within the prevailing political movements and ideas. This is what these reflections and analyses propose to do.

What is characteristic of the cultural situation of our time is, on the one hand, the final Enlightenment originated effort to achieve full happiness on Earth for the total race of men. This is presented in either a marxist or liberal based formula. On the other hand, and simultaneously, we have a secular apocalypse view which argues that it is necessary to overturn basic natural and Christian values in the name of the paucity of resources, so that we might achieve the only ideal that is left, an

earthly continuation of our race on this planet
for as long as possible.

An "orthodox" Christian approach to contemporary politics, then, one that retains explicitly the essentials of the classically defined
doctrines of original sin, creation, the Fall,
redemption, the basics of Christology and the
Trinity, must confront these contrasting, if not
contradictory orientations. In each of these latter, there is a presentation of a Christianity
that denies or changes one or all of these basic
elements, usually in order to achieve the Enlightenment or species-continuation goals of contemporary social theory.[14] And even "heretical"
views must be considered properly "spiritual,"
because they are ultimately rooted in concepts of
man and Earth that choose to deviate from or
deny completely the classical Christian notions.

Christianity is, at the same time, extremely
optimistic and extremely pessimistic. If measured
by contemporary ideologies, it is both at the
same time.[15] This means that it can exalt the
value and power of human freedom. Yet, it will,
at the same time, recognize that this freedom is
what it says it is, namely, a freedom. From this, it
necessarily follows that Christian optimism must
also accept that we are free to choose the worst
as well as the best.[16] If we cannot accept them
both at the same time, then we must believe
something else about the world than that which
Christianity teaches. Christianity, consequently,

will characteristically be able to accept evil and good as realities, without necessarily confusing the two or worse, calling the one the other, without making evil into a counter-god.

Christianity, I think, is optimistic about the potential of the Earth and the cosmos because it is optimistic about what man and his intelligence are about. But its doctrine of original sin, perhaps the one doctrine with the most direct and immediate political consequences, makes it aware that this very optimism, when misplaced, can create an abundant world that is in fact a police state.[17] People and resources are themselves considered good in Christianity so that the locus of their suffering, abuse, or wants is to be placed in will and intelligence, not in the cosmos or the Earth or the body. To be sure, Christianity also holds that there are finite limits to most things, beginning with man's own life. But even these limits must be spiritualized, humanized by being freely understood and chosen. Much of the current non-Christian or heretical Christian thought will be found to deny the way Christianity looks upon human freedom and the capacity of the human brain, while at the same time, in other ways, seeking to remove or change man's natural limits.

The basic Christian political instinct, then, is this rigorous attention to human will and its capacity for choosing good or evil. Hannah Arendt, in her posthumously published volume on "Willing" in her *The Life of the Mind*, even remarked that the very idea of will is practically a Christian invention.[18] This is why the Christian suspects that even in the worst political state, there is good and grace, another theme to which Alexander Solzhenitsyn frequently addresses himself.[19] But the Christian feels likewise uneasy in the best and loveliest places because he is conscious that the worst is not to be identified with external conditions, but rather with choices coming out of the human heart. The worst crimes are often committed in the most prosperous societies by intelligent and well-to-do, educated people.[20] Since the orthodox Christian does not identify his ultimate happiness with any political arrangement of this life even while not denying that this life is of great importance, he is free to accept politics for what it is, a temporary arrangement within a life that is passing away. Yet, this personal life, in Christian doctrine, rises again in the central mystery of the faith, as Paul called it, in the Resurrection. This is a gift that does not depend upon the structures of worldly politics.[21]

What needs to be elaborated, then, is the place where politics fits into a Christian view and, conversely, what happens when politics does not maintain its limited scope as clarified for it by Christianity. Thus, I will argue about man's place among the animals, the meaning of his earthly life, the abundance of this planet, its relation to people and resources. But I shall constantly attempt to preserve the central Christian theme about man's personal transcendence over every political and economic order. For this is the first and the last Christian position. A failure to grasp this would mean a failure to understand the ultimate sources for the limits of politics.

Here, too, I am not interested especially in arguing with contemporary Christian "heresies," that is, with those who deny implicitly or explicitly a basic doctrine held to be central by Scripture, the Creeds, the Councils, or the Papacy. The case of a Hans Küng is thus pertinent here mainly because there has been an effort on the part of the Church not to allow Christianity to be defined in a way contrary to its basic outlines. And so someone may well deny the divinity or humanity of Christ, believe in the coming of a perfect world order, or deny original sin. I am interested in the political consequences of such a denial, but I think it is not my task here to argue about whether various reformed views are the *real* Christianity of tradition. Doctrine is subtle and delicate, perhaps, but it does appeal directly to the intellect, and it can tell when something is divergent from the tradition.[22] Intellectually and politically, the classic Christian positions are more interesting and more true. This is my position and what I shall argue.

Thus, I am concerned to note wherein a contemporary political philosophy is similar to gnosticism or millenarism or pelagianism and why this should be so. But I do not intend to spend time arguing that orthodox Christianity is wrong in order to accept some new kind of political enthusiasm.[23] The orthodox views, the views that the central Christian tradition, Catholic, Orthodox, and largely Protestant, maintained, are far more fruitful and politically relevant than the sophisticated divergent views of our era, views paradoxically often considered to be the real "Christian" ones by a large part of academia and the media. This is why one of the burdens here will be to suggest ways for the student and the reader to know what it is Christianity actually holds. One of the greatest defects of contemporary university education is its failure simply to know the elements of Christian tradition.[24] Ironically, this is not the first era in which Christianity was both accepted and rejected for seeming to be what it was not.

Moreover, this will be an analysis of Christian "spirituality," that is, an understanding of the world, man, and God that results precisely from the "localizing" of politics into its proper sphere. Something can still be said for natural law and free economics. And for this very reason, this will not be a "political theology," as that term is used today, something which seeks to exalt religion by making politics the central human and religious project.[25] Rather, it is radically Christian to believe that while the world can be changed and to some degree improved by men and women, even that this is one arena of their response to salvation, still this is not wholly what the faith is about. Furthermore, Christianity, even though it may not like or approve of them, believes that God can be found in the worst regimes as well as in the best.[26]

The doctrine of the Cross, the fact that Jesus was executed by a political process, means not so much that we can reform every worldly regime, so that no killing of a Man-God could ever take place, but that God is present even where men are at their worst, even where His crucifixion *did* take place. There is more to life than politics, even in politics. Christianity believes this precisely because of human freedom, because God is *not* a politics. Man is the political animal in the universe. The fate of the man who suffers and dies unjustly, or even justly, the normal man or woman who lives a normal life, cannot be exhausted in a common good or in some future earthly paradise for which he is sacrificed by so many modern ideologies.[27] Christianity has something to say to all citizens of all states in all times. And what it has to say is not ultimately political. Nonetheless, politics remains important, even religiously important. What is unique about Christianity in this context, then, is its ability to retain the importance of politics while, at the same time, denying it ultimate importance.

Footnotes:

¹ Dale Vree, *On Synthesizing Marxism and Christianity*, New York, Wiley, 1976.

² Jeane Kirkpatrick, "Dictatorships and Democracy," *Commentary*, November, 1979.

³ Cf. F. D. Wilhelmsen, *Christianity and Political Philosophy*, Athens, University of Georgia Press, 1978.

⁴ "Indeed, one wonders these days whether that old time religion is really so benighted as its mockers make it out to be. Is the anger of these Christians really causeless and their concern for this country mere paranoia? Is 'Armageddon' only some whispered syllables out of an old book? One wonders. Something very intense is going on here right now. Although we won't necessarily see it on TV." Dick Dabney, "Days of Wrath," *The Washington Post*, April 29, 1980.

⁵ Editorial, "A Further Resurrection," *The Economist*, London, April 5, 1980. Italics added.

⁶ Cf. A. Fierro, *The Militant Gospel*, Maryknoll, Orbis, 1977.

⁷ Douglas Jerrold, *The Lie About the West*, New York, Sheed and Ward, 1954, pp. 79, 82-83.

⁸ Cf. the author's "From Politics to Enthusiasm," *Homiletic and Pastoral Review*, October and November, 1971.

⁹ *The Los Angeles Times*, February 24, 1980.

¹⁰ "Ethics Courses," *The National Catholic Register*, April 21, 1980.

¹¹ Alexander Solzhenitsyn, "Misconceptions about Russia," *Foreign Affairs*, Spring, 1980, p. 815.

¹² Robert Nisbet, *History of the Idea of Progress*, New York, Basic, 1980.

¹³ Henri de Saint-Simon, "The New Christianity," *Social Organization, The Science of Man, and Other Writings*, Ed. F. Markham, New York, Harper Torchbooks, 1964.

¹⁴ Cf. John Senior, *The Death of Christian Culture*, New Rochelle, Arlington House, 1978.

¹⁵ Cf. G. K. Chesterton, *Orthodoxy*, Doubleday Image, 1965.

¹⁶ Cf. Russell Kirk, *The Conservative Mind*, Chicago, Gateway, 1953, Chapter I.

¹⁷ Cf. J. L. Talmon, *The Origins of Totalitarian Democracy*, New York, Praeger, 1960.

¹⁸ Hannah Arendt, "Willing," in *The Life of the Mind*, New York, Harcourt, 1978, Vol. II. Chapters 8 and 10.

[19] Addresses of June 30 and July 9, 1975, Washington, DC, AFL, and *Letter to the Soviet Leaders,* New York, Harper's, 1975.

[20] This was Aristotle's view in *The Politics.* Cf. Lloyd Cohen, "Traditional and Modern Views of Crime and Punishment," *The Intercollegiate Review,* Fall, 1978, pp. 33-36.

[21] Cf. the author's *Redeeming the.Time,* New York, Sheed and Ward, 1968, Chapter 7.

[22] Cf. Dorothy Sayers, *The Whimsical Christian,* New York, Macmillan, 1978.

[23] Cf. Jacques Ellul, *The Betrayal of the West,* New York, Seabury, 1978.

[24] Cf. Chapter II.

[25] Cf. Russell Kirk, *Decadence and Renewal in the Higher Learning,* South Bend, Gateway, 1978; Robert Nisbet, *The Decadence of Academic Dogma,* New York, Basic, 1972; J. M. Cameron, *On the Idea of a University,* Toronto, University of Toronto Press, 1978; James V. Schall, "The Christian University," *Homiletic and Pastoral Review,* March, 1979, pp. 17-24.

[26] Cf. the discussion of Jacques Maritain on the barbarous society in *Man and the State,* Chicago, University of Chicago Press, 1952, pp. 71-75.

[27] The idea of collective guilt, the sacrificing of someone because of corporate crimes is not only marxist. The following passage is about the recent Liberian revolution: "The killing is expected to continue. One of the soldiers told the watching journalists that the grandfathers of the shot men had 'suffered us terribly.' He went on to claim that the 'colonizers'...used to cut people's feet with razors to make them dance. 'We shall be killing them every day. Even their children will not live.' This has to be taken seriously." *The Economist,* April 26, 1980, p. 35.

CHAPTER I

On the Non-Existence of Christian Political Philosophy

Those who lived by reason are Christians, even though they have been considered atheists: such as, among the Greeks, Socrates....

—*Justin Martyr*, The First Apology, *Circa 150 AD*

Whatever there be of polemics...(it) is functional within the vision of a man who is convinced that either the principled suppression of the Christian experience by philosophy (by Professor Leo Strauss and the Chicago school) or the reduction of Christianity to mythic or mystic experience whose only authority is itself (Professor Eric Voegelin) drains both Christianity and philosophy of their intrinsic interest.

—*Frederick D. Wilhelmsen,*
Christianity and Political Philosophy,
Athens, University of Georgia Press, 1978, p. 8.

We live in a curious time. We are agreed that our educational and university system has been increasingly dominated, for the past half century, by a pseudo-scientific philosophy that doubted on principle the validity of moral values. Our very constitutional system through the courts, managed largely by a legal profession educated in such a-moral environment, has practically excluded any explicit value or religious criterion from being taught as true. Nor is it difficult to comprehend how radicals of various sorts have managed to write off so easily the United States and western culture as having little sense of strictly moral concern other than their own self-interest.

The Christian Science Monitor can argue, on the other hand:

> As this planet enters the 1980's, the two most charismatic figures on Earth are both religious, even though the public image of each is very different in the West. They are Pope John Paul II and Ayatollah Ruhollah Khomeini. This may well be a portent that religion rather than politics will more obviously influence the course of human events in the coming decade. The response in their respective parts of the world to the Pope and the Ayatollah indicates that each meets a contemporary need.[1]

We are, in fact, an irate generation as we note criticisms about presidents, congressmen, corporations, bureaucrats, and law-enforcement agents, who violate supposed ethical standards, the moral worth of which we are not accustomed or even allowed to justify at a theoretic or religious level.[2] We are, therefore, in lieu of any other standards, coming to accept a sort of poverty ethic which assigns tacit moral justification in practice only to the poor.[3] This latter in some unattended but real way becomes the locus of moral validity for any economic or political enterprise, especially when the "poor" are extended to mean the "exploited," the definition of which is in the hands of some small, usually ideological group.[4]

On both of these scores, Christianity should appear to be in an advantageous position to supply the political philosophy that could recast these moral lacunae into some positive whole which would connect human worth and our moral failures within some worldly achievement. Indeed, if we examine the recent papal, synodal, and episcopal documents, it seems clear that they are attempting rather forcefully to address themselves precisely to these problems of morality and poverty as the central public tasks of our time. Thus it is important to present the best case that can be made for the value of the world and its activities within classical Christian orthodoxy.[5] But, if we examine further the more radical Christian statements proliferating from private and semi-official statements, it seems that Christianity is being presented mainly as the ideology which concentrates on these two areas

—morality and poverty—so that we can revolutionize the present systems.[6]

Yet, whether the rather astonishing corpus of Christian, especially Catholic Christian thought, on the social order is having its desired impact can be doubted. The reason for this is of some significance. Indeed, many Christians are in effect admitting that they have no formal social and political doctrine so that they are free to take on whatever ideological or practical form they wish in order to achieve the goals of the world and of Christianity. These goals, as I mentioned in the introduction, are being presented in terms classically formulated by Henri de Saint-Simon in his "New Christianity," namely, "to relieve the lot of the poor," a theme found in such writers or bureaucrats as John Rawls at Harvard and Robert McNamara, formerly at the World Bank. That today there are considerably more Christians being converted to Marxism (outside of Russia, where the opposite seems to be the case) than Marxists to Christianity should give pause about the real neutrality of all of this. Dale Vree's comment is most pertinent:

> Since Christian intellectuals enter into dialogue (with Marxists) without an obligatory Christian political philosophy to defend, they easily slip into a discussion of political matters which is determined by Marxist categories. Furthermore, Marxists, by the very nature of their belief

system, do not seem tempted by traditional theism, whereas Christians, by the very nature of their heritage, do seem tempted by what they see as an earthly avenue to the new Jerusalem. As a result, the dialogue tends to draw Christians away from loyalty to 'capitalist democracy' and toward an affinity with Marxist political ideas. The cause of communism is strengthened while anti-communism is weakened.[7]

This states the situation and the problem quite well.

An Objection to Christianity

In *Huckleberry Finn,* the hero is washed up onto the Grangerford property on the Arkansas shores to be initially suspected of being an enemy. From Buck, who had just shot off the hat of Harney Shepherdson, Huck Finn learned the two families were locked in a bitter feud, something Huck had never heard of before.

> "Well," says Buck, "a feud is this way: a man has a quarrel with another man, and kills him; then that other man's brother kills him; then the other man's brothers, on both sides, goes for one another; then the cousins chip in—and by and by everybody's killed off, and there ain't no more feud. But it's kind of slow, and takes a long time."[8]

Buck could not remember how long their particular feud had lasted, maybe 30 years.

Anyhow, in the midst of the shootings, both families went to the same church one Sunday morning:

> The men took their guns along, so did Buck, and kept them between their legs or stood them handy against the wall. The Shepherdsons did the same. It was pretty ornery preaching—all about brotherly love, and such like tiresomeness; but everybody said it was a good sermon, and they all talked it over going home, and had such a powerful lot to say about faith, and good works and free grace and preforeordestination; and I don't know what all, that it did seem to me one of the roughest Sundays I had run across yet.

The following week, not unexpectedly, the Grangerfields and the Shepherdsons went out and wiped each other out to end their feud. Huck Finn quickly slipped into his raft with Jim and ordered it out of the place as quickly as possible. He never wanted to see the place again.

No one, I suppose, has formulated the popular accusation against Christianity more quaintly and graphically. Probably no one today reads these lines of Mark Twain without thinking, rightly or wrongly, of some place like Ireland or perhaps Cyprus or Israel. In any case, the essential charge implied is that no relation exists between religion and what believers do. The fact that the Christian faith in particular rather expects men to feud, among other things —we are a fallen race in Christian dogma—is largely ignored. But the assumption abides—if Christianity were true, feuds and wars and injustices ought to be removed. In other words, the criterion of credibility, indeed, the old *preambula fidei,* is today assumed to be public performance. And if it be suggested that a more basic issue is at stake, namely, the real freedom to choose good or evil, we will discover that the response will be—"Away with freedom, then!" The poor, we are reminded, only want bread—the ultimate heresy.

The Evolution of Christian Thought on Politics

The Christians of the early centuries were singularly lacking in a political philosophy and program. They were told by Paul and Peter to obey the Emperor rather than to set up a constitutional government with Bills of Rights or a dictatorship of the proletariat. They also seemed to have expected for a time a rather soon arrival of the next world so that politics, which had to do primarily with this one, could be neglected. The distinguishing of God and Caesar was indeed revolutionary, as was the Parousia, the last blessed things, when it later came to be a this worldly project with the Montanists and Joachim of Flora in the later Middle Ages.

But in their original forms, these Christian innovations had the effect of legitimizing politics by removing from it essentially religious and philosophical elements and goals. The classical objection to Christianity is rooted in this origin and recurs throughout subsequent history in various forms, the objection that Christianity ignores the world. Substantially, then, it is that concern for the next life so enthralls the thought and actions of Christians that they neglect this world and are thereby disloyal to their own political society. A good percentage of history's Christian martyrs, including right up until yesterday, were found guilty on precisely this kind of charge. The Christian doctrines and pieties about humility and poverty, about ultimate destiny for the graced and repentant tended, it was argued, to denigrate the public order. Without full Christian participation, then, the people's energies were deflected from the task at hand. "My Kingdom is not of this world" became the "Opium of the People."

Here, it is not necessary to argue explicitly the counter position—namely, that the Christian solution to the problem of the locus of man's ultimate happiness has been the cause of why men could participate in the public order for its own sake and not as some kind of surrogate for beatitude.[9] It is worth pursuing the question of whether Christians do have a political philosophy, however, since many recent events and theories, frequently originating among Christians themselves, would seem to argue that

Christianity has no political philosophy of its own whatsoever, nor even any basis for one.[10] This is particularly striking as it is proposed among those development theories which hold more or less that God must rejoin Caesar for things to improve.[11]

This is not, in its current formulation, however, the old diplomatic question of whether to deal with *de facto* authoritarian governments in order to gain some minimal degree of tolerance for Christian worship and life.[12] Nor is it the argument about the *forms* of government such that each particular people or age would be free to choose its own constitution or governmental structure. Christian historical experience has known almost every conceivable political form from tribe to world state, from direct democracy to absolute totalitarianism. Christians have held that they ought to be able to live and gain salvation under *any* existing government.[13] Indeed, martyrdom, when it was politically instigated, as it was from the earliest times, including the case of Christ Himself, has been taken as a sign of blessing, even though many persecutions did in fact seem to wipe out formal Christianity almost completely, as happened in North Africa under Islam and evidently seems to have happened in China today or Cambodia, even though the Chinese seem to refuse to use blood and the Cambodian leadership kills everyone in sight. The Reformation, furthermore, proved that governments could change the form of religious worship and, to some extent, the content of belief even among Christians themselves—a lesson already learned by the Constantinian church against the pagans, especially against the Donatists, themselves heretical Christians.

In recent years, there are a number of essays in European Christian journals which argue that specifically "Catholic" social thought is dead, an idea John Paul at Puebla took especial pains to combat.[14] The classic encyclicals were, in this view, seen to be at best merely balancing acts between liberal capitalism and socialism, a kind of overarching hodge-podge which concealed Christianity's own lack of political thought. Christian political parties are in trouble currently because, supposedly, they have nothing distinctive to offer. Clerical students begin their studies of the social apostolate by reading Marx or Lenin or Mao or a number of their offspring with hardly a glimmer of the relation of these schools to classic or Christian political tradition, let alone to modern democratic thought.

Yet, if we reread such a standard and still wise book as Professor Heinrich Rommen's *The State in Catholic Thought* (1945), it is clear that for Rommen, the theory of grace building on nature was central because it was largely "nature" that gave Catholic thought any "state" to think about in the first place.[15] Rommen, however, was quite insistent. Christianity's taking its political and economic thought from experience and reason was itself part of Christian order as well as the link to all men and to creation. In a sense, Christianity did not need a specifically "revealed" and therefore unique political philosophy because men already had the essential outlines of and capacity for discovering what they needed to know and put in practice in the public order.

Even Aquinas, when he argued for the necessity of a specifically *divine* positive law in addition to natural law, left the question of man's temporal well-being up to man. This implied, at first sight, that the socio-economic-political area was not so crucial for salvation. Yet, the actual criterion given in Matthew for salvation—a cup of water to an unknown neighbor—made personal and public life in this world in part determinative of ultimate being.[16] *Grace did not destroy nature* meant the deepening importance for those things that really were "of Caesar." Aquinas and those who followed in his footsteps seemed to have felt that politics ought to be left to man as a proper manifestation of his freedom and what he could create with it.

Augustine, of course, had simply held earlier that we could not and ought not to expect too much of politics, other than a kind of holding action. That Augustine in retrospect seems to have been the more empirically correct in his estimates about what men would do has been one of the disturbing legacies from which Christians of a more liberal and socialist bent have ever desperately sought to escape.[17]

This "escape," moreover, has largely slipped out of the bonds of a Christian discourse, especially in its Marxist guise. The original Judaeo-Christian thesis held that God created man and gave him dominion over the Earth. The "fall" of man changed the original circumstances so that men henceforth worked by the sweat of their brows, coercion entered, children were brought forth in pain. The division of property and coercive government became both evils and remedies for evils. In Medieval Christianity, a line of radical thinking developed through Joachim of Flora in which property division and coercive government and usually family—a tradition by then joined to the Platonic notions of community of wives and property alongside of monastic vows—came to be seen as "removable" obstacles.[18] Sin and evil in the world came to be more tangible, seen as rooted not in men's wills, no matter what form of government, as in classic Christian thought, but outside men, in property division and governmental forms. In the ideal state, then, there would be no property, nor government, nor, logically, any evil as a consequence. In the present state of disorder, however, politics were to be used to rid men of precisely politics.

The utopian project, thus, became actively political or economic. During the Enlightenment and with the theories of Progress, men came to believe it possible, actually possible, to remove evil by political or economic or technological processes, which would eventually communalize property and wither statehood away. Some schools held this must be done violently; others that it must be done with love; others still with votes. Rousseau had taught the French Revolution that men were good, that institutions were evil. Therefore, reorganize the institutions and men would be made to be good, forced to be free. When such strands came to be assimilated into an active political program to be effectuated by men "in history," we had most of the framework of our times.

The project of ultimate happiness, consequently, became political and historical, the two things it was not in classical Christianity. Evil became a "corporate" thing. Even the theologians have come to speak of "social sin," rather than corrupt forms of rule. The older notion of "corporate guilt," associated with the Fall and original sin, has reappeared in our times in theories of property reform and political reconstruction. Myriads of religious types are busy hunting this social sin down in a new kind of Inquisition. The connection of "social sin" with the older theology should not pass totally unnoticed, since the current trend identifies guilt either with corporate groups or with members of politically defined, socially unreconstructed entities, like business corporations.

Any Agenda for Christians?

Several years ago, in controversy with American academic behaviorists, several radical activist theorists argued that since this behaviorism, the established academic orthodoxy, had in its own terms no real ethical or moral concern in principle, it should have no objection to joining radical political movements for the reform of mankind and society. Something of this astonishing atmosphere seemed to be at work among Christians. The Special China Edition of the *Holy Cross Quarterly*, for example, several years ago, seemed to argue in many of its essays that by his reorganizing of China, Mao Tse-tung was in fact "a Christian," so that there was nothing much Christians could do to add to his stupendous success.[19] Though the subsequent events in China have dimmed this particular ideological approach, still there is a considerable Christian literature evidently unable to distinguish what happens in China with the essence of Christianity.

Denys Turner, writing in *The New Blackfriars*, insisted that there was no reason why Christians could not be Marxists, though with some few distinctions.[20] Thus, since both Christianity and Marxism were concerned about reorganizing the world—the only actual task, in Turner's view, lies in getting rid of capitalism, the cause of all evils, the new original sin—it makes no difference what either movement believes about God. If in heaven, the Marxist suddenly finds that the faith is still somehow flourishing there, so what if he erred a bit? And if there is no everlasting, well, the Christian will at least have tossed in his little bit to history. This deftly follows the classic line of Marsilius of Padua, which allowed all the spiritual to the Church, provided it had no effect on the world, which in turn left the world free to organize itself in its own way.

From perhaps another sort of problem, Charles Angell, in his ''The Christian Task in the Middle East,'' wrote:

> All of this leads me to ask today a very simple question: as Christians do we have any agenda, any role, any distinctive contribution to make in the Middle East, or are we simply fellow-travelling appendages of other peoples' causes? Are we a religious force in our own right, or are we simply manipulated as individuals in campaigns of others?[21]

Angell noted sadly that even religious communities were split up over loyalty to Islam or Israel in Jerusalem, that Old Testament scholars seem mainly pro-Islam. A couple of years ago, I remember driving through a very jammed

Bodenstown on Wolfe Tone Day in Ireland. Large contingents of Catholics from Belfast were present. Each week a different faction came to claim the heritage of Wolfe Tone. These were intramural fights, as it were, while the situations in Lebanon, the Philippines, and the Sudan remind us that Christianity and Islam still have much to learn. But in each case, there seems to be no set or basic political approach which would gain unanimity among Christians so that they could be more of a positive force. In the meantime, out of Russia, we hear rumors that what may be the most important Christian revival in our time is taking place, and we are almost wholly untouched by it.[22]

If this facility with which Christians seem to be able to adapt themselves not merely to classic Platonic or Aristotelian traditions also enables them equally to adapt themselves to more radical philosophies—"We need someone to do for Marx what Aquinas did for Aristotle" is the cliché that is as trendy as it is futile—then we will not be surprised to discover a growing skepticism about both Christianity and Marxism.

Professor Stromberg's comments in his excellent review of recent decades are to the point:

> As Marxists grew more spiritual and individualistic, Christianity became more worldly and social.... Christians sought to give their faith a content in this world; Marxists wanted to leaven their worldly creed with a bit of ethical transcend-

ence. Together, they flattered themselves, Marxists and Christians, they can provide a total philosophy, a real amalgamation of both worlds, the mundane and the spiritual.[23]

Professor Stromberg's reflections on the image Christians often presented to the world in recent years are, it would seem, mostly valid. The churches failed to make real contact with the spiritual yearning of the previous decade. What happened instead? "Thus, a familiar personality of the 1960's was the swinging young priest who set off to modernize the Church.... In the later years of the decade, familiar, too, was the revolutionary priest who went wholly over to a position not easily distinguishable from radical or political militancy. The message of Christ, he assumed, was not basically different from that of Marx."[24]

In reflecting on this issue, on why priests committed to Marxism followed uncritically the "most primitive kind of economics," distinguishable only by their fervor, Professor Stromberg felt that it was precisely the lack of a Christian political philosophy that caused them to drift where they might.

The ease with which Christianity as a social ethic or a political position can be absorbed by other causes suggests a basic weakness in its doctrine. Except in the vaguest terms, it lacks a social ethic.... In recent years, they (Christians) have moved with the crowd; they enthusiastically supported both world wars, and just as enthusiastically repented afterwards, vowing eternal pacifism. Biblical passages can be quoted on both sides of most political questions. The only tangible constant of the Christian social message is a passionate hopefulness that encourages expectations of utopia without supplying the means to attain it—and in a way, it is very akin to the mood of youthful revolutionism.[25]

These are hard words and, within the context of public opinion in recent years, largely justified. Professor Hitchcock has, I believe, also traced the ins and outs of this decline and fall.[26] A further aspect of this is the rapidity with which Christian "spirituality" has come to be identified with revolutionary economic or political movements.[27] Some considerable study, I think, needs to be pursued on the manner in which economic facts are being used in theological analyses.

Public and Private Salvation

In making Christianity ever more a this worldly cause, not only have we been leaving the sacred as an autonomous reality in jeopardy, such that men begin to doubt whether this faith is any longer found in the churches, wherein too often what is preached is mostly utopian socialism or statistics, or, if they be in developing countries, nationalism. We have also watched religious people tend to ally themselves with

those worldly ideologies *least* capable, on analysis, of resolving the actual problems they claim
they are concerned about. No one has really
addressed himself to the question of how much
popular ideologies have *retarded* development
and how much Christians have contributed to
this enforced backwardness.[28] The root cause of
this, it would seem, remains the failure to grasp
what is unique to Christianity in relation to
politics. This is the grounding and justification of
the absolute validity of the human person, who
is finite and fallible, and the placing of ultimate
happiness outside of political processes.[29] Paradoxically, politics cannot be politics unless men
first find the answer to their destiny *not* in
politics.

The status of truth today is very vague. Sense
experience is admitted to a point, but there are
no absolute judgments, only theories and opinions with no mechanism for their resolution.
Ultimate judgment is never to be verified. This is
something of a dogma of the modern mind.
Knowledge of truth is thus not important. Yet,
society itself, religious or secular, cannot be
based on this sort of reduction of truth to mere
opinion in which virtue is defined only in virtue
of not knowing the truth. The English Catholic
writer Hilaire Belloc wrote in this regard:

> Let us take the Christian religion as an in-
> stance. That religion has for one essential part,
> though it is only a part, the statement that the in-

dividual soul is immortal—that personal conscience survives physical death. Now if people believe that, they look at the world and themselves in a certain way and go on in a certain way and are people of a certain sort. If they except this, that is cut out, this one doctrine, they may continue to hold all the others, but the scheme is changed, the type of life and character and the rest become quite other. The man who is certain that he is going to die for good may believe that Jesus of Nazareth is God, that God is Trinity, that the Incarnation was accompanied by a virgin birth, that bread and wine are transformed by a particular formula; he may recite a great number of Christian prayers and admire and copy chosen Christian exemplars, but he will be quite a different man from the man who takes immortality for granted....

Heresy is then not a fossil subject. It is a subject of permanent and vital interest to mankind because it is bound up with the subject of religion, without some form of which no human society ever has endured. Those who think that the subject of heresy may be neglected because the term sounds to them old-fashioned and because it is connected with a number of disputes long abandoned, are making the common error of thinking in words instead of ideas.... There is no end to the misunderstanding which arises from the uncertain use of words. But if we keep in mind the plain fact that a state, a human polity or a general culture, must be inspired by some body of morals, and that there can be no body of morals without doctrine, and if we agree to call any consistent body of morals and doctrine a religion, then the importance of heresy as a subject will be clear, because heresy means nothing else than 'the proposal of novelties in religion by picking out from what has been the accepted religion some point or other, denying the same or replacing it by another doctrine hitherto unfamiliar.'[30]

In an age of renewed spiritual concern and a decline of the liberal indifference to truth as such, the view that ideas do not matter, that everything is only opinion, can easily lead to accepting any political theory that proposes a "truth" accomplished by men alone, by their own efforts "in history." Thus, if we repropose the tradition of Marsilius of Padua in a new form —that of reorganizing the world for the poor on any terms—then, whether we have a hereafter or not makes no ultimate difference, since men's energies are to be exhausted in the worldly task which has no particular Christian social ethics to guide it, except a certain enthusiasm that it ought to be done.[31]

Just after World War II, Richard Weaver delivered an address to the Newman Club at the University of Chicago. "What this (dropping the atomic bomb) illustrates to me," he explained,

is that after all the labor of the social scientists, we now know less about human nature than did the men of Socrates' day or the men of the Middle Ages. They recognized that man needs to be protected against himself; and they were interested in setting up safeguards....

The Greeks and the men of the Middle Ages made their failures; but they seem not so egregious as the failures we have made and the failures we may be facing, because our theory of human being has simply ceased to be candid. It is no longer candid because it will not recognize that man has a bad nature too. This is not our whole nature, but it is a part of our nature which has to be looked after sharply. Humanism studies man as expressed through his whole nature, including this motivation; and that is why it seems to some now, as it seemed to Socrates that day in Athens, to have a prior place in the cause of inquiry.[32]

The main problem, then, is not about the dropping of the bomb as the only question of morality. Rather it is moral insight into our being which is capable of rejecting the idea that institutional reconstruction can resolve our problems, as if this is where our problems lie and not in our wills.

The alliance of Christianity with humanism was long hammered out upon the insufficiency of either to present a full view of man in all his aspects and all his destiny. This meant, to be sure, that Christianity was not of itself a complete system apart from original creation and historical experience. Marxism now has deftly laid claim to humanism, while Mao, for a time, came to be seen as the *homo naturaliter Christianus,* by some Christians.

Socrates, it is well to recall, was killed by the best state. This led Plato to wonder if it was possible for the good man to live in any existing state. Our contemporary political mood is such that we insist that there can be no really good man who is not reforming the state, since that is where the origins of our evils lie, presumably. There is no longer any spiritual authenticity that does not pass through politics for many modern minds, usually a politics that *ex professo* denies the validity of the divine. Justin Martyr believed Socrates, though accused of atheism, was a saint. In *The Apology*, Socrates heeded his "voice" which opposed his taking a public business.

Socrates, then, knew he would have perished earlier if he took on public affairs. And Aristotle, after him, left Athens so there would not be two Socrates' on the city's conscience. Socrates went on:

> Do not be annoyed at my telling the truth; the fact is that no man in the world will come off safe who honestly opposes you or any other multitude, and tries to hinder the many unjust and illegal doings in the state. It is necessary that one who really and truly fights for the right, if he is to survive even for a short time, shall act as a private man, not as a public man.[33]

If we reflect on the present state of Christian social thought, we will, I think, not fail to note that, among those who deny the central line of Christian orthodoxy, the view of Socrates is rejected.

Harold Laski once remarked that with the decline of religious faith, this world would become all important. Salvation now becomes a public enterprise through the ideologies of the world. And we are left no specifically religious criterion to decide their validity when we evaporate our social tradition. The poignant conclusion of *The Apology*—"And now it is time to go, I to die, and you to live; but which of us goes to a better thing is unknown to all but God"—has become also the crux of contemporary social philosophy. For the abandonment of private man and private spirituality as an authentic way to God, no matter what the social system, has left us with a worldly salvation that professes to know who are the good and who the evil.

Ironically, then, the ones who claim to know the good and the evil are those who know about faulty political systems which they define in terms of badly distributed property or income, wrongly formed families or governments. It is not an accident that these criteria were originally seen to be the consequences—not the causes—of original sin. Politics thus has become a theology. Throne and altar become very near. Whether such a system is still "Christian" remains the brooding doubt of our century. The feuding, in any case, seems to go on, as does the sermonizing. We shall have many a more rough Sunday, even though we all be *preforedestinated*.

Footnotes:

1 *The Christian Science Monitor,* January 2, 1980.

2 Cf. the following chapter.

3 Cf. below, Chapter VII.

4 Cf. Irving Kristol, "About Equality," *Two Cheers for Capitalism,* New York, Basic, 1978, pp. 171-87.

5 Cf. the author's *Redeeming the Time,* New York, Sheed, 1968, Chapters 4 and 6.

6 Cf. Edward Norman, *Christianity and the World Order,* New York, Oxford, 1979; E. Lefever, *From Amsterdam to Nairobi,* Washington, Ethics and Public Policy Center, 1979.

7 Dale Vree, *On Synthesizing Marxism and Christianity,* New York, Wiley, 1976, p. 8.

8 Mark Twain, *Huckleberry Finn,* New York, Dell, 1960, pp. 146-47.

9 Cf. the author's "Political Theory and Political Theology," *Laval Théologique et Philosophique,* Février, 1975, pp. 25-49.

10 Cf. A. Fierro, *The Militant Gospel,* Maryknoll, Orbis, 1977.

11 Cf. the author's "Conservatism and Development," *Cultures et Developpement,* Louvain, # 2, 1977, pp. 315-34.

12 Cf. the author's "The Modern Church and the Totalitarian State," *Studies,* Dublin, Summer, 1968, pp. 113-27.

13 Cf. Leo XIII's early encyclicals like *Libertas, Diuturnum,* and *Sapientiae Christianae.*

14 The address of John Paul II at Puebla, Mexico, on January 28, 1979, addressed the topic of an authentic Christian social philosophy independent of the ideologies.

15 Heinrich Rommen, *The State in Catholic Thought,* St. Louis, B. Herder, 1945. Part II.

16 Cf. the author's "The Limits of Law," *Communio,* Summer, 1975, pp. 126-47.

17 Cf. John East, "The Political Relevance of St. Augustine," *The Modern Age,* Summer, 1972, pp. 167-81; Herbert Deane, *The Political and Social Ideas of St. Augustine,* New York, Columbia, 1963.

18 Cf. the author's "Monastery and Home," *The American Benedictine Review,* December, 1978, pp. 307-19.

19 *The Holy Cross Quarterly,* V. 7, 1-4, 1975.

20 June, 1975.

21 *The Tablet,* London, September 27, 1975.

[22] Cf. Alexander Solzhenitsyn's addresses of June 30, 1975 and July 9, 1975; P. Gheddo, "Due Testimonianze della Russia di Brezhnev," *Mondo e Missione,* Milano, Marzo, 1975.

[23] *After Everything: Western Intellectual History Since 1965,* New York, St. Martin's, 1975, p. 202.

[24] *Ibid.,* p. 204.

[25] *Ibid.*

[26] James Hitchcock, *Catholicism and Modernity,* New York, Seabury, 1978.

[27] Cf. below, Chapter VI.

[28] Cf. below, Chapter VII.

[29] Cf. the author's *The Praise of 'Sons of Bitches': On the Worship of God by Fallen Men,* Slough, England, St. Paul Publishers, 1978.

[30] Hilaire Belloc, *The Great Heresies,* New York, Sheed, 1938, pp. 9, 11.

[31] Cf. footnote # 20.

[32] Richard Weaver, "Humanism in an Age of Science," *The Intercollegiate Review,* Fall, 1970, p. 18.

[23] # 32A

CHAPTER II

On the Teaching of Ancient and Medieval Political Theory

If man should decide on certain things as being really good, such as prudence, temperance, justice, fortitude, he would not, after having decided on them, consent to listen to anything not in harmony with the really good.
—*The Emperor Marcus Aurelius*, Meditations, V. 12.

But when they had tied him up with thongs, Paul said to the centurion who was standing by, "Is it lawful for you to scourge a Roman citizen, and uncondemned?"
—The Acts of the Apostles, 22:25.

Most people think that only the latest ideas are important, and that's true in science, but in philosophy these ideas that Aristotle had 2,400 years ago are completely relevant to contemporary life and thought, as if he were talking today.
—*Mortimer Adler*, The Washington Star, April 30, 1978.

The San Francisco Examiner (October 14, 1973) had reported a Bay Area survey which unexpectedly discovered that political science had suddenly become popular again on local campuses. This movement was, at a more esoteric level, noted a decade previously. This was the feeling of the Introduction to Professors Laslett and Runciman's *Philosophy, Politics, and Society:*

> We proclaimed (in 1962) a modest revival in political philosophy since the declaration made in the original collection of 1956 that 'for the moment, anyway, political philosophy is dead.' ...We suggested in 1962 that the revival of political philosophy was largely due to two separate but related influences. On the one hand, there was a renewal of interest taken by philosophers in prescriptive discussion of social and political issues. On the other hand, there was the much closer attention which was being accorded to the methods and results of the social sciences.[1]

And Edwin M. Yoder, Jr., wrote of the condition of political science:

> Many political scientists work overtime these days to exclude value judgments from their studies. Political philosophy, with its concern for ideas and values, is necessarily inimical to those who do. It is inevitably the study of the very element so many political scientists try to minimize.
>
> Yet, it is hard to imagine the survival of any political system on a diet of mere data, or in an

atmosphere from which the consideration of political values (justice, freedom, etc.) has been excluded.[2]

So there seem to be new signs of life in the area of political thought.

Needless to say, most government departments have long been in the doldrums with the unspeakable boredom of behavioral orthodoxy and the spate of what was politely called "activism" during the 1967-72 period. This was when the Vietnam War and other assorted causes elevated sociology, psychology, theology, and, for some unknown reason, English departments to the ephemeral rank of popular enclaves in which to study politics.[3] Abruptly, however, the unhappy but headline commanding activities of presidential impeachment and the dire results of losing the Vietnam War came to the rescue of political science as a department in that jungle of competing departments known as the modern university.

This result has been curious, to be sure. The nation announced that it did not want to fight any more foreign wars. It had made practically the same announcement in the 1920's and 1930's, one of the causes many think of World War II. We had made friends with old enemies when Mr. Henry Kissinger, the most famous of the world's professional political scientists, visited Peking and Moscow. Student leaders were applauded for burning their draft cards

—that is, for disobeying the law—and exiling themselves virtuously to Canada—few, evidently, chose Bulgaria, or India, or Kuwait. Iran, Poland, and the aftermath in Cambodia were still in the future. *The New York Times* found at the time that some of the "news fit to print" was found in stolen documents. For this heroic act down came the Pulitzer Prize. Next, so swiftly do our principles seem to come home to roost, came a new Mideast war, with hints that we might need to send troops, certainly equipment, alerts, oil crises. Some wars are better not to fight than others. And, of course, a president came to be a symbol of unjustice for losing tapes, firing people, for disobeying the law.

All of this brought up a special problem, for suddenly "morality" came to be the political fad. And political science was not at all in very good shape to speak to students about something called "justice," even though this particular subject happened to be the very one with which Plato began the whole subject of political thought in the first place. For far too many students, however, the noble Plato in political science has been someone who comes up in a footnote in a chapter on Fascism during the 1930's. The sharp student, in any case, spotted the difficulty quite soon. For if modern political thought was approvingly founded on Machiavelli, as all the textbooks seem to agree—on what politics *does* do, not on what politics *ought* to do, on Max

Weber's value free science—then why was it all right to be angry with a president whose only theoretic flaw, by the criterion of so-called modern political theory, seems to have consisted in being caught and losing power?

Nevertheless, the students in recent years are in political science classrooms not to find the logical consistency of social science research but because they have been morally angry that justice had been objectively violated. There is no other way to put it. In truth, there is really not much fun or point in being angered at a game plan or a linguistic fallacy. Moreover, the students have not been themselves interested in the ancient traditions of legal procedure as it has affected de facto political leaders. No one has explained to them from the moral side why the traditional rules and procedures for achieving justice are so complex and so necessary. They are even surprised to discover that Aristotle's definition of law—"reason without passion"—applies to themselves, especially in judging others.

Unless, then, there is an absolute oughtness in some sense to what the president—and everyone else—should do, a moral accountability based on some certain and universal criterion, since the written law itself, including the Constitution, must also have its moral justification, what grounds did we really have for being angry, when a president apparently tried to follow exactly the program laid down by the texts in political theory on the subject of the invalidity of absolute norms? And to muddle things more, a Mr. Nixon himself would have probably held for an absolute norm.

To be sure, there is recently a movement variously called "post-behaviorism" which demands a radical choice of values for restructuring all men and society according to something usually described as "human needs."[4] In this context, the political radical merely suggested to the behaviorist or the modern that, since he had no objection to values in theory, why not support radical ones? A surprisingly large number of behaviorists have, in fact, actually gone this route. Yet, the radical solution was no real answer, since the very question it brought up was the content of the definition of "human needs." From the viewpoint of classical political thought, these "needs" often look strikingly anti-human as they are proposed. In all of this, the student has been given precious little insight into the notion of political anger, its moral limits and political justification, the way it can lead directly to a supposition of permanent values.

The confusion has been far-reaching. In an odd, presumably relevant article entitled, "The Biological Foundations of Political Science: Reflections on the Post-Behavioral Era," Professor Thomas Landgon Thorson gave a taste of some of what students are invited to consider.

"Man is the product of an evolutionary process stretching back some six billion years," began a popular dogma.[5] Thus, "the Twentieth Century man can see the vastness of time and its overriding significance," something "Plato, Aristotle, Augustine, and Thomas Aquinas" could not have known, while Descartes, Hobbes, and Locke could have known this only vaguely.[6]

We were next informed that "zoologist Robert Bigelow suggests that the only possible way to explain the biologically extraordinary fact of the trebling of size (the measure of increased complexity would, of course, be many times three) of the human brain in a relatively short period of time (by evolutionary standards) is the continued presence of an unusually powerful selection force."[7] This force turns out to be a subtle version of increased cranial activity due to the necessity of survival—something, presumably, that happened about six billion years ago. Next we were informed that man's intelligence is based on this larger brain size, but also that the "men of Philadelphia," whose mere two hundred year old political invention still survives, showed that larger brain size also meant more intelligence.[8] We finally arrived at the astonishing observation that "we must recognize that Plato and Aristotle, for all their towering achievement, were from an evolutionary point of view a step or two from the primitive."[9]

In one sense, probably, it does little good to comment on such confusion. If man really is the product of an evolutionary process starting back about six billion years ago, then we are going to have to have some pretty mathematically dull students to believe that Plato and Aristotle who lived about 2,500 years ago, not to mention Aquinas who lived seven hundred years ago, and even Descartes who lived about three hundred years ago, were just a step from the primitive in a six billion year process. Furthermore, we are going to have to have students who are completely ignorant of the invention of the balance scales to believe either that recent phenomenal progress in knowledge since Rousseau and Madison, caused by this same powerful selective force that once trebled the size of the brain, did not logically result in a considerably larger physical brain size or else that the towering achievements of Plato and Aristotle were not, in fact, some sort of biological miracle. The only other alternative to this jumble of academic confusion is to insist that the student actually read Plato and Aristotle, Tacitus and Thucydides, Aquinas, and Augustine, to discover that they are speaking quite intelligently about very lively issues—like the grounds of justice—no matter how close to the primitive they have been. In other words, the effort to rid ourselves of the discussion of justice by relegating it back on some sort of evolutionary time scale will never do.

The great intellectual crime in our culture is the cutting away of our students—who are themselves by no means totally innocent on this score—from our universal human tradition by opting for some sort of biological or progressive theory which ignores the basic fact that Plato and Aristotle were quite as much men as ourselves.[10] The *Antigone* of Sophocles, another near primitive, presumably, or the trials of Socrates and Jesus are much better grounds for discussions about and understanding of justice than anything our students will find in the theoretical literature or in the newspaper or TV analyses of current problems. Indeed, the reading of the ancient Greeks, Romans, Jews, and Medievals makes one wonder if there has not really been rather a "devolution" in many respects since their time.

What this really means, of course, is that political theory is not very "evolutionary" at all. The ancients recognized quite clearly that corruption and decline were as much a part of its subject matter as growth and virtue. The very greatest thing the student today can be told is that we *can* be worse than our ancestors. We do not *have* to be better, nor are we necessarily so. If any generation of mankind does not at least know that, it is simply being deceived, or more properly, deceiving itself. And even students with voting rights are free to indulge in this latter sort of laissez-faire enterprise.

Testament for the Future

In another survey of political science teaching, Malcolm Scully found that Watergate had touched every course in American Government but that every variety of analysis and reaction to its meaning could be found being proposed on university campuses.[11] Yet, there appears to be surprisingly little evidence in this survey that the real issue this crisis brought up was not about the mechanics of our political system but about the nature and meaning of justice itself. And this question simply cannot be discussed by refusing to demand that we all, students and teachers and citizens alike, return to the classical origins of justice itself, and to its limits. The reason why we are suddenly being forced to return to our past to consider even every-day problems that are the topic of current events, from corruption to foreign policy to defense, is because we have cut our students and ourselves from the ethical and political heritage upon which our public system was founded, a tradition whose essence is the recollection of justice and its limits, perhaps the limits more than the justice itself.

Hannah Arendt thus has remarked in this context:

Without testament or, to resolve the metaphor, without tradition—which selects and names, which hands down and preserves, which indicates where treasures are and what their worth is—there seems to be no willed continuity in time and hence, humanly speaking, neither past nor future, only sempiternal change of the world and the biological cycle of living creatures in it. Thus the treasure was lost not because of historical circumstances and the adversity of reality but because no tradition had foreseen its appearance or its reality, because no testament had willed it for the future.[12]

For in attempting to achieve a "scientific" politics, we have made Aristotle and Plato into primitives with the result that we are, in spite of the valiant efforts of a Professor Leo Strauss, incapable of establishing any reason why we are involved in a continuing drama which has its origins in the kind of ethical condition mankind has borne at least since we know anything of him.[13] Our biological heritage is not enough, or even of much interest in this regard, for clearly it is what is willed that disturbs and angers us. Our students need to know what there is to be "handed down." Otherwise, in a crisis, they find themselves thinking about political ethics with no recognition that their moral criterion is something common to all mankind, including those who have preceded us, who surprisingly often thought more clearly than we ourselves in these matters.[14]

Curriculum Proposal for Political Thought

Most universities, I think, still have scheduled a course variously entitled the "History of Political Thought," "Great Political Thinkers," or some such enterprise. Usually, the history of political theory is not conceived primarily as a history course—the history of Roman law or the Institution of the Greek City-State—for historians are jealous of anything that bears their name without their departmental control. Subjects variously called anthropology, sociology, or behavioral studies also purport some interest in such matters as do classics departments where they still exist.

What I am interested in here, however, is to argue for the absolute necessity for the undergraduate—and not only the student of political science, not even merely the student—to discover again for himself the intellectual and ethical heritage of ancient and medieval political theory, a heritage that will necessarily also touch upon the validity and necessity of metaphysics.[15] This is, clearly, a "more or less" sort of thing. And the very notion of "requirement" is often looked upon askance. Yet, I am convinced that a program of introduction to the core of this tradition will often appear as a sort of revelation to our students who will immediately recognize that it meets precisely that lack of moral and even ontological context which they find missing in contemporary political theory, but which is now so insisted upon in public life.

To be sure, I do not wish to exclude the study of so-called modern and Twentieth Century Political Theory from eventual consideration, though such latter studies are barren and largely unintelligible without a beginning in ancient and medieval theory.[16] Further, I do not wish to suggest that the kind of political theory that arose and flourished after Machiavelli right up to the present is simply not pertinent in understanding where we are. But it is inadequate to confront the deep kinds of spiritual and moral problems that are arising in the fields of everyday politics. This is what the student, even the so-called radical, is looking for, so that he is rightly "turned off" by what he finds in the average presentation of political theory. Indeed, I would suggest here that the intellectual cause of much contemporary radicalism and revolutionary thought, in the peculiar form it has in fact taken, largely is to be explained by a failure ever to be confronted with classical theory in any meaningful fashion.

Furthermore, the failure of the universities to demand a basic minimum of general education which would refuse to grant the noble name of "education" to any student unexposed to and ignorant of the classical thought of our kind—something that is beginning to be more widely recognized—has paradoxically resulted in

a "politicization" of most university courses
themselves. The result is that "politics" escapes
the intellectual discipline of its origins and limits
to become the plaything of every other department in academe. There is a further problem
today. All university students have been legally
declared political adults. The value of the vote of
the teacher and the student is exactly the same,
the same as that of any other citizen. But voting
rights do not as such make anyone aware of
political tradition and political ethic. We must
will our tradition. And this means study and
effort without which our reactions to contemporary "injustice" are frighteningly inadequate,
if not dangerous.[17]

Elementary Guide

What is worthwhile suggesting, then, is
a minimal scheme of matter in classical and
medieval political thought that would serve as
an introduction and a foundation to the moral
level of political theory. We should have no
doubt that this is what is being searched for and
argued about. Perhaps there are two caveats
necessary in this regard.

The first is that political theory cannot by
itself supply what is lacking elsewhere in the
university curriculum. Of its nature perhaps, it
can do better than practically any other field.
This is why Aristotle called it the highest prac-

tical science as it did touch all others. The student who comes to the political thought courses ignorant of theology, philosophy, and history is crippled, as is the student who knows nothing of the history of science itself.[18] We are desperately in need of a generation of students angered at the fact that they have been deprived of their intellectual and moral tradition.

In class, such incidents as the following are common. I asked a student, "Who wrote the *Epistle to the Romans?*" He replied that he had never heard of it, of the New Testament document that speaks of obedience to civil rulers and of the origin of authority. Of another I inquired of the content of the story of the Good Samaritan. "The Good who?" I should like to think such lacunae were mere humorous sidelights. But it is not so. Such students, I think, should be furious at an educational and cultural system that could leave them in such ignorance at twenty years of age. There are encouraging signs that this is beginning to be the case.

A second warning is taken from C. S. Lewis' advice about a truly great book:

> An unliterary man may be defined as one who reads books once only. There is hope for a man who has never read Malory or Boswell, or *Tristam Shandy* or Shakespeare's *Sonnets:* but what can you do with a man who says he 'has read' them, meaning he has read them once, and thinks that this settles the matter?[19]

In other words, classical and medieval theory is based upon a series of books and reflections that are among the greatest mankind has produced. The professor, the university, can do little more than give the student an initial chance at their riches. The failure of education is when the chance is not given. The failure of the student is when he considers it necessary to read only once.

Where to begin? In a sense, Salvador de Madariaga's remarks on the spiritual heritage of Europe seems to be right in place:

> But if the body of Europe may be referred to as a frame of reference composed of three rivers (the Rhone, the Rhine, and the Danube), the soul is the outcome of a meeting of these two mighty streams of tradition: Socrates and Christ; for Socrates taught Europe to respect freedom of thought, and Christ taught her to respect the human person.[20]

What is of significance to the discussion here, however, is de Madariaga's practical proposal, which urgently needs some form of American and indeed worldwide implementation:

> We want to set up a European State but we are dying of too much state about us. We must instill into our youth the feeling of individual responsibility for individual destiny. We might devise means for encouraging such an attitude. We should for instance formally receive as European citizens every new generation; at an adequate time, and during the ceremony present to

each youth a copy of a book bearing the texts from Plato describing the death of Socrates, and from the Gospels, describing the death of Christ, not merely because they are the two spiritual fathers of Europe but because they both perished at the hands of the state.[21]

Perhaps such a rite is too formal, though some formality may well be much of what we lack. Nevertheless, it recognizes clearly what is lacking in our political atmosphere. I believe we must have the corporate courage at least to insist upon an academic requirement which can give the student the liberty of his tradition. For this is what is at issue. We have students and adults who are not free because they have never heard of the Good Samaritan or of the *Histories of Tacitus,* or, finally, of the death of Socrates.

What would be a minimum core of readings that a student should follow to be free enough to begin the great enterprise of classical and medieval theory out of which our ethical standards and instincts in politics have arisen? What is suggested here is a beginning, perhaps a semester or so, probably all the time available to most students. But this beginning is enough to begin well. Further, a professor's comments and reading of secondary analyses should be held to a minimum. What is of prime importance is exposing intelligently the student or interested reader to an actual consideration of the essential tradition. Soon it will become clear that the tradition can bear itself, foster its own interest.

Any student who does not cover and discuss these basic materials during his university years must be considered, must consider himself, in some sense, an intellectual cripple. I do not insist necessarily only on the "great books," which Professor Mortimer Adler made so famous, but rather on a combination which would include reading, discussion, and writing within a context of the flow of ancient and medieval thought. I would say that it is essential to cover all the material, for it is a sort of overall sense of political thought and its abidingness that must be grasped.

The core of what I suggest is a persistent, attentive reading of the following works:

1) *The Peloponnesian War* of Thucydides.
2) *The Republic*, the *Apology*, the *Crito*, and the *Phaedo* of Plato.
3) *The Ethics* and the *Politics* of Aristotle.
4) *The Treatise on Old Age* and the *Treatise on Duties* (Book III) of Cicero. (Penguin Classics have these in one volume.)
5) From the Old Testament: *Genesis 1-4; Psalm 8; Deuteronomy 5-7; Isaiah 64-66; Amos.*
6) From the New Testament: *Matthew 5; 16; 22:15-22; 25; Luke 2; 10:25-37; 14:1-14; John 18-19; Acts 2; 4:5-22; 5:1-11; 5:27-32; 10:34-43; 16:35-40; 17:16-34; 18:23-28; 24:22-25; Romans 2; 13; 1 Corinthians 13; Galatians 1-5; Philemon; James 1:22—2:26; 1 Peter 2:13-25; 1 John 1:5; Revelation 13; 19-22.*

7) Augustine. *The Confessions* should be read but only broadly belong to political theory; *The City of God* is too vast and selections are less than satisfactory, though V. Bourke's *The City of God, Selections,* Doubleday Image, is good. I recommend instead Herbert Deane's *The Political and Social Ideas of St. Augustine,* Columbia University Press.

8) *The Treatise on Law* from the Summa of Thomas Aquinas.

Along with this, and in chronological sequence, I recommend a reading of short treatments, either books or essays, of the political climate of Ancient Israel (perhaps Orlinsky, *Ancient Israel,* Cornell); Rome (perhaps F. E. Adcock, *Roman Political Ideas and Practice,* Ann Arbor); feudalism (perhaps Ganshof or Stephenson or Pirenne); and medieval thought (perhaps Morrall, *Political Thought in Medieval Times,* Harper Torchbooks or especially Christopher Dawson, *Religion and the Rise of Western Culture,* Doubleday Image). It would be well to have available to go along with this a standard textbook such as Sibley, Sabine, McDonald, or on a more theoretical level Charles N. R. McCoy, *The Structure of Political Thought* (McGraw-Hill, 1963). Two little volumes of intellectual background are of especial value in this area: J. M. Bochenski *Philosophy—an Introduction* (Harper Torchbooks,

1972) and E. F. Shumacher, *A Guide for the Perplexed* (Harper Colophon, 1977).

This is certainly a decent amount of matter, but it is not too much for such a project, while it is certainly a minimum for the importance of the matter involved.[22] I do not believe that such a course should be presented to the student under the rubric of "relevancy," for what is at issue is the students' encounter with an ethical-political approach that is itself educative. The very study itself carries us into the questions of justice and injustice, the good man, the best form of government, happiness, government by law, the relation between private morality and public morality, Caesar and God, the death of Socrates and the death of Christ, obedience to the law, why law is to be obeyed in the first place, the question of authority. If students can be guided through such matter, the task is begun and the immediate task is finished. For it is then up to them to realize that all of this requires a second reading, at least a second reading, with an awareness of the abidingness of human good and evil in their political forms.

Moreover, and this is the main point, all of this is itself intrinsically fascinating and, as it were, "sells" itself. Many students today, freed from the immediate ideologies of only a few years ago, are searching for a political theory that puts them back into contact with classical and medieval political ideas, with a theory that again enables them to think of politics as man ought to live it, not as he does live it, yet with the realization that how man does live is important for politics and for thought. Such a project, hopefully, at least might give the student, and everyone interested, an outside chance, a chance to know the naiveté of making Plato and Aristotle "primitives," to know why the Emperor Marcus Aurelius could see the importance of goodness, while the Apostle Paul demanded his legal rights as a Roman citizen. No one should think that we have here a lasting panacea, but rather a sober, exciting recognition of what can happen when man sets out to be just, of what happens when he learns from experience that to be just at all, he must begin to wonder if there is also anything more than justice. And it is from these latter questions that the scope of political theory and Christianity begins to broaden.

Footnotes:

[1] Peter Laslett and W. G. Runciman, *Philosophy, Politics, and Society,* Oxford, Blackwell, 1978, p. 1.

[2] Edwin M. Yoder, Jr., "Fractionalism in Political Science Departments," *The Washington Star,* September 6, 1979.

[3] Cf. Victor Ferkiss, "Theory, Myth, and Ideology," *The Political Science Reviewer,* Fall, 1979, pp. 29-60.

[4] Cf. James A. Gould and V. Thursby, *Contemporary Political Thought,* New York, Hole, 1969.

[5] Thomas Landgon Thorson, "The Biological Foundations of Political Science: Reflections on the Post-Behavioral Era," *The Post-Behavioral Era: Perspectives in Political Science,* New York, McKay, 1972, p. 270.

[6] *Ibid.,* p. 271.

7 *Ibid.*, p. 261.

8 *Ibid.*, p. 262.

9 *Ibid.*, p. 279.

10 Cf. Christopher Dawson, *The Dynamics of World History*, Editor, J. J. Mulloy, New York, Mentor-Omega, 1956.

11 Malcolm Scully, "For Political Science, Watergate Poses Unique Teaching Problems," *The Chronicle of Higher Education*, November 19, 1973.

12 Hannah Arendt, *Between Past and Future*, New York, Viking, 1968, pp. 5-6.

13 Cf. Leo Strauss, *The City and Man*, Chicago, University of Chicago Press, 1964.

14 Cf. John Finnis, *Natural Law and Natural Right*, Oxford, At the Clarendon Press, 1980.

15 Cf. the author's "The Recovery of Metaphysics," *Divinitas*, Rome, # 2, 1979, pp. 200-19.

16 Cf. J. G. A. Pocock, *Politics, Language, and Time*, New York, Atheneum, 1973.

17 Cf. Willard Gaylin, *"Doing Good": The Limits of Benevolence*, New York, Seabury, 1978.

18 Cf. Stanislaus Jaki, *The Road of Science and the Ways of God*, Chicago, University of Chicago Press, 1978.

19 C. S. Lewis, "On Stories," *Of Other Worlds: Essays and Stories*, London, Bles, 1966, p. 17.

20 Salvador de Madariaga, "Europe of the Four Karls," *The Tablet*, London, June 23, 1973, p. 580.

21 *Ibid.*

22 Perhaps it is well too here to suggest a few academic readings along the general lines I have been suggesting, though here, I am more interested in the matter itself than in the justification for it:

1) C. Bay, "Politics and Pseudopolitics: A Critical Evaluation of Some Behavioral Literature," in *Apolitical Politics*, Eds. McCoy and Playford, New York, Crowell, 1967, pp. 12-37.

2) H. R. G. Greaves, "Political Theory Today," *Apolitical Politics*, pp. 232-46.

3) Leo Strauss, "What Is Political Philosophy?" in *Contemporary Political Thought, ibid.*, pp. 46-69.

4) Alfred Cobban, "Ethics and the Decline of Political Theory," *Contemporary, ibid.*, pp. 289-303.

5) Isaiah Berlin, "Does Political Theory Still Exist?" *ibid.*, pp. 328-571.

6) George W. Carey, "Beyond Parochialism in Political Science," *The Post-Behavioral Era, ibid.,* pp. 37-53.

7) Leo Strauss, "Political Philosophy and the Crisis of Our Time," *ibid.,* pp. 217-42.

8) Charles N. R. McCoy, "On the Revival of Classical Political Philosophy," *The Review of Politics,* April, 1973, pp. 161-79.

9) Ferdinand Mount, "The Recovery of Civility," *Encounter,* July, 1973, pp. 31-43.

10) V. A. Demant, "Religion and the State," *Theology of Society,* London, Faber and Faber, 1947, pp. 49-69.

11) Charles W. Anderson, "The Place of Principles in Policy Analysis," *The American Political Science Review,* September, 1979, pp. 711-23.

12) Mulford Q. Sibley, *Political Ideas and Ideologies,* New York, Harper, 1970; George Sabine, *History of Political Theory,* Holt; McDonald, *Western Political Theory,* Part I, Ancient and Medieval, Harcourt.

CHAPTER III

The Effect
of Christian Thought
on Politics

*Thus, while we must resist with all our power,
the secularizing of theology—that is to say, the
reduction of the Christian religion to a concern simply with the things of this world and our life on this
planet—we must do all in our power to work out...a
theology of the secular—that is to say, an outlook
which sees the things of this world and of our earthly
life as redeemed by Christ and destined ultimately to
find their place in the final transfiguration of all
things in him....*

—E. L. Mascall, The Christian Universe,
London, Darton, 1966, p. 159.

If it be valid then that we must have some
sense of the Christian tradition, that Christianity
is not merely a political mobilization theory to

refashion the world, that there is no "revealed" politics, even though revelation clarifies what politics is, can it be therefore maintained that the propositions of Christian orthodoxy have no normative influence on politics? The history of Christian political thought has contained both Augustine and Aquinas. This means, in principle, that there is a pragmatic way of looking at politics based on what fallen men really do, a method associated primarily with Augustine.[1] Likewise, there is a more positive approach, associated with Thomas Aquinas, which grants a good deal of autonomy to man and to the world, though "autonomy" should not in this context be seen somehow in opposition to the divine.

Neither the Thomist nor the Augustinian view, undoubtedly, contradicts the central orthodoxy of Christianity. What is worthwhile presenting at this point is the most optimistic and positive case that can realistically be made for a humanly organized world within the limits of the kind of beings men are. We will not argue here that such a world must or even might come about. But there is within the Christian analysis a case to be made for a better world order, one more international, yet more local too, one that does respond to the exigencies of poverty, to the need for good institutional systems.

Nevertheless, such an intellectual system must also account for man's sins and his weaknesses. Likewise, it must not confuse politics and salvation. States are not saved. Persons are. In stating what Christians do in politics, how they conceive this area, the intention is to remain primarily within the Thomist tradition, which derives its principles of economics and politics from "reason" and not from "revelation." Yet, this same tradition itself recognizes the intrinsic incapacity of politics, often, to achieve its own ends, let alone specifically religious ends. This is why we must probably speak, to be accurate, of the Christian *effect* on politics, rather than Christian politics as such. Russell Kirk caught something of the trend of both of these aspects:

> Another cause of Christianity's success was that its appeal unconnected with political systems, became universal. "Indeed," Jacob Burckhardt wrote, "the great advantage of the religion whose kingdom was not of this world was that it did not set itself the task of directing and guaranteeing any definite state and any definite culture...." Most of all, the new faith taught people how to restore harmony in their souls, in this earthly life; and it offered them the promise of the Life Eternal.[2]

This paradox must always be at the heart of Christian political thought.

Human economic and social relations in any era and nation involve a complexity of goals, pressures, conflicts, exchanges, and destinies whose sum total, whose full comprehension are beyond the grasp of any man, indeed of any given group of men, of even the whole race of men. The knowledge component of such relations alone, even apart from the corresponding problem of what to do with it, represents what is probably the single most complex "apparatus" known in the universe, more so probably than the complete comprehension of the laws of the cosmos itself. Undoubtedly, the political, economic, and social relations are more complicated and opaque to human knowledge than the structure of the physical universe because of the infinite, continuous variability connected with freedom and knowledge. In this sense, the Christian affirmation of the validity of the human intellect really to know and the consequent freedom of the will, these are a rejection of any political determinism or, indeed, any closed system.[3]

Man cannot, then, wait to know or act in politics until he has made some sort of complete statistical summary of all the possible interconnected aspects of political life. There are some technological mechanisms which seem to imply that this is possible, but this usually means a control of knowledge and freedom, rather than a complete comprehension of all factors. Usually, indeed almost always, man must act on partial knowledge and comprehension. The necessity of this kind of action, of action with partial knowledge projected into an unknown future, this is indeed the major issue of all politics."

What happens in fact in political life is a process of experience, experimentation, abstraction, reflection, analysis, order, judgment, and action, a process that is continually repeated, checked, rethought, as life in time proceeds. But while paying the fullest respect to the concrete details, to the raw materials of political experience, the mind also tends to see patterns and levels of procedure with which to reduce the blunt data it received to manageable proportions. Only when this is done can man dare to fashion the as yet immediately unknown future, the future which is proceeding directly out of the past and the present.

Now, as this initial or continuing organizational process goes along, the question of "ethics" must begin to be asked about politics. At first sight, this might not mean anything more than that some alternatives must be rejected, some accepted. So if we do not have some kind of deterministic philosophy, as we do not in Christianity, choices of political action must be made. And because these are precisely choices, we are responsible for them. We assign praise and blame. We try to establish institutions wherein this accountability can be manifested. So over and beyond the aspect of fact and knowledge, the relations of men, society, and nations contain within their sphere the problems of right and wrong, of moral and immoral, of good and evil. And such questions arise, not as we might expect, out of some alien divine or mythical imposition of duties, but rather out of the relations themselves considered as components, as it were, and factors in human existence. The killing of the innocent or the guilty, the promotion of trade, the alleviation of poverty, the eradication of disease are seen to be ethical or unethical because of their connection with man and his importance. In a real sense, then, the Christian grounding of the value of the human person as something of worth and significance is itself what ultimately gives politics its seriousness and its nobility.

Man, the Political Animal

The problem of why man is important is, of course, legitimate and demands the attention of the philosophical and theological disciplines beyond politics. In a sense, with these sciences themselves becoming politically oriented, politics is left without its ultimate basis. Politics begins with the fundamental proposition that man and his tasks are worthwhile, supremely worthwhile, though not ultimate and not exclusive. Other things are important, even in this world, besides politics. Politics differ from the theoretical sciences on the one hand and art on the other. The theoretical sciences, particularly metaphysics, stand to reality as receivers of what is not created or determined by them. They seek to know for its own sake and to react on the basis of what is given. Art, on the contrary, is free both in regard to what it creates and as to how it achieves its goals. The artist, to be sure, is dependent on matter and time as necessary substrata, but his artistic production is wholly dependent on him. Politics occupies a middle ground between the theoretical sciences and art.

Politics, then, accepts man as something given by nature, a creature whose essential outlines—his tendency to knowledge, to society, to family, to creativity—are not the original results of human creation. But politics, once having accepted man for what he is, becomes free with regard to the many ways in which human lives can be lived, developed, and modified. There are and should be varieties of human cities and communities. On this foundation of the acceptance of man from nature so that he is not a mere artifact, on this principle of the primacy of the human person, politics can separate what is for and what is against man, how human life can be lived now in one way, now in another. Politics can ask, therefore, about the ethical in public life because ultimately this too is for man.

Nevertheless, the question of the ethical in all human life and especially in that kind of ethics called, since Aristotle, "politics" is often equated in the minds of many with what might be called the "static-providential" view of morals. In this view, what is meant by an "ethical'' decision is calculated to be some formula or code which contains all the ready-made solutions to concrete problems. The ethical is then considered to be some prophetic insight into what will or should be, so that the decision of politics is merely an eye-witness report of the future, as it were, seen in the eternal solutions.

Ethics in this sense, of course, eliminates any real responsibility on the part of man, something Christian theology necessarily endeavors to prevent. Indeed, this view eliminates man altogether, for man is precisely the political being in the universe. He is that being whose primary definition, whose unique cosmic distinction is to act on and in the world freely to create the human city, to transform the world in the pursuit of his destiny. This is how Christianity has always looked upon the original mission given in *Genesis.* Any ethical theory which jeopardizes the very possibility of man's responsibility, which undermines the reality of risk and decision in the creation of the earthly community, is clearly to be rejected.

The Multiplicity of Ethical Choices

With this in mind, then, an important theoretical problem arises. Not any particular political question in any given political society concerns us here. Rather, we want to know what is meant by an ethical or moral decision in political life at any level, local, national, or international. We know that men do get angry, and they do constantly blame or praise political actions as worthy or unworthy. This in itself suggests that they implicitly consider such actions based on a freedom that could have been different. Otherwise, the praise and the blame, the drama of politics would mean nothing. Perhaps the first thing that must be recognized in this respect is that, while man can only make one decision at a time and act on it, nevertheless very seldom, if ever, is there just one "ethical" alternative open to him before he acts. Action, clearly, is in the singular. We do not do seven things at once. No one can choose two courses at the same time. Until one or the other is decided upon, no action results.

Yet, the prerequisites to a given action are almost always multiple. This may sound a bit confusing or paradoxical, but the theory of it deserves attention. Indeed, it would seem that a considerable amount of the tension and hatred existing in the world today arises, psychologically, because every determination in political life is believed to be between good and evil, so that the critics of any given policy can, with apparent intellectual impunity, consider any opposing policy to belong to the category of the simply unethical, the evil, or the immoral. This is a simplistic view of catastrophic magnitude. Ultimately, I think, this mentality is rooted in a refusal to accept the human condition, a refusal which is at the bottom of any theory of "permanent revolution." Practically, without a theory about the legitimacy of many, if not most, alternatives to our own views, we cannot have those parliamentary institutions, procedures, and manners that underlie any peaceful combination among human beings.

Yet, in saying that alternatives in political life cannot be always categorized as good or evil, that an alternative policy may likewise work out all right, I do not wish to suggest that there are no choices between good and evil in ordinary political life. History and contemporary politics are full of them. There are, then, many possible ethically good decisions, both in regard to promoting wise policies and in regard to eradicating an admitted evil. Furthermore, an ethically good political decision may not in fact bring about either the promotion of the good or the avoidance of the evil, which is in fact its human intent. To understand why this is so, then, provides a clue to one of the deepest mysteries of man, the mystery of finitude. Christianity's influence on politics will suggest that good and evil are real factors in human life, not just arbitrary or changeable particulars. But by the same token, it does not imply that good and evil, in terms of personal values and relations, are the sole reason why men do not live in some kind of paradise. Moreover, the notion of finitude also explains why each free alternative open to man in political life does not necessarily involve only the choice of good *or* evil. Choices may well be between good and good, or even evil and evil.

There is a theory in ethics, a theory which seems to be largely the case, that each human choice in the concrete, that is, each actual decision about what a man or a nation is to do or not to do, is ethically good or evil. The concrete choice is good or bad. Now, that looks like we are saying that man is free to decide *a priori* whether a concrete choice is ethically good or bad, to hate it if bad, to praise it if good. But this is not exactly the case. What needs to be suggested rather is that, while it is true that every choice is ethically good or bad in ordinary life, this does not and cannot mean that there is not a multiplicity of alternative choices in each given case which would also have been good or bad. The usual alternative to an ethically good political choice is another good political choice, not an evil one. The consequence of this view is that we cannot judge the opposition to an ethically good political decision to be *ipso facto* evil, nor can we judge any alternative to an ethically bad choice to be automatically good. It may be evil also. On the other hand, this does not mean that simply because a series of alternative political choices may each be good, each in its own way, that there is nothing to argue and dispute about. Man is free to create the kind of ethical and political life he "wants," so that it does make a difference to him which one alternative he and his fellows do in practice choose. Christianity has always held that there are degrees of both good and evil. Often, the greatest dramas in politics, as in life, are precisely over questions of the precise degree of good or evil.

Politics and the Expansion of the Human Potential

At this point, then, the problem arises from the ethical theory that man should always choose not merely the ethically good, but the ethically best. Why this is a problem is of some importance, because it introduces the issue of *development* into political ethics. Indeed, this very idea of human development has often been the avenue in which utopianism has re-entered modern politics, the idea that we can somehow reorder society to make men "perfect." It is curious, in fact, how difficult it is to retain the fine distinction between what is possible and what is indeed beyond human potential on this score. Many a good thing was once considered impossible, after all. For Christianity has held that men can and ought to improve. It has also held that there is no heaven on earth. So towards what do we progress? Is there an inner-worldly happiness that is not beatitude? How are the two related?[4]

The following example may illustrate some of the difficulty. Suppose that one hundred and fifty years ago, some government decided to introduce a comprehensive health plan for its citizenry. Ethically, this would have been a noble and compassionate decision. The motives would have been concern for public health and concern for the sick. The government seemed to be the logical instrument to try the experiment. At the time, however, the type of medical care at hand would have been dependent upon the state of medical knowledge and practice. The therapy of bleeding would still perhaps have been in use, the cleanliness of instruments minimal, medicine primitive. The result of such a system would have been that many of the remedies prescribed under the medical system, itself ethically good, would have been, as we now know, medically detrimental. Thus, if a doctor practiced the same methods today on a patient, he would be prosecuted for malpractice or even murder. Therefore, we can see that an ethically good political choice for the time stood under the judgment of development and knowledge. The ethical judgment is itself subject to the pressure of the greater good. This means that an ethically good judgment can become an ethically bad judgment, if continued in the face of changing circumstances. Ironically, in this regard, advocates of the people's medicine in China today, as well as someone like Ivan Illich, from his own point of view, are in fact arguing that we should return to a simpler medical profession and level, precisely in the name of the greater good.[5]

Politics, in any case, does involve the maximalization of the human potential. There are times when this maximalization can become obligatory. Political decision, therefore, is ethically good when it actually does choose some alternative that is feasible and workable for the problem at hand. But the decision always stands under the further test of knowledge and development of the human person. Christian political thought has always held that this is itself a limit, a judgment on politics. Man is thus not free in the public order to refuse to develop or employ those essential means by which a fuller human life for the actual men and women on Earth is possible. This is, after all, what gives most Third World critics their moral passion and ethical justification insofar as they respect the possible, which they do not always do. Nevertheless, since it is not often absolutely clear just what particular policy or means really does foster this greater good, or with what priority one goal should be attacked in preference to another, we can accuse few of the alternatives proposed by men in public life of being ethically evil, especially in every respect. There are almost always a multiplicity of good alternatives, each of which is ethically possible and good, at least in its general orientation.

Therefore, we cannot and should not polarize political alternatives as simply good or bad. This brings an alien element into political life which is detrimental to its normal fabric because it insists on categorizing as black or white what is merely grey. And if something is grey, the truth is that it is neither white nor black. In this connection perhaps, the Inaugural Address of Thomas Jefferson on March 4, 1801, seems pertinent: "I shall often go wrong through defect of judgment. When right, I shall often be thought wrong by those whose positions will not command a view of the whole ground. I ask your indulgence for my own errors, which will never be intentional, and your support against the errors of others, who may condemn what they would not if seen in all its parts."

The Question of Evil in Politics

The further question of evil in politics is an important one.[6] The fact and concept of evil is a mystery with ramifications of the most profound nature in philosophy and theology as well as in politics. Further, it has long been my impression that few men are familiar with or even sympathetic toward the effort to face up to the reality of evil in the world. Undoubtedly, a Christian by virtue of his belief will be apt to recognize both the reality of evil and the error of refusing to do what can be done to confine it. A Christian will not, if he be orthodox, believe that evil can be "removed," since he sees its origin in the human heart and will and not in some economic or political arrangement. Thus, any political arrangement will be expected to betray its signs somehow. Yet, a kind of tragic flaw seems to be operative in this area. Too often evil is in fact multiplied in the world when men fail to allow for its presence. On the other hand, too easy acceptance of evil and its conditions saps the energy out of any movement designed to remove or lessen it.

Most of the actual choices in politics, we have maintained, are between feasible, good ethical choices, each of which has something to be said in its favor. Further, ethically good choices in politics may not actually accomplish the good that really needs to be achieved in the concrete situation. Human life has a principle of development and evolution according to which man is more and more capable of accomplishing certain goals and goods, the most obvious ones being in the areas of health, welfare, and technical knowledge. The ethical point of this development is that while man can make good choices in imperfect situations—that is, in circumstances where his knowledge, technical capacity, or voluntariness is less than complete—still there is a sense in which he must morally be striving so that these imperfect tools and techniques he must employ may be improved. Beyond this, however, lies the fact of evil. This gives rise to the peculiar phenomenon in politics that a politician may quite possibly be faced with a series of alternatives, each of which is judged to be ethically evil in practice. The question arises, then, where is the ethically good choice, especially when the choice not to act at all also involves grave evil?

To answer this question, it is well to recall the structure of the argument that concludes to the necessity of government in the first place.[7] The fact of a multiplicity of human persons joined together in various groupings for human purposes, all interacting on one another is a given datum. This interacting complexus cannot be simply chaotic. By that we mean that the very interrelation of men to one another in the pursuit of their welfare and goals requires a practical, living principle of order—a principle which itself is dependent upon the dignity of the human person and what grounds this dignity—by which these groups and individuals so involved can achieve their earthly purposes in some kind of harmony. The central line of Christian thought about government has always argued that this necessity comes from nature, that is, this natural need is presupposed by any specifically Christian revelation.[8]

Government, as a philosophic conclusion, then, arises out of this objective situation. That is, some institution within the society with decision-making functions is required. This institution can take a wide variety of historical forms—the ancient philosophers usually discussed this under the terms of monarchy, aristocracy, and polity and their corruptions and combinations—but in some sense it is needed for men to be complete, be fully what they can be. This institution will have the precise function of looking to the interrelation of subjects and their organized activities as such, and this not to any particular purpose except insofar as it is a help to their overall order. This is why the purpose of government was called "a common good."

All of this, of course, presupposes that human freedom and consequently human creativity are widespread and legitimate factors in human society. The purpose of government, therefore, is the good of this order, the good of actual people and actual groups of people interacting on one another in concrete life. The function of government is to choose and to decide among existing, possible alternatives, which set of rules, which public policy, which political outlook can best achieve and define the good of this or that particular people. In this sense, government makes visible to a people what they are, because it embodies those choices they have in fact made or allowed in their name. The level of government, however, is such that it deals with real subjects and with real governments besides itself. In such a context, both internally and externally, there can and, as history clearly records, do arise situations in which the alternatives are so injurious that none of them seems permissible. Yet, the very nature of government and of human life is such that it must continue, choices must be made even in the face of the most anguishing alternatives.

In this context and on these hypotheses, then, we can attempt some answer to the original question about the conditions of ethical choice in politics. The issue is important because it provides a principle which prevents man from ethically believing it morally good to abandon a world, which for man is ultimately the political world, in which evil alternatives do exist. Here, it is not intended to deny the right to emigrate or the right to escape from absolutist states when possible, but to delineate the objective condition that remains. The positive side of this ethical problem is relatively simple. That is, a politically ethical decision should select alternatives that are good and workable whenever this is possible. The more negative side of this question can be stated in this way: The ethically good choice is the judgment of the political authority in favor of that alternative which seems to involve the lesser evil in a context which attempts to alleviate it or minimize it. The paradox of this political fact is that the political choice of an admitted evil can be ethically good as a choice because, to state the principle briefly, a greater evil is prevented by allowing the lesser one, when that is prudentially the only way open to the political leaders.

In politics, even though most choices are for the most part good, still there are probably few complex choices which do not involve some degree of derangement or disorder which contribute to some presence of evil consequences. Yet, what is suggested here is that the political choice is a moral choice; the political order is not intrinsically corrupt because of its involvement with actual evil, except in the case of the government which chooses it positively and wants to promote it actively. The reason that the political order is not corrupt is that the nature of the political complexus, what it is in itself, must take all things that really exist into account, among these will be some degree of evil in human society. In other words, the choice to ignore the presence of real evil is politically and morally fatal. On the other hand, the choice to allow the lesser evil, which is what a political choice can involve, will not, *ipso facto*, prevent the lesser evil that must be allowed from having its bad effects. These effects will sooner or later have to be faced politically. And they will usually be used as a sign indicating corruption on the part of those who allowed them in the first place.

On the international level especially, then, this is particularly important and tragic simply because the complexity and difficulty caused by evil are so cumbersome to comprehend and control. Indeed, it seems possible to maintain legitimately, by virtue of the expansion of evil caused by its lack, that a real governmental authority on a world level is now imperative. We can argue that there is a relation between the growth of evil and the lack of government in the world, though it still may be argued, in view of other factors, that a legitimate choice exists to delay its full implementation. Furthermore, it is possible to fear that the organization of the world against human dignity on a world scale is precisely the greatest potential secular evil the human race can face.[9]

The Problem of Finitude

Nevertheless, while there is such a reality— or more exactly, such a lack of reality—known as evil present in the world caused through human choice against human values, and while it is true that this has a profoundly disrupting effect on the relations of men and nations, still by no means can it be implied that everything disorderly is directly the result of human moral evil. It is tempting to believe this, as it does make the world much less complex if we can attribute the vast disorder we see in national and international life to evil. It would justify our guilt and our effort to find a political evil in every shortcoming. In contrast to the category of evil, however, it is well to pay some attention to the category of finiteness. The two, evil and finiteness, are not unrelated. Indeed, the coexistence of the possibility of both evil and finiteness is perhaps the profoundest of philosophical problems.[10] This is really the problem on a metaphysical level of whether anything good which is not God can exist simultaneously with him.[11]

The point, however, is that finiteness, which is itself a good, is also responsible for much of the disorder in the world, as well as for much of the good. We cannot equate evil and disorder without further qualifications. This is another way of saying that man has a real task in the world itself, that the existence of God does not obviate the existence of man. Man's place and task in the world are, therefore, significant. They involve essentially the eradication of the cruder limits of finiteness by knowledge and experience. The world is there to be put in order by man.[12] This is the primary political and social mission of the race precisely as the mortals who will pass through the world. This means too that man is dignified by God precisely by not having been given everything in a complete form. A good deal of the inflexibility and difficulty we experience, then, is due to the fact that man only slowly learns to attack the real problems before him because he it is who must learn to cope with his own life on Earth. One generation begins to solve the problems the previous age suffered under.

Yet, a new generation may forget or ignore the lessons of the previous ages. There is no necessary progress. And this is why the study of history is always fruitful, for men before our time really did know things, things we may well not know.

The limits of finitude, consequently, are expanded by labor and patience, by knowledge and memory. At this point, one further theological observation is worth making. If a man thinks that all of the suffering and disorder in the world are due, with no further qualification, to human evil and not also to finiteness, then he will end up logically by calling the human condition, as such, evil. He will probably even rebel at being a man at all since that involves, in part, the recognition of finiteness as a good, not an absolute good, but a good nonetheless. Indeed, I think, a good part of the political turmoil in recent years has been the result of precisely this intellectual confusion, a point we shall pursue in the following chapter.

The Common Mission of Man

In concluding these initial remarks on just how much and why we can grant anything to politics, some lines of thought in contemporary theology which have general pertinence to politics are worth reflection. The recognition of a common mission of man on Earth is the primary ethical and religious imperative that we do have as a race. The pursuit of this mission provides in theory the basic possibility for reconciling the powerful forces that can wreck or enrich the life of man on this planet. But as this is such a central question, it is not only the locus for the greatest hope but for the greatest controversy and struggle. Thus, it is also true that politics is not our highest good as such. It is a value, a high value, but not the very highest, so that politics itself stands under the judgment of human transcendent vocation and destiny, something that relativizes all politics.[13]

Christian theology has long been used for the valuable distinction between grace and nature.[14] The general purpose of this distinction was to clarify the levels of human and religious destiny. The level of creation was considered to refer to natural cosmic, planetary, and human modes of activity. These modes were considered to be good—adequate for man but not the highest destiny to which he might be called. The supernatural level referred to the special call of the trinitarian God to associate man in God's eternal life. The means to achieve this destiny were provided by the reality of Christ. By virtue of this distinction, Christians have religiously felt able to meet with men of all faiths on a common temporal ground. The so-called natural order was considered to be open to human reason. Thus, following the principle that grace builds on nature, it has been long held that the Christian effort in the natural order was at least contributory in some preliminary sense to Christian belief. The Christian was thus not religiously free to ignore the demands of this Earth, even though these demands were not everything. On the other hand, to make the accomplishment of the earthly mission itself to be what religion or ideology was primarily about was seen to be idolatry, for it was possible to make the organization of the Earth to be the ultimate reality. And this was the ultimate deviation from the Christian God.

For various reasons which Christian theology itself considered, the distinction between grace and nature has come to be understood in a different way. Formerly, it was sometimes held, though the Church never officially taught this, that the unbaptized were in the "natural" order, while the baptized were in the "supernatural" order. There was a way of speaking which talked of man's natural acts and of his supernatural acts as apparently separate. It is better to say, however, that there is not now and never was in our actual history a "purely" natural order, although a natural order was theoretically possible in another kind of creation open to God's possibilities. In this present order of creation, the whole race of men in Adam from the beginning is called to eternal, trinitarian life. This is, in a way, the classical Augustinian view that the supernatural is now what is "natural" to this particular race of men, that there is, ultimately, only the City of God or the City of Man.

The consequences of this way of looking at things are significant for the Christian. In Christian theory, a man's eternal status is determined primarily by his personal response to the divine call. But this call comes to man in his finiteness and sin, in the context of his temporal life and task. This is precisely where the divine and the natural meet in Christian thought. Man is a creature who is a *tabula rasa* in the beginning. He knows through his contact with the Earth, through his material needs and encounters. Through his experience with the Earth, through his physical contact with it, he learns to know others, to realize that of all the things he experiences, persons are the most important. These are the beings who respond to his own call, whom he learns to work with, to be with, to love. The Christian person's response to God is judged, as it is indicated in Matthew and John, by his relations with his brothers. All men belong together. They all have the common heritage in the face of their finiteness, the heritage of increasing and subduing the Earth, so that the vocation to the Earth in the light of an ultimate destiny is a major and determining factor in their lives. Man was not given everything from the beginning because what he actually did with the Earth made a real difference to himself and to his brothers.

All of this suggests, in other words, that the mission of man on Earth, even though it is not itself to be confused with Eternal Life, has ultimate consequences through each personal life. Thus, no effort to foster value is, in itself, apart from the divine purposes for men. This divine purpose, ultimately, is the intention of associating man with God in realizing the destiny of the terrestrial world and through that destiny to realize the relation of men to one another and to God. Christianity has never believed that men could give themselves their ultimate destiny.[15] But it has believed that in the acceptance of the gift that has been offered, there would be a renewed vitality even in the temporal order. Men cannot, then, ignore or escape their ultimate destiny. They must finally choose, which means that the free choice to refuse the kind of world envisioned by God in his natural and divine law would also have consequences in the public order. The effort to make the world to be human can thus have an anti-theist sense.

Participation in programs to transform the Earth for the physical, cultural, and spiritual benefit of man is a part of the human task and no person or nation can avoid it, provided the concept of man on which it is based is valid. There is a commonly agreed basis on which men from the various cultures and religions and nations can act, assuming this be not itself a denial of any further destiny to man.[16] The effect of Christianity on the political order, then, consists in both recognizing what is and what is not potential for man, in confronting evil and finiteness within a common Earth. But it is also a radical appreciation of the consequences of freedom, the possibility of creating a world for or against man and God. The common mission of man to Earth is not itself beatitude, even though it is serious and the arena of much of our relationship with God.

Men do reach God outside political orders, which do not absolutely confine them. The transcendent itself defines and limits politics. In a sense, the ultimate effect of Christianity on politics is a limiting one, one that frees man by removing from politics what politics cannot deliver. In this way, politics is left to be politics and not a substitute religion. At the same time, Christianity accepts the importance of the world and its betterment as a religious element in the destiny of each person. In other words, at its orthodox best, it avoids both the temptation to make politics and its earthly destiny an absolute and the opposite one of reducing the meaning of the world to a mere nothing. We are left with a world that is important and worthwhile, then, without having to make it everything.

Footnotes:

[1] Cf. H. Deane, *The Political and Social Ideas of St. Augustine,* New York, Columbia, 1963; Reinhold Niebuhr, "Augustine's Political Realism," in *Perspectives on Political Philosophy,* J. Downton, Editor, New York, Holt, 1971, pp. 243-57.

[2] Russell Kirk, "The Genius of Christianity," *The Roots of American Order*, LaSalle, Illinois, Open Court, 1974, pp. 147-48.

[3] Cf. Josef Pieper, *Scholasticism*, New York, McGraw-Hill, 1960; *The Silence of St. Thomas*, Regnery, 1957.

[4] Cf. Robert Nisbet, *History of the Idea of Progress*, New York, Basic, 1980; J. B. Bury, *The Idea of Progress*, New York, Dover, 1932.

[5] Ivan Illich, *Tools for Conviviality*, New York, Harper, 1971.

[6] Cf. the author's "On the Scientific Eradication of Evil," *Communio*, Summer, 1979, pp. 157-72; "Displacing Damnation: The Neglect of Hell in Political Theory," *The Thomist*, January, 1980, pp. 27-44.

[7] Cf. Yves Simon, *The Philosophy of Democratic Government*, Chicago, University of Chicago Press, 1951, Chapter I. Cf. also the author's "The Necessity of Government," *The Commonweal*, November 26, 1954, pp. 215-17; "Government without Bother," *Thought*, Summer, 1961, pp. 277-88.

[8] St. Thomas, I-II, 91, 4.

[9] Cf. Oscar Cullmann, *The State in the New Testament*, New York, Scribner's, 1956, Chapter 4. Cf. also following chapter.

[10] Cf. the author's *Redeeming the Time*, New York, Sheed and Ward, 1968.

[11] Cf. footnote # 6. Cf. also the author's "The Rediscovery of Metaphysics," *Divinitas*, Rome, # 2, 1979, pp. 200-19.

[12] Cf. the author's "The Cosmos and Christianity," in *Redeeming the Time, ibid.*, Chapter 4.

[13] The statement of John Paul II on the clergy and politics in 1980 falls within the liberal tradition of Christianity of acknowledging a difference of vocation and goal of the priest and the politician.

[14] Cf. Etienne Gilson, *Reason and Revelation in the Middle Ages*, New York, Scribner's, 1966; Henri de Lubac, *The Mystery of the Supernatural*, Herder, 1967; Frederick D. Wilhelmsen, "Faith and Reason," *The Modern Age*, Winter, 1979, pp. 25-32; E. L. Mascall, *The Christian Universe*, London, Darton, 1966.

[15] Cf. J. M. Bochenski, "Man," *Philosophy—an Introduction*, New York, Harper Torchbooks, 1972, pp. 80-82.

[16] Cf. Jacques Maritain, *Man and the State*, Chicago, University of Chicago Press, 1952, Chapter V. Cf. below, Chapter 8.

CHAPTER IV

Atheism and Politics

Religion is only the illusory sun about which man revolves so long as he does not revolve about himself. It is the task of history, therefore, once the other world of truth has vanished, to establish the truth of this world.... The criticism of heaven is transformed into the criticism of Earth, the criticism of religion into the criticism of politics.

—*Karl Marx, "Critique of Hegel's Philosophy of Right,"* in The Marx-Engels Reader, *New York, Norton, 1978, p. 12.*

During the immediate post-World War II years, the major task of Christianity was often looked upon as finding for itself a justification to be involved in the world. This justification was largely hammered out, in Catholic circles, in *Mater et Magistra, Pacem in Terris,* in the Church in the Modern World and Religious Liberty Documents of Vatican II, in *Populorum Progressio* and *Octogesima Adveniens.* There has been, however, a concerted effort to attack the central

Christian judgment that the world itself is a passing place, not of ultimate importance, a place wherein certain basic divine traces and values are seen to be operative and even normative. There has been, then, an effort to identify politics and atheism. From a Christian point of view, what are we to make of this? Socrates, we pointed out earlier, was called an "atheist," as likewise were the first Christians, because they would not worship the Roman gods. Why is it now that atheism in the form of a political movement to refashion the world can be so attractive to many Christians, particularly to many intellectuals, especially those who do not actually have to live under any atheist regime? This is, I think, the darker side of the principles which were discussed in the previous chapter, namely, that human freedom does allow a political world to be constructed, one which would be against the basic values contained in human nature and in revelation. Neither historically nor philosophically do I think we can long deny this possibility, so that some attention must be given to it in any consideration of Christianity and politics.

Among certain strands of cultural thought in recent years, then, it has become almost obligatory to assume that atheism is the primary and necessary result of a presumed Christian "failure" to produce a "just" social order of this world. Christianity, as I have suggested before, does believe in and feel itself obligated to work for a just and abundant public order in the nations and the world. But atheism, in this curious view of its origins in a Christian failure, has itself essentially political origins. Furthermore, it is presumed that the public order atheism does produce, when it is itself in power, is in fact "human."

Thus, there is no need for religion or, more likely, there is clearly need to remove its influence as a prerequisite to civil peace and good. Therefore, we read that someone like the late Mao Tse-tung eliminated poverty and exploitation in forty years, but what have Christians done in two thousand? The implied pragmatism sanctioned in such an affirmation, aside from its intrinsic ideology, of course, is rarely recognized. Nor is there any real untangling of the complexities of actual history or reflection on the means by which such marvelous results were achieved in China. Only for the Christian, apparently, are the means and ends problems of principle and not of tactics. Atheism, it is suggested, is to be judged by economic and political "development." The proof of its truth is its "success," defined by the goals it sets itself.

Or else we may be told, with even less historical accuracy, that the reason people are atheists is because Christians—who are unaccountably pictured to be totally responsible for what happened in the European and colonial past—have not practiced what they professed to preach. Atheists, it is even darkly hinted, are busily building a perfectly human and humane world order. Christians have lost their chance in a kind of holy ideological war, so that the only thing left for them to do is join forces with the atheists to better this world. Chesterton's famous aphorism that "Christianity has not been tried and found wanting but tried and found difficult," is hardly even understood. So we should either further secularize Christian doctrine, so that Christianity really means only what the atheist means, or so spiritualize the Christian faith that it is a totally abstract, other-worldly, private phenomenon. Neither of these extremes, of course, is the central Christian tradition. Further, in admitting that atheists *can* have good will, it is often concluded that they all, especially the most powerful, in fact *do* have good will, so that the main task we have is a kind of rational dialogue rather than a penetrating and critical analysis of what atheists are, in truth, doing when they are in control. Somehow, only Christians are permitted the privilege of sinning against their own light. Paradoxically, Christianity is the only faith or philosophy that has an adequate analysis of how men can in fact go contrary to what they profess to believe.

That Christians individually, even rather often, do not do as they ought is, of course, a proposition of the Christian faith itself. In this, we are always reminded of Paul's other law in our members drawing us to what we would not do. Atheists of whatever variety, on the contrary, who do not "do" what they ought according to their own tenets, are exempt from this Christian problem. In other words, atheism is precisely the claim to be able to do whatever one wants or must because man gives himself his own law and his own being. Seen collectively, this means that the atheist state cannot sin against its own light such that it must defend its empirical record against obvious failures and violations by re-writing history, by finding someone else at fault —some exploiter or some traitor within its own ranks. Self-confession in the atheist tradition is either impossible because there is no sense in confessing to oneself or coerced in order to keep the public record of political purity in-tact. The famous anxieties in, say, *Darkness at Noon*, on this point, should not be forgotten.

In confronting the atheist, then, Christianity makes two rather infuriating claims: The first is that there will be no human, decent, honorable public order without faith, even though, as we suggested previously, the public order is largely a matter of reason. John XXIII put it as well as anyone in *Mater et Magistra:* "No folly is more characteristic of this modern era than the absurd attempt to reconstruct a solid and prosperous temporal order while prescinding from God, the only foundation on which it can endure" (no. 217). The second is that Christianity is really not about worldly politics and order as its direct and principle concern. And this ultimate "arrogance" and simultaneous "unconcern" of Christians are what perplexes the atheist most about believers, because it is seen as a denigration of man and the world, a disbelief in human powers. When these latter are defined as "all there is," faith will seem like a horror to the atheist, who can only operate at a very low level of reflection, as Professor Schumacher brilliantly pointed out.[1]

The Christian Possibility of Unbelief

However, the Christian tradition of "See how they love one another" as a motive of astonishment for believing—since it is not normal even to atheists that men so love—must also leave us wondering about what happens when we see believers who do not love one another. "See how they shove one another," one wag once put it. Atheism is, in a way, an attempt to find a real substitute for Christian love as a cohesive force in society. The human tendency to blame others for our own faults in this regard, to project our guilt on others, is as old as the story of Adam and Eve.[2] "The man replied, 'It was the woman you put with me....' The woman replied, 'The serpent tempted me...' " (*Genesis* 3:12-13). Yet, before we go too far in assigning unbelief to the faults of believers or to the honesty of unbelievers, we cannot forget that Scripture itself, especially the *Gospel of John,* reveals another context which must make us seriously hesitate in this popular assigning of the cause of atheism principally to the failure of Christians. Paradoxically, we can also argue, even with more cogency, that the major cause of atheism may well be precisely the *virtue,* the *truth* found in belief and faith. The unsettling motive not to believe, as Christ intimated in his Last Discourse, was the very content and context of his coming and message—"If I had not come, you would have had no sin..." (15:22).

Consequently, throughout the events and conversations in the middle chapters of *John,* Christ's words and actions are met with both unbelief—"Though they had been present when he gave so many signs, they did not believe in them..." (12:37)—and also belief. Sometimes, the signs did result in faith, as with the Samaritans. Yet, after the multiplication of the loaves·and fishes, after they wanted to make Jesus king because of this satisfaction of human needs (6:15), Jesus went on to question the disciples' motives for faith: "You are not looking for me because you have seen the signs but because you had all the bread you wanted to eat" (6:26). So too in Capharnaum, after he spoke of the Spirit who gives life, Jesus said, " 'But there are some among you who do not believe.' For Jesus knew from the outset those who did not believe....

After this, many of his disciples left him and stopped going with him..." (6:64-66).

This constant theme recognized that belief is not coerced and that the signs of God can be received by a choice against God. This is mindful too of the troubling passage in *Matthew,* where Jesus cured the man with the withered hand before some Pharisees. The very next passage was: "At this, the Pharisees went out and began to plot against him, discussing how to destroy him" (12:9-14). Such passages leave little room for naiveté in these matters. Such passages too are not technically about "atheists," but about theists who refuse to believe that Jesus is the Messiah. However, they do serve to correct any innocent notion that unbelief *must* be caused by aberration in the believer alone. Atheism is always choice and can be a choice against the good, especially the kind of good that man is from the hand of God, from the kind of good by which man has been redeemed.

The Atheist Project

Modern atheism has become actively political. We should not, I think, miss the profound import of this. Atheism has not always been political or activist or zealous. Indeed, most of the classical atheists believe that a little religion was useful in controlling the masses. It kept them quiet. But the very evolution of modern thought has seen atheism become militant, to insist that it *must* be believed. Atheism has felt the need to impose its views, to forbid competing visions. There is no doubt, as Paul Hazard pointed out in a striking passage, that the path to atheism led through the logical inadequacies of modern philosophies, which in their turn were substitutes and secular imitations of Christianity. At bottom, there is something very Christian about modern atheism, even in its unbelief. At the end of the 18th Century, Hazard wrote of its conditions:

> Not only, now, was Christianity rent asunder; it began to dissolve. All that remained was a herd that looked for happiness in this mortal life, and with no very high standards of happiness at that. It was now no more to them than worldly well-being, natural comforts and, sometimes, just pleasure. They were not even atheists, for that would have meant they denied something. They were now, just nothing, nothing at all. It was everyone according to his conscience, and conscience there was none.

> Over and above the duties imposed upon them by the fact that they were part of society, they were not conscious of any others. All they thought of now were not duties, but rights. Tens of thousands, hundreds of thousands, millions... lost all notion of the Divine, whether as a starting point or as a goal.[3]

The major project for atheism in the 19th Century was to discover a meaning to history, in man himself, that would replace the transcendental meaning embodied in religion. And in an evolution from Rousseau, to Hegel, Feuerbach, and Marx, such a project was found, "the humanization of man and the socialization of nature" so that the project of politics was to create the man totally dependent, quite literally, upon himself alone.

The Christian Reaction

For the Christian, however, it is often difficult to take the modern atheist seriously. There is something healthy in this, in a way. Christianity means nothing if it does not mean man's own inability to create and save himself and this world. Men have real responsibility and real knowledge, but these arise primarily because there are already order and value in things and in others. Christianity is chronically anti-Pelagian, unable to conceive a totally man-made, man-oriented universe, except as something fundamentally anti-human. This enables the Christian to let go, not to think all is lost because all is not achieved. While the Christian believes in an ultimate happiness, he does not think it must be achieved in this world so that persons are more important than the worldly human task. They are not just instruments to some future society. Thus, it is no tragedy that our politics are so unsatisfying, for Christians should be rather surprised that politics should satisfy them. Indeed, the freedom of politics—its metaphysical freedom—is precisely its incapacity to solve man's most intimate and ultimate needs and goals. But atheism does not have this liberty. Rather, it must produce—produce something it cannot deliver. Atheism, for all its lofty philosophy, is strangely pragmatic. The production of a "better" society is the only value it can discover. When it takes control, it must forbid apparently any proof that its goal is not being achieved. Intellectually, it is no accident that the principal alternative to the City of God has come to be the City of Man.

The Christian can—indeed, must—admit that man does not control the sources either of grace or of nature. He knows and receives what he does not make—he can "make" and does make things, but he does not "make" himself. This means that man is free to discover that "man did not make himself to be man," as Aristotle said. For the atheist, man makes himself to be man— by his labor for the marxist. To be man, then, is, in the atheist sense, actively to remove those very institutions, values, and realities that do *not* arise from a definably human origin. Marx, in a powerful statement, said he wanted the eye and the ear even to be "human," so that everything we saw, tasted, heard, and touched with our senses revealed only man. The "revolution," the very act of removing divine law and natural institutions, is an act of conquest *for* man.

Perhaps, for Christianity, it is better not to speak of "man" or "humanity" or even "persons" as some kind of neuter collective, but rather of John, Paul, and Mary in this context. The Word Became Flesh—and this means the Word was Jesus. Jesus is Himself, the Son of God, not John, Paul, or Mary. Each person has his own autonomy. The City of God, of which Augustine spoke, was composed, not of abstract concepts, but of individual persons, with names and tangible lives, each with his own sex, history, will, intelligence. There is an irreducible absoluteness in the person that cannot be comprehended by pure thought, nor is it the result of human labor or even natural evolution. Every person is "called" to be, to be only him or herself. Everyone is a mystery even unto himself. Christian thought cannot help but think of precisely each humanly unique person who has an opening also unto the world, to himself, to his fellows, to God. His happiness is not "collective." It must bear on him in his own person. So only persons with names like John or Mary can be and be happy or sad.

The Atheist World

Atheism, on the contrary, cannot admit a cause of uniqueness outside man himself. Marx, in a memorable passage, wrote:

A man who lives by the grace of another regards himself as a dependent being. But I live completely by the grace of another if I owe him not only the sustenance of my life but if he has, moreover, created my life....

The Creation is therefore an idea very difficult to dislodge from popular conscienceness.... The creation of the Earth has received a mighty blow from geogeny—i.e., from the science which presents the formation of the Earth, the coming to be of the Earth, as a process, as a self-generation. *Generatio aequivoca* (spontaneous generation) is the only practical refutation of the theory of creation.[4]

Needless to say, this naive dependence on a dubious theory of spontaneous generation puts marxism on a very unsteady scientific basis. But it also serves to emphasize that the reception of our being from another, the being a "dependent being," may well be the only way to discover what we are, as Christianity has always held.[5]

The denial of Creation posits this production of ourselves as a problem. We presuppose nothing so that our collective work, being only a human product, results in beings who owe nothing outside themselves. The suspicion that there might, indeed, be more to reality than man was what caused Marx to try to remove any natural institutions—state, property, family— that were not subject to man's own control. Aristotle had said that if man were the highest being, politics would be the highest science. And it would be the "science" of making man to be man, and thus to define his good, the good that can have no outside check from creation. Man could not object then to what he made himself to be. He would be what is to be.

Politics, then, would become the creation of man and his own happiness, subject only to his own definition and action. The kind of being formed by those totally controlling the state would be *ipso facto* "human," because it owed no further allegiance except to man himself. Marx, indeed, seems even to have held that we quite literally share in the same human being—the "generic being"—in some sense so that individually we possess all there is, all we have made. Again this is a kind of Christian heaven without either God or even our own unique type of personalities. What is thus lacking is precisely a notion of community that can bear both diverse personalities and their common relationship to one another.

All of this, of course, is rather heady stuff. Marx would seem strangely out-of-date were his influence not so widespread today as a result of the exercise of political power. Yet, we deceive ourselves when we underestimate the attraction of marxism to many contemporaries. Furthermore, all we have to do is examine carefully the astonishing programs trying to be effected in, say, Cambodia, Vietnam, China, and in parts of Africa and Central America, to see how marxism guides political perspectives. Christians instinctively believe that there are as many doubters in atheist villages as there are in Christian ones. No doubt this is true. In fact, Solzhenitsyn frankly states that no one in Russia believes in marxism as a truth or a faith, and marxism is not the only form of political atheism. I once asked an English journalist who had recently returned from several years in Moscow, if Solzhenitsyn's observations were substantially correct. He said he believed they were. This leaves us in an anomalous position. The true believers in marxist atheism today, perhaps aside from the rulers of certain countries, are most often those who do not live in an atheist society.[6]

Be that as it may, the contemporary success of marxism as an atheist politics has been its ability to commandeer the idea of building a totally just society on this Earth, this as the highest ethical mission of man, with no further qualification. In this sense, it is a kind of heretical millennarism. That, on the contrary, the principal cause of underdevelopment today, of why the poor are not actually better off and freer than they are, is probably the general belief that "socialism" of some untried form will solve our problems; this is a fact that few leaders, religious and civil, seem to grasp.[7] Thus, we see "poverty" translated into ecology and reduced or forced control of consumption, "chastity" becomes restricted to mean no or little birth, "obedience" becomes coerced mobilization for quick development according to ideological norms. It is odd how in giving up Christianity, the various forms of modern atheism bring its values back in a distorted form.

The Ecological Version

We should be alive, also, to the growing struggle between the marxist form of atheism which believes in the economic and political restructuring of human nature and society over against the bio-conservationist form which wants to restructure man from the inside of his very body, again according to some pattern of "man" conceived norm that is not dependent on any prior "intelligence" in the original creation of the human person. This is why more and more humans are becoming defined as non-human—the very young, the very deformed, the very sick, the very old. The reason for this is that there is nothing absolute in man except the good of his on-going species. Christianity holds, of course, that there is something wrong with man, with John, Paul, and Mary. We are, in a way, witnessing the end of 18th Century optimism and seeing the re-emergence of a secular form of original sin. A "new Adam," a new "man," a new "heaven and earth" are indeed Judaeo-Christian terms, ones that the tradition has recognized need the most precise definition. Yet, such ideas in their "atheistic" formulations have largely come to predominate in the public order as to what we must be about.

This means, I think, that the form of public discourse we had hoped would typify the "mature" modern world—the dialogue of men of good will—is probably no longer the actual context of our future. This does not mean that we cannot or ought not to "dialogue" even with men of "bad" will. Nor does it mean a clear black and white situation. But neither can we ignore the lessons from our scriptural and historical traditions that warn us to know what disbelief can do when it is active in its efforts to establish its position as the only publicly permitted one.[8] The atheist presence in politics is now so pervasive that the object of politics will largely center about removing precisely any distinctively Christian—and therefore non-man-made—elements from the public and private orders. A major sign of this will be, in western societies at least, the legitimization as legal and "human" precisely those actions defined by Paul in *Romans* as vices. Already, it is becoming less and less politically possible to give a Christian definition of "vice," except when formulated in ideological terms about social structures. The import of this should not be lost, however, for in allowing that vices be called "good" in the public order, we are implicitly and politically removing the natural, that is, the non-man-made, norms from creation. We act to make good what is not naturally good. And we enforce this as a public norm.[9]

The Christian has already lost, throughout a good part of the world, any right to public existence. In China, Vietnam, Cambodia, Cuba, he does not even seem to have the right to his own thoughts. Elsewhere, he is driven underground or, if above ground, strictly controlled, as in most Muslim countries. The optimistic notions of Vatican II about religious liberty are largely dead letters for Christians in too many areas. The problem during the next years, I suspect, will largely consist in a gradual denial of those specifically Christian truths that are not shared, even in word, by all men. There will not just be the ignoring of the political relevance of Christian truths, but the active attempt to remove their political consequences. These will be legally held to be directly inimical to the kind of self-made man, enforced on the public by law and propaganda.

Faith as Its Own Guide

The reaction of Christians to all of this, it seems, should not be to transform Christianity into a pale imitation of what opposes it. The present Pope appears to understand the dangers of this kind of a temptation. That is why he wants Christians clear on the real nature of religious and clerical life, how it is not a counter-politics.

Christianity has its own validity, its own way of looking at the world and its projects.[10] That much of Christian political philosophy comes from what is called "nature" should not lead us to expect that everyone will agree with it. Christianity, moreover, does not believe that God *cannot* come, cannot act among men unless they *first* establish a just society. The historical action of God has generally been—by definition, almost— towards unjust men within disordered societies, for there are, as Socrates saw, no other kinds.

Roger Heckel put it well:

> It has become a slogan to affirm that Jesus died because he resolutely opposed the injustices of Roman and Jewish religious and political authorities. Without denying the partial truth of this affirmation, it is at least as true to note that he died because he deceived the hopes of the people and by this rendered possible the exploitation of their spite against him. But the ultimate cause of his death is not human, it came from a divine love which freely delivered itself to the end....
>
> The liberation of Jesus did not await, as a necessary precondition, the freedom from the other servitudes (economic, political, religious, psychological, cultural).... The faith increases with its own rhythm.... There is no necessary and simple parallelism nor direct proportional relation between the progress of faith and progress in other liberations.[11]

This is why Christianity behaves according to and acts upon its own sources, with its own methods and legitimacy, for its own goals and values. God's spirit breathes as it will—and also in unjust societies. Jesus' message is the glory of the Father, the transcendent life given to each person to share the life of the Trinity. Consequently, it is not something that can be politically confined or defined.

Christianity, then, is not necessarily opposed to a "perfect"—or at least, a more perfect—earthly kingdom. What it is sure of is that this happy result is not its direct mission or goal. It is sure that most men who have ever lived have not lived in such a blissful, perfect system. Further, the creation of this system does not justify sacrificing the present lives of men, with their own values and worth. In being loyal first to the Kingdom of God, all this may be added, graced. If we return to the *Gospel of John* once more, we again see the remarkable dimension in which it was written:

> I tell you solemnly, you are not looking for me because you have seen the signs but because you had all the bread you wanted to eat. Do not work for bread that cannot last but work for the food that endures to eternal life.... Now the will of him who sent me is that I should lose nothing of all that he has given to me, and that I should raise it up on the last day. Yes, it is my Father's will that whoever sees the Son and believes in him shall have eternal life and that I shall raise him up on the last day (6:32-37; 39-40).

Now, in the context of atheism and politics, these are powerful words, for they recognize not only the limits of bread but that its very abundance may be used against God. Jesus' sign was not accepted in the way he intended, but it was seen rather as a move for a good social order wherein men have free bread.

Furthermore, the first thing we were to do was not a political, but a religious act. The project of the perfect kingdom will be achieved—the raising up on the last day—but not by us.[12] This eternal life shall reach each person in his mysterious uniqueness—to John, Paul, and Mary, to Shakespeare's "which can say more than this rich praise.../that thou alone art thou." The contemporary joining of politics and atheism, then, has forced us to reflect upon the uniqueness of theism in its orthodoxy—a theism we also believe to be precisely a humanism, an incarnation, a condition of being first loved, then loving. Consequently, on account of this, we do not merely or even mainly have a "justice" or a man-made world. Christian humanism, at all points, accepts creation and *re*-creation.[13] Our generation is not "spontaneous," but chosen.

Christianity accepts, contrary to a Marx, that the sun about which it revolves is *not* man himself. Therefore, man—John, Paul, and Mary —is free, precisely from himself to be himself. The ultimate and best argument against atheism remains the one that suspects man in his individual personhood, even in his fallenness, is better than "self-made."[14] The ultimate loneliness, the ultimate alienation is from himself as something already given to him. And politics is thus not an atheism because it does not make man to be man. That man can be better than he seems is a proposition intrinsic to the faith, to its notion of human freedom. That man can "create" something better than what it is already to be a man, this is despair, despair of what and who we already are—John, Paul, and Mary.

The criticism of theology is transformed into the criticism of politics—Marx was right. What atheism has taught us is that without classic theology to check politics, what disappears is precisely man as we have known him. What the New Testament teaches in this regard is that God is not restricted to our politics because God is neither an "atheist" nor a politician, if it can be put in that way. That is, nothing of what is given to Christ will be lost because faith does not depend upon our works, our making ourselves to be human. And in understanding this, we can, as we shall see in the next chapter, know how the whole cosmos has meaning for us, that other side of the atheist human enterprise that seeks to subsume even nature into itself.

The Polish marxist philosopher, Adam Schaff, ended his book, *A Philosophy of Man,* with these words: "Independent of conscious choice, under the pressure of the needs of life and the longing for happiness, the words of the good poet are being translated into all languages: 'We want on Earth a happy life.' "[15] The New Testament says rather, "Seek ye first the Kingdom of God and all this shall be added to you." This is indeed the difference between atheism and Christianity in politics.

Footnotes:

[1] Cf. E. F. Schumacher, *A Guide for the Perplexed,* New York, Harper Colophon, 1977.

[2] Cf. Dale Vree, " 'Stripped Clean': The Berrigans and the Politics of Guilt and Martyrdom," *Ethics,* July, 1975, pp. 271-87.

[3] Paul Hazard, *European Thought in the 18th Century,* New York, Meridian, 1963, p. 434.

[4] Karl Marx, "Economic and Philosophic Manuscripts of 1844," *The Marx-Engels Reader,* R. Tucker, Editor, New York, Norton, 1972, p. 12.

On this whole issue of creation, cf. S. Jaki, *The Road of Science and the Ways of God,* Chicago, University of Chicago Press, 1978; Josef Pieper, *The Silence of St. Thomas,* Chicago, Regnery, 1957; "The Origin of the Universe," *The Economist,* London, April 12, 1980, pp. 67-71.

[5] Cf. Frederick D. Wilhelmsen, "The Christian Understanding of Being," *The Intercollegiate Review,* Winter-Spring, 1978, pp. 87-94.

[6] "As growling bulldozers and hammering soldiers constructed a tent city around them, hundreds of Cuban refugees celebrated an emotion-filled Roman Catholic mass today, singing 'Glory, glory hallelujah' and shouting, 'Long live free Cuba.' "

"For many of these children of the revolution, the religious service held in a small sun-baked stadium (in Florida) was the first they had ever attended." *The Washington Post,* May 5, 1980.

[7] Cf. below, Chapters 6 and 7.

[8] Cf. the author's "The Missing Element in Catholic Social Thought," *Social Survey,* Melbourne, July, 1975, pp. 165-71.

⁹ Cf. Joseph Sobran, *Less Catholic than the Pope?* New York, 1979.

¹⁰ Cf. John Paul II, Address of January 28, 1979, at Puebla.

¹¹ Roger Heckel, "Foi et Justice: Théologique, Magistère, Spiritualité," *Fides et Justitia,* Roma, 1976, pp. 48-49.

¹² Cf. Eric Mascall, *Theology and the Future,* New York, Morehouse-Barlow, 1968.

¹³ Cf. Jacques Maritain, "Christian Humanism," *The Social and Political Philosophy of Jacques Maritain,* Notre Dame, University of Notre Dame Press, 1976, pp. 155-70.

¹⁴ Cf. the author's *The Praise of 'Sons of Bitches': On the Worship of God by Fallen Men,* Slough, England, St. Paul Publications, 1978.

¹⁵ Adam Schaff, *A Philosophy of Man,* J. Lindsay, Trans., New York, Monthly Review Press, 1963, p. 139.

CHAPTER V

On Taking Possession of the Whole Universe

The message which the Bishop of Hippo addressed to men is to the effect that the whole world, from its beginning until its final term, has as its unique end the constitution of a holy Society, in view of which everything has been made, even the universe itself.

—*Etiénne Gilson, Introduction to Augustine's* The City of God, *Doubleday Image, 1958, p. 21.*

According to modern physics, the universe began with a big bang, in which space and matter made a sudden explosive appearance—from literally nothing. There was a moment when all the material eventually used to create every star and galaxy could have been held in the palm of an infinitely small hand.

—*"The Origin of the Universe," The Economist, London, April 12, 1980, p. 87.*

Christian political philosophy has been both denied and affirmed, as we have previously suggested. Somehow, it contains within itself a vision of the world, yet its major thrust is to tell us that the world is insufficient, of little importance in comparison with the life of God offered to men in the Trinity.[1] The ordering of the world is not to be ignored, however, as the atheist challenge incites us to recognize. For the very life of God has "naturally," as it were, the effect of peace and harmony among men, never forgetting that men can freely reject even the whole universe. Generally speaking, there is in the Judaeo-Christian tradition not merely an emphasis on this Planet Earth, but on the whole cosmos itself. Indeed, it is at this very point that Aristotle's theory of knowledge as being the other fits most naturally in with the idea of revelation. I shall argue later on, in fact, that any hope to create in truth an abundant society among men will have to pay attention to this cosmos beyond us.[2]

In a sense, then, the Earth itself, however vast and varied it is, is only a beginning. If atheism, in its own way, seeks to explain the whole universe in terms of human powers, Christianity, for its part, while recognizing the unique place of man in the cosmos, places both man and cosmos in the same higher order.[3] We are not accustomed, I think, to talking about, taking account of the cosmos in our social philosophy. However, I think we must, and here I shall offer some initial approaches to precisely this question of how social order, cosmos, and human destiny fit together.

Whether man thinks too niggardly or too grandly has ever been a major question in the history of human culture. The whole modern era probably, as Professor Nisbet has suggested, has perhaps thought too grandly, while today we are becoming so locked into ourselves that we are in great danger of losing any higher vision at all.[4] Cowardice and pride are both expressions even of the spirit. In *The Social Contract,* Jean-Jacques Rousseau remarked, to this point:

> When Nuñez Balboa took possession, on the shores of the South Seas, of that ocean and of all South America in the name of the Crown of Castille, was that act sufficient to dispossess the inhabitants of the country, and exclude all the princes of the world from settling there? At that rate these ceremonies might have been multiplied extravagantly, and the Catholic King, at one stroke, might have taken possession of the whole universe. (I, x, 1762)

Such are, indeed, caustic words, yet with a certain grandeur. Nonetheless, the "taking possession of the whole universe" is a thought, a project even, that deserves rather more attention than even a Rousseau was prepared to give it. At first sight, of course, it might seem to be pure arrogance to suggest any intrinsic relation between the race to which the King of Castille belonged and "the whole universe." Yet, a case can be made that it might be undue, even culpable, humility to think in terms of anything less.

The human problem—what is man to do with himself on this Earth?—and the cosmic problem—what is the meaning of the universe? —have always been felt to be related, even when no rational order was admitted. The indifference of the cosmos to man—we think of Pascal—evidently seemed to define his aloneness, his unimportance, even bred a kind of defiant elegance in the hearts of some of the braver of our kind. Greek cosmology was held to have reached an impasse with Socrates, so that it turned to ethical and political questions, areas over which man was said to have some control, precisely because there was no cosmic meaning.[5] Humanism, then, came to have many roots in a kind of cosmic despair, as with the post-Aristotelian Epicureans and some Stoics.[6] Man escaped the universe to himself alone, or, with the Stoics, he became a kind of spark within the divine order itself, indeed perhaps he became the order.[7] His emotions were to be "apathetic," conformed to what did happen so that a man could be master of the universe by not letting it affect him.

Judaeo-Christian scriptures, on the other hand, were full of the cosmos.[8] Only, they seemed to reverse the Greek priority. The heavens shouted the glory of God, while the cosmic order was "for" man. For Aristotle, the mind was to know all being, to be sure, but man was the lowest of the intellectual creatures, as indeed he was in scripture. The Prologue of the Gospel of John, however, proclaimed that, "In the Beginning was the word, and the word was with God." This word became flesh and dwelt amongst us. Christianity is full of the universe from creation to resurrection to the parousia. And while there have been numberless attempts, ancient and modern, to eliminate in scripture its utterly realistic implications, the instinct of the faith has stubbornly clung to the fact that it was precisely *this* cosmos that God created, this Earth into which the Son of Man did come, this universe that will be transformed. Paul did not hesitate to tell the Colossians that Christ is "the image of the invisible God, the first born of all creation; for in him all things were created, in heaven and on Earth, visible and invisible..." (1:15-16). How to understand such a passage has not been easy, especially within the scientific and darwinian revolutions in which theological and scientific truths were believed to have been diametrically opposed in a biblical view. That science and religion are necessarily opposed to each other on this score is, however, much less clear today.[9] In our times, it is atheism, not faith, that must be enforced for political reasons, which must accept spurious theses in science to reinforce its doctrine.

In Christianity, the condition of the universe, its structure and purpose, are considered to be related to man. Whatever be the age or size or dynamism of the cosmos, that is not of itself adequate to minimize (or maximize) man, who has that unique quality of intelligence that distinguishes him from the other creatures of physical creation. "We have seen," Stanislaus Lyonnet has written,

> that St. Paul and the Bible conceive the redemption of the universe only in function of the redemption of man himself. Without the redemption of man, we would have neither the redemption of the body nor that of the universe. Thus it follows that every pretention to prepare by our own work a redemption of the universe which would not be ordered to the redemption of man would be entirely illusory.[10]

So Christian scriptures, creeds, and liturgies do have vast cosmic overtones. The Nicene Creed proclaims: "I believe in One God, the Father Almighty, maker of heaven and Earth, of all things visible and invisible." Paul wrote to the Romans that "Creation waits with eager longing for the revealing of the sons of God: for creation was subject to futility, not of its own will but by the will of him who subjected it in hope, because the creation itself will be set free from its bondage to decay and obtain the glorious liberation of the sons of God" (8:19-21). The Third Canon of the Roman Mass speaks of sanctifying "the whole universe."

The redemption itself as a dogma holds that Jesus Christ, the Son of God from all eternity, became man in precisely this world, on this tiny spinning planet, the third from our Sun in our Galaxy, in a definite place and at a definite time, when the whole world was at peace, in Bethlehem of Judea, in the reign of Caesar Augustus. Orthodox Christianity, moreover, holds that this particular cosmos, vast as we know it to be, need not have existed at all. But since it does exist, it does betray an order curiously pertinent to the rational creature man, however tiny he might at first sight appear to be. The universe, thus, is not "necessary," but dependent upon an abiding creative act, that need not have taken place. Since it did take place, nevertheless, it is ordered in a manner that responds to man's freedom and knowledge.[11]

A Received Existence

Within this cosmos, furthermore, the human race has a special place in that destiny which is of primary importance. The relation of man and God includes the cosmos. Pius XII put the matter well: "Now mankind cannot, without guilt, reject and put out of mind the coming and stay of God on Earth because it is, in the economy of providence, essential for the establishment of order and harmony between man and what he possesses, between these possessions and

God."[12] The cosmos exists because men exist. Whatever be the cosmological sequence of birth and death of the stars and the galaxies—a sequence at both terrestrial and astral levels we have more and more pieced together—men have "dominion" over the world for their purposes. Yet, their purposes are ultimately illuminated by the reason why God created the universe in the first place—namely, to associate other free creatures in his own inner, trinitarian life.[13] Thus, there is a direct relation between the physical evolution and structure of the universe and the combined intelligences and personal destinies of the total human race, of all intelligent creatures, in fact.[14]

Certain strands of modern theology, to be sure, have tried in recent times to "demythologize" Christian thought so that it would "conform" to modern science, or at least to what was believed to be modern science. However, in the meantime, both science and theology have largely demythologized themselves so that we are now rather in a period in which science, faith, and human society find themselves converging on each other in a remarkable fashion. Indeed, during the past decade, it has begun to appear that the scientific enterprise itself, almost unchallenged for three hundred years, will not itself survive without some "faith" in the purpose and destiny of the universe and the relative place of man within it.

No one, obviously, proposes some kind of automatic or simple connection between these areas that have often gone their separate ways in the modern world. In a sense, to propose an ordered, logical, necessary relation would be to propose either a determined world or a divine knowledge directly available to men, both propositions the Christian faith explicitly rejects. On the other hand, there are things we do know, others that are revealed, yet others gradually figured out by so many minds reflecting on the human condition, so that to deny any co-relative intellectual relationship between reality and mind would be a kind of stubborn skepticism.[15] Intellect does know. The being that is its proper object and source is non-contradictory. We need not wonder, with Descartes, then, though even this thought is a healthy exercise, whether perhaps some evil principle is delivering us the wrong information through our senses, such that the certitude of our mind is wholly falsified.

Thus, things ought to "converge," as Newman once put it, if they do fit together, so that it is possible to take a new look at the interconnections of reality.[16] Whatever else the classic Thomist position on nature and grace meant, at least it insisted upon this non-contradictory relation of God and cosmos and mind and human destiny. The finite mind was intrinsically limited, to be sure, but "limitation" is a real good and a real knowledge, nevertheless. Christianity allows for something less than God. Indeed, it rejoices in it.[17] Eric Mascall emphasized this basic point:

> In every finite being, then, its existence is a real, though received, activity, communicated by a creative act of the God who himself is absolute existence, who is "all that he has." *Esse* (being) is *esse a Deo* (being from God), but it is also *esse ad Deum* (being towards), for the final end of every creature, the purpose for which it exists, is to glorify God, by manifesting in its operations, in *actu secundo* (second act), the nature which it possesses in *actu primo* as the sheer gift of God.
>
> Subrational beings glorify God involuntarily, and this is something not to be despised; but rational beings have the even greater privilege of glorifying him by the free and loving offering of their service. This is an offering they are free to make or withhold; therein lie both the greatness and wretchedness of man.[18]

That creation is a gift as well as an order open to finite intelligence is a truth, flowing from trinitarian theology, that grounds all cosmological and societal thought and science. Indeed, if creation is to reflect the glory of God in its own way, this will mean that it will be in precisely those things that are closer to gift that there will be the most intimate contributions to the order of this world within itself. This is also why Christianity has insisted on seeing a direct and fundamental relation between sanctity and the condition of the world and men.

Space and Christianity

Undoubtedly, the two most dramatic events of the past half-century have been the Moon landing and the awareness of the worldwide social condition of men, especially that epitomized, as we pointed out earlier, by the word "development." These two "events," in several ideologies, are often put in opposition to each other, while, in what is perhaps the newest ideology, ecology, the conflict is quite open. Man's good supposedly wars against the "limits of growth." Many, therefore, will passionately argue that the space efforts are deflections from the primary purposes of man on Earth, from his own general conditions. There has been, furthermore, a remarkable shift of interest within theology from individual to collective salvation, from individual to corporate guilt. "What doth it profit a man to gain the whole world and lose the life of his soul?"—this famous question has, for many and varied reasons, come to be de-emphasized, if not condemned. The thrust of this de-emphasis has been, in marxist terms, "the socialization of the world and the humanization of man," this seen to be the project for making all things of strictly human origin. This is, as we have previously seen, the classic atheist-humanist position.[19]

The highest form of atheism, to recall, is precisely the one that proposes an "intelligence" to the cosmos—a human rather than a divine intelligence.[20] From a less optimistic viewpoint, man's task is held to be that of conforming to an ongoing cosmic and terrestrial process whose social purpose is for this race of men to last as long as possible within the cosmos against increasingly hostile cosmic circumstances. Both views have in common an elevation of the *species*—itself an abstraction—over the individual persons, John, Paul, and Mary.

The relation of human intelligence to *this* cosmos, however, is a key one both for the purposes of human society and human destiny within it. If the Christian proposition about the cosmos being "for" man be true, it will follow that our knowledge of the universe will be essential to our understanding of what we are and what we can do. In a very real sense, the great intellectual temptation of our era is to denigrate or neglect space and cosmos in favor of a very narrow view of human planetary history and purpose. At first sight, this will seem to contradict the emphasis on creation being "for" man. But in fact, if the age, structure, and vastness of the universe are properly objects of our human intelligence, then the riches and challenges of the universe are calls, attractions that cannot permit man to rest at knowing too little. If, in one sense, it is sufficient to know God alone, as it is, in another the adventure of the universe in time is connected with man's own dignity, which is proper to him from his origin and grounded in his proper knowledge. Arthur C. Clarke, I believe, put it quite well:

> The Moon is only the first milestone on the road to the planets and the stars. And space exploration comes none too soon in man's history. For civilization cannot exist without new frontiers; it needs them both physically and spiritually. The physical need is obvious—new lands, new resources, new materials.... The spiritual need is less apparent, but in the long run it may be more important. Man has an impulse to explore, a yearning for adventure, a need for novelty along with the more respectable forms of scientific curiosity.... Contact with a contemporary non-human civilization could be the most exciting thing that ever happened to the human race.[21]

Christianity, to be sure, would rather believe that the ''most exciting thing that ever happened to the human race'' was the Incarnation, in which the Son of God became a member of this human race, a dweller in *this* cosmos. Science fiction, in fact, is full of theological overtones about other ways in which the Deity might come to this cosmos. But all this does not deny our fascination with the thought of encountering other intelligent races in this same universe, other races which also are from God.

Since Christianity believes in an ''orderly'' universe—an order both within the world and one embodying its overall relation to its origin—

a reflection of God is naturally present in it. The universe is *not* God, of course, but in it, in some finite yet extraordinarily fecund way, this order will be like unto God's interior life, like its source. Medieval theology spoke of this in terms of "footprints" and "images" of God in creation. But there can only be one God, so that what is not God can only be "like" him. This created order will require the free participation of men, of each individual as a member of the race, a bearer of true intelligence. Yet, the relation of the cosmos to God seems to be a non-deterministic one. That is, some anti-God cosmic order is also possible and conceptual in some sense, such that God "adapts," as it were, to the way men individually and in groups in history use their freedom. Indeed, the "seriousness" of the universe and of human life in particular is founded on this centrality of human choice, which can reject God's order as it appears in men and in the cosmos.

Cosmology and Social Thought

In order to connect cosmological speculation with contemporary social thought, then, with politics, it is well to consider the kinds of speculation that are about. We know, for example, that some 80-90 billions of people have so far lived on this particular planet, Earth. If the Christian doctrine of immortality and resurrection be true, these same human persons do abide and have a presence outside of God. As far as we actually know, ours is the intelligent race in the universe, so there may well be some correlation between our own fecundity and the striking vastness of the universe. The evolution of the stars, however, their enormous cycles of energy formation, expansion, and contraction leads us to believe that there is an unlimited source of power in the cosmos. The myriads of stars in the galaxies leave much probability that other civilizations either have or do or will exist in the cosmos. Further, it is not impossible, some hold it likely, that other civilizations could be in communication with each other or could be seeking contact with us. Much of the controversy over UFO's is rooted in this assumption. This proposition that we are being sought out, which Arthur Clarke felt to be exciting, could in fact be something less than welcome. C. S. Lewis once remarked: ''...If we encounter in the depth of space a race, however innocent and admirable, which is technologically weaker than ourselves..., we shall enslave, deceive, exploit, or exterminate (it); at the very least, we shall corrupt it with our vices and infect it with our diseases. We are not fit yet to visit other worlds.''[22]

C. S. Lewis, of course, began such reflections with the fact that our relation to the cosmos is first a theological one. He was never willing to ignore the choices we as a race have made. Lewis suggested that in modern times, both the absence of other life in the universe and its near certainty have been used against Christianity. He insisted that we speculate spiritually about what we might find. We could find, for instance, a race innocent, one with no wars or wickedness, no Incarnation or Redemption. He felt we would probably destroy such a race. On the other hand, we could find a race like us with good and evil within it. These creatures might have had some historical event or visitation designed to make them better, a way perhaps different from ours. Or else we might find a race in need of Redemption but not yet receiving it.

Conceivably, also, Christianity is designed for the whole universe.

> For if they are rational, capable of both sin and redemption, they are brothers, whatever they look like. Would this spreading of the Gospel from Earth, through man, imply a preeminence for Earth and man? Not in any real sense. If a thing is to begin at all, it must begin at some particular time and place; and any time and place raises the question, "Why just there and just then?" One can conceive an extraterrestrial development of Christianity so brilliant that Earth's place in the story might become prologue.[23]

Finally, as many current films seem to imply, it is possible to conceive of a diabolical race, one which has no single spark of good, one which has definitely and finally chosen against God, the ultimate City of Man of Augustine. This is something we should quite prefer to avoid at all costs. What if we should encounter such a race, not at all impossible in Christian terms? These reflections of C. S. Lewis are still important, for they serve to keep at the center of discussion the Christian notion of the purpose of the cosmos, its relatedness precisely to free creatures, who can choose for or against God, a choice that will touch on how the cosmos will look to man.

The Purpose of the Rest of the Cosmos

Professor John Hick has taken up many of these issues from another angle.[24] Hick has sought to combine eastern and western cosmologies and theologies to account for the purpose of the universe. He has denied or minimized certain classic Christian doctrines such as hell and, to some extent, the once and for allness that gives ultimate seriousness to the Christian view of man and universe.[25] The result is an effort to account in a new way for the meaning of the cosmos. C. S. Lewis had no difficulty in imagining a diabolical race existing in this cosmos, on some planet in some solar system. Indeed, strictly speaking, Christian theology could imagine that ours might eventually turn out to be such a race and place, though with some remnant escaping this dire fate.

As I have suggested before, in another connection, a good many of the contemporary speculative questions in genetics about sex, human uniqueness, human lifetimes, which were found in Thomas Aquinas to be problems connected with death and the afterlife, are now appearing as part of contemporary scientific speculation.[26] Geneticists wonder about launching the same genetic corpus and make up in each generation—an Einstein for every age, sort of thing. They talk of making a whole race exactly like one individual. There is hope of expanding the life span greatly, even so as to eliminate the need of birth.[27] In considering the radical modification of the human corpus, in proposing the begetting processes be replaced by other forms of being-making, in expostulating on sending human nuclei elsewhere, we are again confronted with the direct relation of man and the cosmos, and the relation of this kind of man and some intelligence that keeps him or wants to keep him the kind of being he is from nature.

Similar speculation can be taken up from another angle, as Professor Hick has shown. What if we admit the possibility of reincarnation, for example? What if we are given another "chance" morally to change our lives in another existence until we all become "good"—or"bad?" —even if it takes billions of incarnations of ourselves? The other side of such reflection is that it seems to give a direct moral "purpose" to the vastness of the cosmos. The infinite spaces that "frightened" Pascal would then be more accommodating. An orthodox Christian view, while admitting the tenuousness of this problem—though as Professor Hick has shown, there is more and more evidence of a type we are wont to admit in our enlightened moments—would not hold it necessarily wrong, on the face of it, if the physical universe is connected with a post-resurrection physical life of the particular human persons we are, though this is certainly not a perpetual reincarnation theory. This seems to be rather close to the literal meaning of much of Paul of Tarsus.

Thus, if it is true that the inner life of God is the direct object of ultimate creation and happiness, the evident fecundity of God in making this incredibly vast universe would not a priori exclude the billions and billions in the race of men who do exist, in Christian theology even after death, from using it.[28] Indeed, there seems something quite logical and fit about it. One of the principal mysteries of this universe is precisely its incredible variety and fecundity. Some are scandalized by it all. Many want to exclude it from our social calculations. We assume it has no meaning for us, yet that position might well have a too narrow base because we assume that the billions of humans that have existed and will exist—the other intelligent beings if there indeed are any—no longer count in the cosmic computation. If we imagine that the four billion or so human brains now alive and functioning be added to those of the past and the future, then the combined "mind power" confronting this universe from the creature side does serve to bring its creativity into human proportion in some curious way.

Moreover, there is the problem of "possible" lives. The medievals used to wonder about human beings who might well have been conceived, but who were not. Each person lives an actual life, a life that seems determinative of ultimate spiritual status. If the Christian view of the Resurrection is to make sense, if there is a proper "City of God," as Augustine called it, then the cosmos itself must bear room for continuing encounters and endeavors that would be even more significant in a sense when there were no future chances of a fall. There seems to be no reason why ultimate encounters with God would not mean also more intimate encounters with the world and with others of our kind. Indeed, this is essentially what Christianity claims when the doctrinal formulations are translated into ordinary language.

That there is some correlation between cosmic vitality, resurrection, and the number of one-life, intelligent persons already on this, if not other planets, makes more sense than Professor Hick's effort to introduce reincarnation theory into Christianity. The classical and orthodox thesis remains not only more romantic, but even more cosmological, if it might be put that way. On the other hand, the contemporary question is not so much with the relation of cosmos and resurrection, but rather the relation of the cosmos to the status of man in the present condition of human life on Earth. Some types of contemporary theology, notably that which goes under the rubric of "hope" and "liberation," wish to combine this-worldly political and developmental tasks with the kind of destiny Christians attribute to the parousia, so that there is to be one unbroken continuum. This, presumably, gives the present earthly tasks a direct hand in ultimate redemption of the universe. But to do this borders on a pelagianism, the idea that man can do everything by himself. Often, too, it is directly atheistic in its formulations and implications. But it should not pass without comment that marxism and other radical views in recent years have felt it necessary to add an ultimate cosmological vision to their social philosophy. In this sense, it is doubtful if Russian space efforts are exclusively military or scientific. They have this metaphysical aspect to them.

The Reach of Our Knowledge

Moreover, the scientists themselves are not indifferent to the problem of the meaning of the cosmos to man. With Professor Carl Sagan, there is even beginning a new kind of appreciation of cosmos in our culture. Professor Richard Feynman, who is fascinated by the beauty of nature and its minute order and curious disorder, has written:

> The biggest mystery of physics is where the laws are known, but we don't know exactly what's going on, we don't know the strategy.... We get reports from the experimentalists.... And we try to analyze the information. We may even suggest a new experiment. But we're still waiting and hoping for the big strategy. Then maybe we'll really understand how wonderful is nature.[29]

The other side of this vastness and complexity of nature is that the human mind is the ultimate wealth, the ultimate watcher on the physical universe. The universe is not merely "created" by God and therefore in some vast sense, "finite," but it is also to be regarded by minds that belong to finite persons, if it might be put that way. This means that the vastness of the riches of the universe are open to man according to his intelligence as it works, reflects on the universe. This too, I think, is why we cannot forget that Aristotle defined man as that being with a brain and a hand. That is, our intelligence is not just abstract. It touches the world, this world.

We are, therefore, not "short" of anything except brains and goodness. This is why recent conservationist and ecological movements are philosophically so dubious, since they tend to limit the potential of man to present knowledge, which is only a bare fraction of what it might be.[30] These movements should be viewed not as scientific analyses but philosophical views of man. Their science is a product of their philosophy, not vice versa. I shall return to this contemporary doomsday mentality in the following two chapters. New minds, new persons, then, make the universe of man, indeed, the universe itself, more, not less rich. Buckminster Fuller has written:

> In this century we have learned that the energies are not running down but are in fact reassociating themselves. We can now assume that man is getting onto the energy of the universe itself, which is eternal and inexhaustible. This brings about a completely new way of looking at economics. I would simply say that anything we need to do that we know how to do, we can afford to do. The concept of conservation that I was brought up with was that the universe was running down and that anybody who expends energy is to be looked at askance: we were going to be made bankrupt by that man. This is simply not so.[31]

The conclusion to be drawn from this will put a different light on the relation of the cosmos, God, and human society.

Historically, of course, religion has often been looked upon as an escape from the world. Emphasis on other-worldly values was thought, usually wrongly in modern political thought, to deflect man from working hard enough in this world. However, it turns out today that the primary crisis is of a spiritual, not secular nature. The question is not why is the world so small, but why is it so incredibly large? Human society is tempted to withdraw from the challenge of the cosmos either theologically—that is, not facing its import for precisely our kind of salvation wherein our choices decide how we shall relate to it, for better or worse—or socially—that is, concentrating on inner-worldly ideological success, which conceives the human enterprise almost exclusively in corporate sociological terms.

Professor Edelson wrote, summing up various strands of astronomical reflections:

> ...Astronomers have found the records of cosmic bodies whose properties are strange by terrestrial standards. There are the pulsars—burnt-out and collapsed stars.... There are the black holes.... There is the flotsam of the universe: clouds of gas and dust that are the birthplace of the stars...and there are quasars, star-like objects brighter than a thousand million suns....
>
> Of all these wonders, the quasars are the most wonderful..., because their very existence has led to what could be the most exciting finding of all: the discovery of the edge of the universe.... Beyond the (quasars), say the astronomers, there is nothing to be seen. Mankind has arrived at the outermost rim of the universe, a point in space-

time that is as close as scientists will ever be able to come to observing both the boundary and origin of the universe.

And so it appears that astronomers have achieved a new and more precise understanding of how the universe began, and of its evolution from the beginning, perhaps 13 thousand million years ago, to its present stage. They understand more clearly how stars are born, evolve, and die.[32]

Mankind is involved in this universe both by its actual living in it and more particularly by its knowledge and technique. As the questions of man's control over his own nature, his relation to extra-terrestrial life and matter, his organization of his own terrestrial life, and his relation to God in the cosmos and transcending it converge, it seems clear that these relationships are not solvable in total independence of one another.

Thus, if we place our emphasis on the physical or moral well-being of man, we discover we cannot project or protect either without the inexhaustible riches of the universe or without some intellectual reason why man should remain precisely man. If we emphasize God and contemplation, we recognize that our universe is itself affected by our moral choices. We see too that the order of the universe, its purpose, relates to our own finiteness. We who have minds capable of knowing all being find ourselves to be yet mortal. Do we need to propose a pantheism or an ever-recurring incarnation theory for ourselves to account for our permanence and our relation to the vastness of the cosmos? Such a thesis would question certain fundamental elements in orthodox Christianity that seem far more to the point in their present form. And if we propose that the structure of society leads by our work to the humanizing of the universe, do we allow this structure to be open to what is not merely human, to what is in accord with reason or even revelation?

A Christian View About the Possession of the Universe

The proposition that man is "to take possession" of the whole universe, then, can and, it seems, ought to be put forth and argued in orthodox Christian terms. The crisis of confidence about human numbers and social well-being is in fact grounded in a pessimism that is not warranted by the inexhaustible riches and vastness of the Earth and cosmos, a theme that will presently be treated further. Our pessimism is primarily a philosophical question about choice, what man is, what we want him to be.[33] On the other hand, the importance of the universe itself and of each rational person in it is only retained if this human freedom is maintained to have an effect on the cosmos and other men in relation to God. The divinity does not remain inert in the face of the human cosmic reality. Rather it does continue to act according to its own inner nature as that flows forth into creation. There can indeed be other intelligences in the universe which are not divine, something our own existence proves. Our race may somehow be destined for a mission beyond this particular solar system. Technological means for this, while still exotic, are no longer inconceivable.

Yet, our relation to our own members and to other intelligences, should we encounter them in whatever their theological status, depends upon what we conceive to be the reality of God and the status we have before Him. This is not a side-issue even in the minutest part of space, for it is precisely the non-essential, orderly, yet gift structure of the cosmos that enables it to reflect our relation to God and each other through it. Mankind does need a cosmic frontier, even if it is to solve what it conceives to be its own social and economic problems. But this frontier will not itself be the solution. That will remain fundamentally spiritual, even amidst the vast riches. This is why the size or age or complexity of the cosmic order does not lessen the central meaning of human personal destiny within this order. Spirit is not to be a question of size, great or small, but of intelligence and choice.

"If cosmology is exciting to some, it is disturbing to others," Timothy Ferris wrote.

There is apprehension that, should the universe prove finite, it would be diminished in grandeur. This is probably unfounded; the riches of the Earth were not diluted by the discovery that it is a small planet on the skirt of an average galaxy. A deeper anxiety rests with the old question of how far science should be pushed. To measure the span of the universe would be an audacious act. It could be expected to renew the debate over whether science has gone blundering where it does not belong, reducing the very sky to a set of equations. It is true that many scientists act as if that were their purpose—to explain everything flat and then shut up shop—but most of them don't. They know that to understand how the universe works is not the same as to understand the universe.... Profound insights into the greatest things do not dispel our sense of mystery.[34]

Understanding and mystery go together. This is but a reformulation of the reasons that the medievals gave for the notion that grace builds on nature. The ultimate resource in the physical universe, to repeat, is the human brain—intelligence. And this intelligence belongs to persons who are born and die in time. It would seem to some, as Professor Hick argued, that the permanence and spirituality of the intelligence and personality must conclude to a theory of reincarnation to account for the meaning of the universe and for the awesomeness of a failure of moral choice within it.

Classical Christianity, however, has insisted upon the absoluteness of our own one and given life, on its abiding uniqueness and consistency, on the importance of this radical choice for its own destiny, a power that it does have. What Christianity insists upon is resurrection and a God who responds to the freedom in rational beings in His own way, a way that makes God's own good, His inner life, present as an unexpected and uncomprehended factor in cosmic and personal reality. This is called variously grace or divinization. But it means essentially that even the apparent smallness of our planet and our lives on it is not apart from the purpose of creation itself, a purpose found also within the cosmic order and God's abiding gift relation to it. We live in a time of convergence, while vaguely believing things fall apart and disperse. How the universe, our society, even God look to us, then, is also revelatory of what we are, of what we choose to be, of how we make our world "appear," as Hannah Arendt once put it.[35] Too often we appear like Rousseau's King of Castille—claiming a world but not going out of our own closets. That it all fits together is the Christian challenge and faith.

Footnotes:

[1] Cf. the author's chapters on "Cosmos and Christianity," and "The Trinity," *Redeeming the Time,* New York, Sheed and Ward, 1968.

[2] Cf. also Herman Kahn, *The Next 200 Years*, New York, Morrow, 1976.

[3] This is St. Thomas Aquinas' explanation of the Eternal Law, in I-II, 91, 1.

[4] Cf. Robert Nisbet, *History of the Idea of Progress*, New York, Basic, 1980.

[5] Cf. Charles N. R. McCoy, *The Structure of Political Thought*, New York, McGraw-Hill, 1963, Chapter I.

[6] *The Stoics*, Edited by J. Rist, Berkeley, University of California Press, 1978.

[7] Cf. Ernest Cassirer, *An Essay on Man*, Doubleday Anchor, 1944, Chapter I.

[8] Cf. the author's "The Old Testament and Political Theory," *The Homiletic and Pastoral Review*, November, 1979, pp. 64-72.

[9] Cf. Eric Mascall, *Christianity and Natural Science*, London, Longmans, 1956; A. C. Crombie, *Scientific Change*, New York, Basic, 1963; S. Jaki, *Science and Creation*, Edinburg, Scottish Academic Press, 1974.

[10] Stanislaus Lyonnet, "La rédemption de l'universe," *Lumière et Vie*, Juin-Août, 1970.

[11] Cf. Eric Mascall, *The Openness of Being*, Philadelphia, Westminster, 1971.

[12] Pius XII, Christmas Address, December 24, 1955, *The Pope Speaks*, Winter, 1955-56, p. 306.

[13] Cf. the author's "Apocalypse as a Secular Enterprise," *The Scottish Journal of Theology*, #4, 1976, pp. 357-73.

[14] The medieval speculations about the relation of the number of humans in relation to the fallen angels showed how seriously this problem has been felt.

[15] There is some effort to reestablish this relation of mind and reality in Karl Popper's *Unended Quest: An Intellectual Autobiography*, London, Fontana, 1976. Cf. also J. M. Bochenski's chapters on Law, Knowledge, and Truth, in *Philosophy—an Introduction*, New York, Harper Torchbooks, 1972; Harry Blamires, *The Christian Mind*, Ann Arbor, Servant, 1978.

[16] Cf. John Henry Newman, *The Idea of a University*, Doubleday Image, 1959, Section I, University Teaching. Cf. also C. S. Dessain, *Newman's Spiritual Themes*, Dublin, Veritas, 1977.

[17] This is, of course, the theme also of G. K. Chesterton's *Orthodoxy*, Doubleday Image, 1957.

[18] Eric Mascall, *Existence and Analogy*, London, Longmans, 1949, p. 184. Cf. also John H. Wright, "The Eternal Plan of Divine Providence," *Theological Studies*, March, 1966, pp. 27-57.

[19] Cf. Chapter IV. Cf. also the author's "Some Remarks on the Current Problematic of Theoretic Atheism," *The Homiletic and Pastoral Review*, October, 1972.

[20] Cf. also E. B. F. Midgley, "Concerning the Modernist Subversion of Political Philosophy," *The New Scholasticism*, Spring, 1979, pp. 168-90.

[21] Arthur C. Clarke, "The Fascination of Space," *Dialogue*, # 1, 1970, pp. 52, 54.

[22] C. S. Lewis, "Onward, Christian Spacemen," *Space Digest*, March, 1963, p. 58.

[23] *Ibid.*, p. 59. Cf. also Gilbert Meilaender, *The Taste for the Other: The Ethical and Social Ideas of C. S. Lewis*, Grand Rapids, Eerdmans, 1978.

[24] John Hick, *Death and Eternal Life*, London, Collins, 1976.

[25] Cf. the author's "Displaced Damnation: The Place of Hell in Political Theory," *The Thomist*, January, 1980, pp. 27-44.

[26] Cf. the author's "Human Destiny and World Population," *The Thomist*, January, 1977, pp. 92-104.

[27] Cf. J. Lederberg, "Experimental Genetics and Human Evolution," *The Bulletin of the Atomic Scientists*, October, 1966.

[28] Cf. Karl Rahner, "Open Questions in Theology," *Journal of Ecumenical Studies*, Spring, 1978.

[29] Interview, L. Edson, "In Search of the Quark," *Dialogue*, # 1, 1969.

[30] Cf. Peter Drucker, *The Age of Discontinuity*, New York, Harper Colophon, 1978.

[31] Buckminster Fuller, "Energy, Past and Future," *Dialogue*, # 4, 1973, pp. 74-75. Cf. also Herman Kahn, *World Economic Development*, New York, Morrow, 1979; Norman Macrae, "America's Third Century," *The Economist*, London, October 25, 1975, Supplement.

[32] "News about the Universe," *Dialogue*, # 1, 1976, pp. 16-17.

[33] Cf. Ben Wattenberg, *The Real America*, New York, Capricorn, 1976.

[34] Timothy Ferris, *Harper's*, June, 1976, p. 42.

[35] Cf. Hannah Arendt, *The Life of the Mind*, New York, Harcourt, 1977, Vol. I, Part I, "Appearance."

CHAPTER VI

Revolutionary Spirituality

The saints are not what most certainly scandalizes non-believers, but rather it is the tremendous fact that all Christians are not saints.

—Paul Evdokimov,
"L'Uomo Nuovo," Monastica, #3-4, 1975.

At first sight, it will seem unusual to follow a reflection on the relation of the universe to Christianity with a rather formal discussion of spirituality within Christian social thought. To be sure, Christian social thought has always and properly contained within itself a spirituality and an insistence on the primacy of the spiritual.[1] However, formal ascetical and mystical theology were never seen, especially in the atheist and revolutionary traditions, as directly pertaining to them. Under the pressure of the totalizing influence of certain aspects of marxism, however, this situation has changed so that Christian mystics, especially if they be heretical, are now often considered by certain marxist writers to be pioneers in human earthly freedom as defined within their ideological scope. It is important, it seems, to pay some attention to this movement in any complete Christian political and social thought.

When John Paul II clarified the priestly status by forbidding priests to be politicians, he contributed positively to the theory of church and state. Of this, *The New York Times* wrote: "From the viewpoint of the Roman Catholic Church's effectiveness, a policy of keeping priests out of elective politics makes considerable sense. A priest who is a full-time politician is, to that extent, less available to preach and administer the sacraments."[2] It has been precisely this latter view that has been under considerable fire from those ideological versions of Christianity that seek to identify the spiritual with the material more closely, more politically. "But as soon as the traditional Christian commits himself to the liberation of the workers and the peasants in tasks of an educational or political nature," Segundo Galilea wrote, "he finds himself in a way exiled. The categories of his faith—sin, salvation, charity, prayer—do not inspire or illuminate sufficiently his commitments."[3] This leads to a form of spirituality, "revolutionary spirituality," which seeks to transform Christianity into a worldly enterprise, or at least one in the sense of placing the worldly aspect of Christianity at the heart of what men do.

The central spiritual problem facing each modern man is, undoubtedly, whether he can forgive God for making precisely *this* world when, presumably, as we saw earlier, he might have created one which either lacked evil or left no doubts about the ultimate reconciliation of what man had wrought with what God has created and redeemed. Perhaps the fundamental root of modern intellectual atheism, to repeat, lies in its bold proposal to construct a "better world," "a more just world" than the one nature and redemption have given to us. The evident fact that man is free to produce a world in defiance of God, both in his personal and in his corporate life, is what gives spirituality its depth and earnestness. Too, it is what connects our interior and exterior lives. "If we imagine the world," Herbert Butterfield has written, "as a world of generally righteous men with—at any given moment—only one especially wicked nation in it, we shall never envisage the seriousness of that situation with which Christianity sets out to deal."[4]

In classical Christianity, neither nature nor redemption were "works of men."[5] Modern atheism, however, has come to view this intrinsic "formability" of the world which, because of its "incompleteness," appears to give man a special *vocation* in it, as precisely an "alienation." This is so because atheism interprets the principles according to which men *ought* to govern personal and earthly orders to be received from outside man's own autonomous formulation; thus he is alienated. The world created by man in the name of natural or Christian values is seen, in this view, to be an "alienated" one wherein man's authentic future is found to be frustrated by religion and metaphysics.

What needs to be done, consequently, is to "overcome" all the alienations in order to restore man to his authentic self, so that all in the universe will *belong* to man as if from no other source. The definition of happiness, so dominant in Greek and Christian discussions, comes to be realized when man has created his own city, even his own self, by *eliminating* what has been assumed to be given from outside his realm. Why man lives in darkness, in this view, is because he has dreamed of a "heaven" wherein his highest desires were to be fulfilled. But if this "heaven" is a gift of God, as Christians maintained, then it cannot properly be said to be man's. Indeed, its very illusion is what prevents men from "working" to produce a completely "human" and, therefore, "happy" world.

Exterior and Interior Spirituality

The contrast between what I have chosen to call "exterior and interior spirituality"—the reform of man by reforming his institutions or the reform of institutions by a change of the heart, a change due to a "something beyond" man— must, eventually, both in logic and now in practice, reach the crucial barrier of classical mystical and ascetical tradition, which held that religion ultimately was the experience of *God as God,* an experience that relativized all other duties and relationships.[6] Christian spirituality especially has recognized that the things of man in this world were legitimate and necessary. There was a Second Great Commandment as well as a First. But the primacy of esteem and order has always gone to the First Commandment. Even though to Caesar were to be rendered what was Caesar's, still obedience was due to God rather than to men. This meant, indeed, that we were even to obey a Caesar because his authority came from God. As a result, Christianity contains within itself a vivid realization that a fundamental disharmony may exist between what men do and what God wants them to do. This is, of course, implicit in the Christian belief in human, personal freedom, which gives to each person, no matter what his specific temporal economic or political circumstances, the choice of loving God or refusing to do so. The Christian "hell" contains only those who choose not to love God and is a judgment on the world which proposes values other than those given through the Father. "Others he saved, himself he cannot save"—the taunt to Jesus on the Cross—means both that men are saved and that they choose to be saved in the way it is given to them to be saved. The "legions of angels" were not requested or sent. To choose a way of salvation other than Christ's way is to choose not to be saved, even if the choice is proposed, as it inevitably is, as "being fully human."

For long centuries, there has been a kind of collision course between two types of spirituality, a course that is coming to its inevitable conclusion in contemporary social theory. These two "spiritualities" partake of one another to some degree, but essentially they are in conflict because of an effort to substitute the primacy of contemplation for that of concrete political and social action in the world as the main concern and criterion of Christianity and of virtue. The belief that the contemplative life was the "superior" life has roots back at least as far as Plato and the Psalms. Man's meaning is God so that he cannot be man unless he worships God. Contemplation is not of man's making, but a response of a free creature to a reality transcendent to the world which calls to him. When man ceases worshiping God, he does not merely become pure "man," he becomes something quite lower than man. He becomes intelligence turned against God and himself. This is where ultimate "struggle" and "conflict" in the world lie, as ancient ascetical tradition always held.

Ascetics and Political Promises

Nevertheless, man is made for this world also, as we have noted in previous discussions. How are his twofold ends to be reconciled? Is he always to live in tension even in his worldly task because of the very nature of his personal freedom to accept or reject the specific kind of redemption offered to him, a redemption that did not so far give to most men who ever lived a full or even "adequate" earthly life in terms of health or riches or even actualized intelligence? Or is it perhaps possible to *identify* what man does in the world with the worship of God? For such a project to remain "Christian," of course, some distinction between the world and God would have to be retained, but the idea of a "spirituality" devoted directly to God and not to the world would have to cease as it would distract man from the real focus of his energies. The moral virtues of justice and temperance would become the speculative virtues, for they would be "creating" human happiness and value.

All of this, consequently, would involve incorporating "history" into spirituality so that "reading the signs of the times" would come to be the primary task of active contemplation, signs which found their meaning within the economic or political conditions of men. Further, these "signs" would be discussed according to some ideological criterion of what the social and political world "ought" to be and look like. "Revolutionary spirituality," as I have called it, would then be pure "contemplation" because it would be pure action designed to produce a man-made world in which all the presumed "evils" would be eliminated by reorganizing social "structures" and cultural values—perhaps even ultimately genetic configurations. This would "end" history, which began when man was found to be "unhappy," due to the "exploitation" of one man over against another, to the dividing of property, as Rousseau put it.

In *The Waning of the Middle Ages,* Jan Huizinga wrote: "For at all times the vision of a sublime life has haunted the souls of men, and the gloomier the present is, the more strongly this aspiration will make itself felt." [7] There is a connection in the contemporary world between those who have what I like to call "a vested interest in making the world's prospects appear as dire as possible" and the rise of "revolutionary spirituality" as a project to make the world totally prosperous, human, and spiritual. Traditional Christianity did not expect so much of the world, however much it might have expected of it, as we saw in the last chapter. Man's true home was beyond this life and any attempt to suggest, as the millenniarists did, that paradise might be found in some Third Age was rejected as both illusory and belittling for the promises made to men. But the "project" of the modern world

—the Protestant, scientific, and industrial revolutions—made it seem that a far more happy place could be built in this vale of tears than men were originally prepared to expect.

The contemporary effort to "revolutionize" spirituality, thus, arises from the so-called failure of the modern world to achieve its promises. Marxism is not the "cause" of modernity, but just one more theory about how to make the world better. The Third World with its masses has become for many the "dire" and "gloomy" present which has reintroduced the vision of a sublime life. And this has come about precisely as a spiritual project which identifies "mysticism" with action in the world. The various movements to make the Second Commandment the "only" Commandment, the "materialist" reading of the Gospel of Mark, the "human" personality of Jesus—each of these is an interpretation or effort to break down the Christian barrier of mysticism and charity which insisted on making God transcendent over both personal life and history such that man's most important tasks were in communion with God no matter what the worldly condition, still without denying its importance.[8]

That most of these new "revolutionary spiritualities" are marxist in origin and atmosphere should not surprise us since, as was pointed out, marxism retains the atheist premise of a secularized Christianity, the idea that we can actually deliver to man complete happiness as a project in this world. The "failure" of the earlier "revolutions" is to be redeemed by the marxists who bravely promise to achieve that abundance and order and happiness offered to man at the beginnings of the modern era. And that the advocates of this new "revolutionary spirituality" should be most often representatives of the so-called "Latin" traditions should not be surprising, either. Indeed, the present vogue of "liberation" theology is not unconnected with the Reformation and the post-Reformation attacks on the Catholic Latin World as being unfit because of its theological failure to inaugurate and bear those concrete movements which gave economic and political power to northern Europe for four centuries.[9]

The bitterness and often self-defeating attacks of contemporary Third World—especially Latin American—theology on the capitalist world are, in a sense, attempts to vindicate itself against the suspicion that precisely because of the beliefs and manners embedded in this Third World, it was incapable of becoming properly "modern." The lack of a true "Protestant Ethic," which founded and justified work and saving, the basis of progress, has now come to be an essential element in all "revolutionary spiritualities," under the aegis of political reform or theology. This new revolutionary spirituality, however, does not follow the basic individualist trend of the earlier movement. It is much closer to a kind of neo-mercantilism which makes the state the organ of progress and spirit, once it is under ideological control. Too, there is a kind of clericalization of the left with priests and bishops more in its forefront than practicing politicians or economists. But it is one which proposes, as marxism originally did, to avoid or remove the 19th Century evils of capitalism taken to be the reality of the 20th Century world. The irony of this is not only that it will undoubtedly fail to deliver its new promises because of its economic and political presuppositions, but it will further confirm the post-Reformation thesis of Max Weber that the "religious" beliefs of this world were what kept it in servitude. The change to marxism merely is a modernized version of the old absolute state, though, it must be admitted, a much more dangerous version.

In any case, the proposition that the uniting of spirituality with a certain view of economics and politics would produce a world of happiness for the masses of men is what is exciting and disrupting Christian circles today. What we are witnessing is an attempt to combine the essentials of the marxist outlook with religion in order to achieve a world in which no evils exist, a world identified with God's action in the world, such that worship and adoration of God are bound up directly with identifying oneself with this "prophetic" world process. Luther's destruction of the monasteries in order to give to all men a "calling" in the world is finding its modern resonance in this new spirituality which tends to identify martyrs and saints with those involved only in political and economic actions.[10] A member of a Parisian parish was said to have complained that the only "poor souls" that were ever prayed for in his Church were those living in the Third World.

Culture and Class Struggle

The elements of this new "spirituality" are important to spell out in some form if only to reveal their relationship to classical Christian thought. Perhaps the first element is the belief in what Ernesto Balducci called "the alternative culture."[11] Italian marxism in particular has been hard at work for almost a half century, following its founder, Antonio Gramsci, with the problem of "culture." This notion of culture means literally the imposition of a marxist outlook on every human expression, including religion. There is a "marxist" explanation for everything. Christians opting for "socialism" or "communism" take up the whole language and background of the marxist problematic with the hope of aiding the marxist goal and of influencing it in a Christian direction, or better, of identifying the Christian position with the marxist goal. The "alternative culture" thesis accepts the

notion that the Church has been allied with
"capitalism" and "domination." In this "alternative culture," there is a deliberate shift of
social emphasis from the person to the group or
collectivity. Individual genius is downplayed. Indeed, it is looked on as domination. All great
works of art, literature, or religion come to be
interpreted as collective expressions. Authority
arises only from below. The well-being and
views of the basic "group" become the spiritual
center of life. Under the rubric of "the poor" or
"the underprivileged," the collectivity is the
source of value and grace as interpreted by the
political "prophets."

The "alternative culture" proposes a first
step in the depersonalization of society which
reverses the progress toward the person as the
center of ethical and spiritual life that has been
seen to be the distinguishing hallmark of Christian social life.[12] The distinction of things, the
sense of "inequality" that characterizes all truly
free and spiritual expression of men and women
is deliberately downplayed by means of an
"equality" theory which holds that unity consists in eliminating differences among cultures
and persons.

A second element in this shift strives to
Christianize the essential marxist values—the
class struggle and hatred in particular—as
capable of Christian acceptance and promotion.
This means, consequently, a suppressing of the

notion of a *common good* in favor of a class who bears the sign of history.[13] Spirituality consists in reading the movements of "history." This is why the category of "prophecy" and "discernment" takes on a new dimension. And the "prophecy" is precisely reading where history is, as if the divine message were mediated directly through contingent events, almost as the old astrologers used to read the stars.[14]

The effort to justify conflict and class struggle involves a complete reinterpretation of the central Christian notion of love and suffering. Generally, the defenders of a "revolutionary spirituality" propose the "scientific" basis of the class struggle such that it is not subject to intellectual criticism nor to the individual will as to its real existence. Since "history" and, therefore, the human future depend on the continual evolution of the class struggle to eliminate the oppressing classes, then Christian charity cannot avoid the "violence" of the struggle, cannot arise above it all to achieve a good beyond class decision, at least until the oppressors be eliminated. Leo XIII's notion in *Rerum Novarum* (1891) that capital cannot do without labor nor labor without capital, in this view, involves a misunderstanding of history. The determinism of the so-called objective historical process of conflict, which presumably leads to a better world in history, where all domination would cease, justifies the abandonment of "charity" in favor of a "justice" that revolutionizes and reorganizes society along the lives of the ideological pattern.[15] Thus, A. Durand wrote:

> The profound novelty of this point of view in relation to the earlier is evident. No longer do we have the choice between refusing or accepting freely the class struggle. We are within it; we are in it in diverse ways, more or less immediately, according to our own class, social status or category to which we belong. To be implicated in the class struggle does not depend on the free will of the subject.[16]

This shift, naturally, places "reconciliation" in the future, out of the hands or competency of individual persons to change.

Incorporating Classical Mystical Writers to Revolutionary Spirituality

Segundo Galilea, moreover, has attempted to bring the central Spanish mystical tradition, represented by John of the Cross, into the orbit of this liberation or revolutionary spirituality, where it seems most out of place. To understand how this is accomplished, it is useful to cite the élan seen to be motivating recent Christian social and spiritual thought in this context. B. Kloppenburg has noted that the real question is "the relation that exists between the eschatological dimension of Christian salvation and human temporal progress."[17] The drive to unify these two enterprises into one whole is what gives impulse to contemporary efforts to form a revolutionary spirituality on the basis of action in the world. This would serve to eliminate the old tension between active and contemplative spirituality and would raise political and economic action on the model of revolutionary thought to the highest rank of sanctity.

For Galilea, John of the Cross can be seen as a precursor to such social and political efforts at liberation because he began the internal liberation of man by his ascetical and mystical doctrine. Since the exterior is merely a continuation of the interior, modern spirituality can take up and add the content to the "process" that John of the Cross left at the interior level.[18] Mysticism now follows an application of Nadal's "in actione, contemplativus," which would make the actual participation in the revolution—freeing the poor from unjust structures—to be the worship of God.[19]

Pluralism and Praxis

Robert Hale, moreover, has recognized the similarity that exists between the old "integralist spiritualities" which sought to deduce concrete social principles from natural law and the New Testament and the new spirituality which, in its own way, is a new integralism of the left, also deducing political justification from scripture.

The "revolutionary" approach, however, first had to deny to the older spiritualities any effect on the concrete social order except as an expression of spiritual "domination." Usually, the notion of cultural or spiritual "pluralism" was used in the beginning to deny any specific Christian social outlook. This quickly became a one-sided affair in which "pluralism" meant not plurality of political forms or options guaranteed by a constitution but rather the legitimacy of the revolutionary or marxist view within a constitutional or religious structure whose principles were alien to its real spirit.

From this, then, it was but a short step to identify the marxist option with the one best capable of reforming the social order, a task seen to be the prime expression of Christianity and the wave of the future. The new spirituality found it necessary to reject the early connection between politics and religion which, supposedly, supported the capitalist system, only to find it necessary to bring the connection of religion and politics in the back door. This latter was done through the guise of the prophetic voice in the collective group. The "call" of the progress of history was seen as the establishment of the eschatological kingdom. There was no break between this world and the next except in a mere time sequence.

"What is the common root of these expressions of integralism?" Hale asked.

Probably they consist in the conviction that the religious experience as such, insofar as it is an intimate communion with God, who is the Light and the Truth, is not able not to illuminate in a decisive way the truth found also in human affairs. To know the Creator is to know the creature. The Christian *gnosis* can, then, embrace every dimension of reality. Thus, the saint, the mystic, the man of prayer will have a decisive word to speak regarding also the social-political field of human life.

It would be interesting to confront this integralist spirituality with the theology of prophetic charism, granted that also the prophet tries to read the historic movement, the 'signs of the times,' in the light of the Word. But the prophetic intuition is a charismatic gift and therefore transitory, while this spirituality has the character of establishment. The prophet aligns himself on the part of the poor and of the oppressed, while this spirituality enjoys the esteem of the dominating classes. The prophet, in his spiritual poverty, feels the demands to deepen cultural and political mediation while integralist religiosity feels itself, in its spiritual riches, dispensed from such work.[20]

Thus, what is constantly characteristic of this new revolutionary spirituality, as was the Catholic spirituality as seen by Max Weber, is a lack of any specific or worldly function. The political-economic efforts come from *a priori* ideologies described as "scientific" in order to hide their contradiction with the basic thesis and positions of classic Christian spirituality, and any influence it might have on what a person really is. Religion and spirituality, then, come to have the function of conforming man to the revolution's inevitable progress, just as religion was said to make Christians conform to capitalism in the 19th Century.

The attempt to rejoin political with eschatological happiness reaches, then, its ultimate expression in transforming "spirituality" into a prophetic *praxis,* which sees God's work as forming a worldly kingdom to alleviate the poor and exalt the weak, a project, as we noted earlier, in Henri de Saint-Simon's "New Christianity."[21] In a way, however, it is remarkable that this confident literature on revolutionary spirituality should appear at a precise moment in history when a whole series of Russian Christian writers are appearing in the name of the more classical norms of Christianity.[22] For the Russians, the notion that history is to bring about a better future for mankind is the most merciless concept recently taught since it justifies horrible and continual suppressions in its name.

Furthermore, the silence of Christians before the *de facto* violations of human freedom and dignity in actual marxist and revolutionary states is a scandal so deep that western Christians and Third World Christians proposing to solve their problems by this same ideological cast seem to betray the very name of Christianity. Indeed, some writers, like Piero Gheddo, see the ideological power of marxism to be so formidable because of the failure of western Christians to grasp its spiritual import and performance. Gheddo thinks that this failure will mean that all the structures of Christianity will have to be practically eliminated merely to survive in the ruthless absolutism that is to be imposed on more and more human beings.[23] And ironically too, as Octavio Paz has argued, the world has ceased being beholden to this future and its equality in which all is justified. There is a splintering effect such that all peoples are claiming their differences and separatenesses and are unwilling to see the future as a justifications for the abuses of the day.[24]

"Christianity," Luis Arostegui has remarked, "is the definitive revelation within human monotony."[25] This monotony of the revolutionary movements, however, serves to point out a basic challenge to their very suppositions in spirituality. The progress of Christian social and spiritual life is ever toward personal diversity and uniqueness.[26] The variety and differentiation of gifts are an essential part of the action of God (1 *Corinthians* 12:7). Men do not and are not supposed to have the same gifts and talents. What is going on in the world is not a salvation of the "world" by human effort, but by the newness of God's rule. Furthermore, God's effect is not to make men suddenly perfect, not to change their basic freedom. If men are scandalized because Christians are not all saints—and therefore have lived in and produced imperfect social orders—it means that they have not understood what Christianity is about. There are "saints," to be sure, but Christianity is for men mostly as they are, even though it encourages them through their freedom to be better. The present effort to erect a spirituality of a future perfect social order is merely the corporate expression of the refusal to accept the kind of salvation actually given to men, a salvation that calls them first to seek the kingdom of God.

Rudolf Schnackenburg wrote in this context:

> In contrast with these various Jewish hopes, the Gospel of Jesus that the Kingdom of God is at hand brings a new and special revelation. Jesus explicitly repudiates the idea of a Kingdom that is purely national and affected by the dreams of political freedom. He shares the apocalyptic notion of a universal cosmic Kingdom which God of his pure grace will inaugurate, but he dissociates himself from all calculations and imaginative descriptions. He is at one with the Pharisees in insisting that God's rule imposes serious moral obligations on men but he rejects the Pharisaic interpretation of the Law and its legalistic piety. He will have nothing to do with any particularisms and is, therefore, distinguished from any special sects of the elite.
>
> He is conscious that he has been sent particularly to call sinners. His teachings of salvation

which link up with the preaching of the prophets, especially that of Deutero-Isaiah, may be
characterized positively as the definitive proc-
lamation of God's reign, as God's greatest and last
offer of salvation, which calls, of course, for
men's response in conversion and belief in the
Gospel, individual service of God and earnest
moral effort in order to 'enter into the Kingdom
of God.'[27]

The endeavor to link theology, metaphysics,
politics, and science in one unbroken sequence
of the active creation of men—which is the hope
behind all revolutionary spirituality—fails to preserve the newness and gratuity of the kind of
salvation men have been offered. It also fails to
preserve any objective look at the reality of
politics. The Russian writers have insisted on
keeping the primacy of the spiritual life because
they have realized clearly in suffering what kind
of a worldly order results from the identification
of politics and religion, or better, of politics and
the effort to identify man's happiness with its
accomplishment. Only a belief in the personal
dignity, freedom, and responsibility of each person, no matter what the social order, can give
hope for a more Christian world.[28]

A Normal Christian Spirituality

Undoubtedly, it is not unchristian to long for
a better world. We are strangers and pilgrims in
this one, as Scripture often reminds us. Further-

more, some social systems are better than others. From the time of Plato and Aristotle to the descriptions of Gulag, we have recognized that there were good and bad sorts of governments of various types and degrees of evil and good. However, Christianity is unique in that it proposes a resurrection of the *body*, not the future organization of the state, which, as we pointed out earlier, came primarily from reason, not scripture. This means that Christianity addresses itself to a more fundamental kind of hope that can be conceived in planning for and in the world. Moreover, Christianity, in rejecting both pelagianism and manichaeanism, does insist that evil does exist even if it be not a counter-deity, that there are things that cannot be reconciled with the good.[29] This means that the personal standing and uniqueness of each man before God is what determines his destiny, not his social system.

Further, it means that each person has a direct relation to God, expressed in prayer, no matter what be his worldly condition. There are, as Solzhenitsyn insists, times when men must resolve to have nothing to do with evil, which expresses itself today in political form proposing a good social order.[30] A spirituality that does not retain its sense of transcendence, its own autonomy must, as we see in the efforts to erect revolutionary spirituality, become subordinate to the historical processes now seen as a prophetic evolution of God's will, but with no critical capacity to see that the newness of God is not allied with men's ways. There is no more serious issue in Christianity today than that of preserving an authentic spirituality free from its subordination to the historical ideologies that are seeking to subsume spirituality into themselves for their own purposes. "What Christians most need in our day, therefore," E.R. Norman wrote,

> is to see that the complicated mixture of the Infinite in the structures of time is explicable according to the spiritual interpretations of religious tradition—and does not require them to turn, instead, to the inappropriate explanations of secular culture. Both in daily life and in the worship of the Church, the prevailing emphasis upon the transformation of the material world has robbed men of their bridge to eternity.[31]

The fact that the barrier of spirituality must be broken is but a recognition of the ideologies of the spiritual subtility of the issues involved.

Forgiving God for the kind of world he made means also forgiving him that we are not yet all saints. What this means is accepting our humanity as it is, as God evidently accepted it. We are not to create a perfect kingdom but to love God. We are called to charity, not to class struggle, which is in no way a "scientific fact," as many pretend. But neither is charity a "scientific fact," but rather a way of redemption that is beyond reason and expectation. The newness of redemption is precisely the freeing us from the temptation to create our own world, our own paradise, because God did not first bequeath us one.

Spirituality, in other words, is not being scandalized that God's ways are not our ways, in recognizing that we are none of us yet saints. All social orders and systems will reveal the human condition, the same radical problems in different proportions and degrees. Within each social order, in ways we do not always know, there will be the freedom to love God within a human world that is not perfect. The Russian Christians are right in warning us that the marxist path is anti-human because it is anti-God, the path of their ideology. But these same Christians feel, too, that it is among them that the presence of God is most vivid today because they need no longer have any doubts about the anti-humanity of the marxist or utopian or revolutionary premises. The "revolutionary spirituality" of Christianity is still its "grace," its refusal to save us in our own ways.

"Lord, has the time come? Are you going to restore the Kingdom of Israel?" He replied, "It is not for you to know the times or dates that the Father has decided by his own authority..." (Acts, 1:20-21).

"Asked by the Pharisees when the Kingdom of God was to come, he gave them this answer, 'The coming of the Kingdom of God does not admit of observation and there will be no one to say, "Look here! Look there!" For, you must know, the Kingdom of God is among you' " *(Luke,* 19:20-21).

If we do not know and the Kingdom of God is already somehow among us, we must be alert to the fact that what God is doing must not be identified with what we do. The mystic, the ascetic is about God's business. And it is around this that the scandal of the saints arises. "There are people (a great many of them) who are slowly ceasing to be Christians," C.S. Lewis wrote, "but who still call themselves by that name: some of them are clergymen."[32] The ceasing to be Christians and the remaining have to do with our capacity to perceive the word of the Kingdom that Christ did give us. The liberation that was promised to us was not from the "non-saints." Fortunately, it came to all of us in the way we are. "The greatest need in the Church today is the contemplative life of monks and nuns," John Senior wrote in welcome words. "...Don't be put off by the false humility and inverted snobbery of the carnal man who sneers at prayers and says it's for mystics, not for ordinary men. The ordinary man is made for heaven and the only way to heaven is the Cross."[33] These are the words of the real revolution of Christianity and its spirituality.

In the beginning of the Gospel of Mark, we can read: "The time is fulfilled and the Kingdom of God is at hand: repent and believe in the Gospel."

The New Testament does not speak of making a perfect social order so that unbelievers might, on empirical grounds, believe. It says that Christ rose from the dead. This is the revolution, the basis of the kind of spirituality that remakes man and the world, a spirituality to which we must finally return if we are, as we shall see in the following chapter, to confront the poor in a Christian way, while remaining loyal to the spirituality that is not dependent for its meaning or content on the ideologies of our time.

Footnotes:

¹ Cf. Jacques Maritain, *Man and the State,* Chicago, University of Chicago Press, 1951, Chapter VI.

² "Priests and Politics," *The New York Times,* May 8, 1980.

³ Segundo Galilea, "Politics and Contemplation," in *Mystical and Political Dimension of the Christian Faith,* Geffre/Guttierrez, Editors, New York, Herder and Herder, 1974, p. 20.

⁴ Herbert Butterfield, *Christianity and History,* London, Fontana, 1957, p. 160.

⁵ Cf. Denzinger, # 373ff.; # 1520ff.

⁶ Cf. the author's "Interior and Exterior Spirituality," *The American Ecclesiastical Review,* September, 1975, pp. 490-503.

⁷ J. Huizinga, *The Waning of the Middle Ages,* Garden City, Doubleday Anchor, 1924, p. 34.

⁸ Cf. I. Colozzi, "Cristianesimo e Ideologia nel Pensiero Italiano Contemporaneo," *Sacra Dottrina,* #78, 1975, pp. 328-29; "Primato di Dio e Cristianesimo 'non-religioso,' " *La Civiltà Cattolica,* Maggio 15, 1976, pp. 313-22; D. Vesce, *Per un cristianesimo non-religioso,* Milano, Feltrinelli, 1976; Fernando Gelo, *Lecture materialiste de l'Evangile de Marc;* D. Del Bo, *Il Dio della Felicità,* Roma, Rizzoli.

⁹ Cf. Max Weber, *The Protestant Ethic and the Spirit of Capitalism,* New York, Scribner's, 1958.

¹⁰ Cf. Luis de Serra, "Réncontrer le peuple," *Convergence,* # 2, 1974, pp. 12-15; V. d'Asienzi, "Cristiani e Marxisti di nuovo a confronto," *Il Tetto,* Gennaio-Febbraio, 1976, pp. 108ff.

[11] E. Balducci, "Bilancio di un decennio," *Testimonianze*, # 181, Gennaio-Febbraio, 1976, pp. 22-30.

[12] Cf. *Pacem in Terris*, # 9.

[13] Cf. J. de Fabrègues, "La politique et la foi religieuse," *Revue des Travaux de l'Academie des Sciences Morales et Politiques*, # 2, 1973, pp. 45-59.

[14] Cf. F. Urbino, "La vita spirituale come tentazione," *Concilium*, # 9, 1975, pp. 124-36.

[15] Cf. the author's "The Experience of Hatred," *The Way*, London, October, 1977, pp. 288-300; "The Love of Enemies," *Spiritual Life*, Winter, 1977, pp. 228-37; "The Re-Discovery of Charity," *Spiritual Life*, Winter, 1979, pp. 195-203.

[16] A. Durand, "Lotta di classe e prospettive cristiane della reconciliazione," *Concilium*, # 9, 1975, p. 49. Cf. also G. Girardi, *Cristianesimo, Liberazione umana, Lotta di classe*, Assisi, Cittadella, 1972.

[17] B. Kloppenburg, "Evangelización y Liberación según el Sinodo de 1974," *Medellin*, Junio, 1975, pp. 216-22.

[18] S. Galilea, "San Juan de la Cruz e la Espiritualidad Liberadora," *Medellin*, Junio, 1975, pp. 216-22.

[19] For a more standard interpretation of Jerome Nadal, Cf. J. Conwell, *Contemplation in Action*, Spokane, Gonzaga University Press, 1957. Cf. also the commentary in the *Jerusalem Bible* on James 2:5, about the poor.

[20] R. Hale, "Integralismo Spirituale," *Testamonianze*, Febbraio, 1976, p. 45.

[21] Cf. Henri de Saint-Simon, "The New Christianity," *Social Organization, The Science of Man, and Other Writings*, Trans. F. Markham, New York, Harper Torchbooks, 1965, pp. 81-116.

[22] Cf. the journals *Kontinent*, Paris, and *Russia Cristiana*, Bergamo. Cf. also Alexander Solzhenitsyn, "Western Misconceptions about Russia," *Foreign Affairs*, Spring, 1980, pp. 797-834.

[23] Cf. P. Gheddo, "Cosa insigna la caduta del Vietnam?" *Mondo e Missione*, Milano, Gennaio, 1976, pp. 49-53.

[24] Octavio Paz, "L'irruzione del presente," *Il Popolo*, Roma, Giugno 1, 1976.

[25] L. Arostegui, "Vida terrenal del cristiano en clave teologal," *Rivista de Espiritualidad*, Octubre-Diciembre, 1975, p. 480.

[26] Cf. G. Meilaender, *The Taste for the Other: The Ethical and Social Thought of C. S. Lewis*, Grand Rapids, Eerdmans, 1978.

[27] R. Schnackenburg, *God's Rule and Kingdom*, Trans. J. Murray, London, Burns & Oates, 1963, pp. 349-50. Cf. also R. Cullmann, *The*

State in the New Testament, New York, Scribner's, 1956; H. Schlier, "The State according to the New Testament," *The Relevance of the New Testament,* New York, Herder and Herder, 1968, pp. 215-38.

[28] Cf. Battista Mondin, "L'atheismo, nuovo 'partner' della missione?" *Fede e Civiltà,* Gennaio, 1976, pp. 22-26.

[29] Cf. Lazek Kolakowski, "Le diable pêut-il être sauvé?" *Contre point,* Paris, #20, 1976, pp. 129-39.

[30] Cf. Addresses of June 30, 1973, Washington, and July 9, 1975, New York.

[31] E. R. Norman, *Christianity and the World Order,* New York, Oxford, p. 84.

[32] C. S. Lewis, *Mere Christianity,* New York, Macmillan, 1952, p. 176.

[33] John Senior, *The Death of Christian Culture,* New Rochelle, Arlington House, 1978, p. 160.

CHAPTER VII

Christianity and the "Cures" of Poverty

*We believe that the developed world every-
where has a moral responsibility to help the poor
of this world to become reasonably well off (or at
least what we have called 'middle income'—neither
affluent nor poor). We do not believe that the
developed world bears any overwhelming moral
imperative to decrease gaps, the large differences
in the average incomes of nations. It is probably
desirable to do so but only as a relatively low-
priority objective.*

—*Herman Kahn,* World Economic Development,
New York, Morrow, 1979, p. 465.

*The notion of transferring control over the
means of production to the people or to society as a
whole is an empty slogan. It says nothing about what
people are to take charge of production. It gives no
more than the faintest guidance about what policies
they should follow. And it tells nothing about how
the leaders and policies can be changed by those*

human beings who are their victims. The failure to answer the query quis custodiet *(who will watch the rulers), I think, is the fatal flaw at the heart of the whole socialist remedy for human ills.*

> —*Barrington Moore, Jr.*, Reflections on the Causes of Human Misery and Upon Certain Proposals to Eliminate Them, *Boston, Beacon, 1972, p. 71.*

Since so much of the opposition to Christianity as well as turmoil within it evidently appears to be connected with the social problem, with the poor of the world, it remains necessary to examine this question itself on its own terms. A Gallup Poll commissioned by the Scottish bishops revealed that sixty-seven percent of the Catholics agreed that "richer nations have a duty to accept a lower standard of living for the sake of the poor nations."[1] Likewise, a Joint Statement by the Secretariat of the World Council of Churches—Vatican Commission on Justice and Peace (SODEPAX) in Geneva worried:

> What is the responsibility of the Churches in this debate? Unfortunately, the forthcoming UNCTAD Conference is meeting with much less enthusiastic response among Christians than either UNCTAD III (Santiago, 1972) or UNCTAD IV (Nairobi, 1976), even though world economic problems have become much more pressing. This is largely due to the fact that success has hitherto been so meager (precisely because of the unwillingness of the industrial countries, largely Christian in tradition, to make real and meaningful concessions.)[2]

Both of these statements are typical in revealing the theoretical presuppositions of religious thought when it seeks to confront the poor of the world to whom it normally feels a special obligation. Today, we can no longer call religion precisely the "opium" of the people, but rather there is a sense in which "poverty" has become the "drug" of religion, such that anything spoken in the name of its presumed relief is assumed to be ethically and morally healthy.

The Scottish question, for example, in examining sympathetically the formula given, does not seem to be aware of the rather massive evidence that a lower standard of living in the richer nations would in fact *harm* the poorer nations.[3] The surest way to make the poor poorer would, ironically, be for us to do what the sixty-seven percent in good conscience preferred on moral grounds. Further, the question gives no clue about the difficult problem of the capacity of the poor nations to absorb and use aid in a really productive way. Consequently, to ask normal people the question as posed is in fact a deception, if they are not likewise informed of the economics of this not so simple issue. Moreover, the western Christian nations may no longer be the models or best at teaching the poor how to develop. As Herman Kahn wrote, "...the Neo-Confucian cultures of Asia are actually better at economic development than the traditional Western cultures."[4]

The SODEPAX statement, moreover, is based evidently on the doctrinal assumption that changes in "social structures," rather than changes in moral ethos, work habits, social philosophy, or religious attitudes, are what will aid the poor. Some structural change may, no doubt, be needed, especially as political and economic organization has often been based on social ideologies most detrimental to development. One of the most important changes in the world today, especially in the developing countries, though not there alone, is an intelligent move in the direction of less government and more emphasis on individual incentives and human proportion.[5] The impression in the Joint Statement gave the feeling that "Christian" nations are at fault *because* they do not endorse certainly highly questionable social theories about wealth distribution. Indeed, in the Statement's own terms, it could undoubtedly be better argued that the cause of the Third World's poverty is *not* the failure of the Christian tradition, but a failure rather of this same poor world to imitate precisely those Christian values and standards that did cause development, something the Japanese and neo-Confucian cultures have managed to do very successfully. The economic miracles that are taking place in the world—from Japan to the South Asian non-marxist countries—seem to suggest that the main cause of any lack of development is the selection of the wrong western models and ideologies by the leadership of the Third World, who made historically fatal errors in believing the myth that some form of socialism was the wave of the future and the proper path to development.[6]

The much agonized subject of the lot of the Third World has in modern times been dominated by liberal and socialist theories, themselves notions that arose largely out of the Enlightenment tradition in opposition to classical and medieval theory. This ameliorative concept which transformed man's central project from religion to economics and politics proposed, indeed, that the Christian tradition was itself against modernity both in terms of rights and development. Professor Arthur Schlesinger, Jr.'s statement is not untypical:

> In fact, the great religious ages were notable for their indifference to human rights in the contemporary sense—not only for their acquiescence in poverty, in equality, and oppression, but for their addiction to slavery, torture, wartime atrocities, and genocide.
>
> Christianity, for example, assigned to earthly misery an honored and indispensible role in the drama of salvation. The trials visited on mankind in this world were conceived as ordained by the Almighty in order to test and train sinful mortals.[7]

Thus, "suffering" was no longer to be acquiesced in. The passivity in the face of it became the "original sin" in a world from which evil could not presumably be removed by proper social and technical action. Rousseau it was who taught social thought that a structure, property division, was what put men in chains, whereas the orthodox tradition, with Augustine, had held that evil was not to be located in a worldly organization outside man's own heart.

New Analyses of Poverty

The degree to which many religious people have come to accept the liberal or socialist theses about world poverty is well-known. In this context, however, too little attention has been paid to a change in intellectual atmosphere that can only be described as remarkable. The costs and mistakes of the various liberal and socialist experiments and policies, because they have actually been tried, are now capable of more empirical analyses. Religious leaders, Protestant and Catholic, have been slow to grasp this, though Jewish intellectuals have not. Indeed, a good deal of the change can be attributed to Jewish sources.[8]

The dimensions of this change can, perhaps, be best ascertained from two remarks, one English, one French, which serve to suggest the import of this newer intellectual climate. At the beginning of one of its informative reports on a British election, *The Economist* wrote:

> The historian, Lord Blake, said recently that, for the first time since the War, the British Con-

servative Party had the tide of public opinion run-
ning in its favor. ''There is a wind of change in
Britain and in much of the democratic world,'' he
wrote, ''and it comes from the right, not the
left.''[9]

Similarly, in France, Jean-François Revel, reflecting on Jean Daniel's justification for the ideological policies of *Nouvel Observateur*, wrote:

> The error of the French non-communist left
> has been to take as its point of departure for every
> political action the hypothesis of the ineluctable
> and progressive liberalization of communist
> regimes existing in the world, and of communist
> parties in western Europe. As a corollary, the
> socialist regimes of the Third World also would
> be expected to resolve the problem of develop-
> ment and of socialism with a human face in the
> same way....
>
> What Jean Daniel refuses to see or pretends
> not to see, is that the left is enclosed in a nar-
> cissistic arrogance in which it is a sacrilege in
> its eyes to pose the true problem: the economic
> validity of socialism, the roots of totalitarianism,
> the profound reason of the permanent shock of
> the socialist-communist alliance, the acceleration
> of Soviet military expansionism, an honest eval-
> uation of liberal socialists and social democracies,
> of the socialist authoritarian regimes of the Third
> World, the persistent links of the western Com-
> munist Parties with Moscow, the recognition of
> the errors and lies which have been accepted by
> us in our view of the USSR, China, and Cuba, of
> decades of indulgence towards them.[10]

What is becoming evident from such remarks is that new grounds presently exist from which to evaluate the kind of development theories that have dominated the Third World thinking in the area.[11] What is equally clear is that the implications of this thinking have not yet begun to penetrate contemporary religious and cultural centers, which are still mostly locked in the older theories of liberal, socialist, or liberationist orientations.

In order to appreciate the scope of this shift of perception, then, it is well to stress that our contemporary formulae for development—birth control, education, land reform, change in social structures—do not, in fact, explain the development that took place in previous centuries nor less that taking place in those areas of the world where development is taking place. As Professor P. T. Bauer of the London School of Economics wrote, the great transformations took place not from the above-mentioned accepted canons but from the agency of cash crops. England developed most before it had compulsory universal education. Bauer suggested the personalist basis of this newer approach:

> But poverty, whether domestic or international, is not as superficial a phenomenon as many development economists would have it: poverty cannot be solved by the application of more money, more resources, a "better" education, or even a trauma that sets the stage for a revolt of the masses.

Much of the development aid literature since World War II on which far-reaching policies have been based implies that basically everyone is alike and that poor people differ from rich people only in having less money.

Massive evidence, including the experience of aid, makes clear that this is not the case, that income and progress depend very largely on personal, social, and political factors, and not on physical or financial resources.[12]

This would suggest that a reconsideration of the religious and philosophical outlooks over the world which underscore and support redistribution and development theories becomes a first consideration for the prospects of "curing" any actual poverty. Poverty, in other words, may well be caused mainly by our theories on how to remove it, and if not poverty, then loss of political and civil freedom.

This seems, then, to mean that the modern liberal or socialist projects as they have been understood in the modern world militate against real development which depends rather on strictly personal values and initiatives within an economic and political framework designed to allow and aid and reward newness and growth that comes into the world because of human intelligence and energy, the only real source of wealth in the world, ultimately the only "resource." Professor Kenneth Minogue has described the precise background which contrasts so much with the newer conservative approaches to development:

> Liberalism develops from a sensibility which is dissatisfied with the world, not because the world is monotonous, nor because it lacks hero- ism, or beauty, nor because all these things are transient, nor for any other of the myriads of reasons people find for despair, but because it contains suffering.[13]

The consequence of this view, clearly Enlightenment in origin, is that suffering comes to be a "political" problem whose end is action mini- mizing such identifiable suffering. Indeed, suf- fering comes to be itself identified with "what can be removed."

Liberalism, then, "is good will turned doc- trinaire; it is philanthropy organized to be efficient."[14] And the generic sympathy for the various suffering "classes" and types, all deper- sonalized categories—workers, race, peasants —converts actual politics "into a crudely con- ceived moral battleground."[15] Poverty becomes merely the root cause of all suffering, the source of vice, something it never really was in the clas- sical Christian tradition, which did not distin- guish man essentially according to his income levels. Thus, when someone is beaten or robbed by a member of a "suffering" class, there is no personal responsibility. Retributive justice be- comes reduced from persons to classes. Culpa- bility lies not in the doer but in the class and system that "causes" poverty.

Modern politics, therefore, must first be reduced to "fighting" poverty. And, thanks largely
to J. A. Hobson and Lenin, this struggle no longer
takes place mainly at home where there is a
growing ideological suspicion that the resident
"poor," the old-line workers, have in fact joined
the exploiters. Barbara Ward recently embraced
this kind of a position:

> The term "workers" does not represent a
> valid category any longer.... When, for example,
> Mr. George Meany (the late AFL-CIO President)
> receives more than $100,000 a year as a special-
> ized laborer, he cannot be compared to a textile
> laborer in Bangladesh who today is paid only
> a starvation wage. Save for a few exceptions,
> the workers of the North Atlantic today are as
> wealthy as were the employers of Lille in 1890
> when compared to their operators.[16]

This again, however, is based on its theoretical
presuppositions that the poor in Bangladesh are
poor because of the wealth of the workers of the
North Atlantic area. And this is not true, at least
not in the way implied.

Professor Minogue went on to argue that the
concentration of all value on the alleviation of
suffering is not merely dangerous as a dubious
political project, but also one that makes religion
seem at odds precisely with the higher cultural
values that transcend economics such that the
presentation of religion as an aid to moderniza-
tion may in fact be tantamount to its own subtle
undermining:

If the great issue of our times is how to prevent malnutrition among Asians and Africans, then the events of scholarship must seem very far from the battle. Who would elucidate a text of Chaucer when his duty lies out in the monsoon region? How futile experiments in painting techniques must look when the survival of the species is in question! Artistic movements are implicitly reduced to the role of entertainment, and Flaubert, torturing himself for a week over the structure of a sentence, can only seem absurd. Universities have traditionally followed the trail of truth; but truth is an irrelevance in a world crying out for "science in the service of man." Here is a menace more insidious to religious institutions than any debate about evolution.[17]

Thus, Professor Minogue here touched both the crucial question of what policies in fact alleviate the poor and the more basic one of whether religion in opting for a this-worldly social ethics has not forgotten its more important duty and strength.

Tradition and Progress

The proportions of the cultural and religious background to valid development, then, have been well argued by Professor Hodgson at Oxford. The question is whether fundamental scientific research is, over against technology, itself an exportable item to other cultures, and if so, on what basis. This is, no doubt, one of the most delicate topics of all in today's egalitarian atmosphere. Hodgson, however, cited a growing number of studies that suggest that something in western culture is distinct and unique without which basic scientific study is not able to flourish.[18]

Professor Hodgson's position is worth much reflection in this regard:

> Science is hard to export.... The reason for this is profound.... Science cannot take root in a mind unless certain clear, instinctive and strongly held beliefs about the material world are already present, in particular that it is rational and orderly and follows definite and quantifiable laws that can be discovered by the human mind, that it is worth mastering and can be mastered....
>
> ...This very special set of beliefs about the material world that alone made science possible was first brought into human history as an integral part of the Christian revelation. The belief in one God, the Creator of heaven and earth, at once assures us that the world is rational and orderly. The belief in the divine freedom implies that we cannot hope to find out about the world by pure thought, but must make experiments. The incarnation shows us the dignity of matter, and Christ's injunction to feed the hungry provides a moral impetus to carry on with our scientific work....
>
> The implications of this for the development of science in alien cultures are profound. It takes a very long time, certainly several generations, to implant those beliefs which alone make science

possible. It is necessary to accept this and be prepared for a long period of growth to eventual maturity. A further corollary is that Christianity and science are now seen to be in mutually reinforcing partnership in the process of development.[19]

The significance of this position is not only that classical theological and missionary activities may in fact be the best way to help the poor—a position against which much of Protestant and Catholic liberation and missionary theory has currently set itself—but also that the basis of any real help to the poor lies in a social philosophy based on what is most unique in reality, the newness of the human person, his unique historicity.[20]

In this sense, the personalist emphasis of classical Christian social thought, recalled by a Maritain, represented by John Paul II, seems to provide in an unexpected way the link both to the newer kind of thinking on development and to the intellectual presuppositions that would show its values and limits. Jacques Maritain's "Confession of Faith" is well worth recalling in this regard:

> The pursuit of the highest contemplation and the pursuit of the highest freedom are two aspects of the same pursuit. In the order of spiritual life, man aspires to perfect and absolute freedom, and therefore to a superhuman condition.... The function of law is a function of protection and education of freedom....

> To my way of thinking, the pursuit of freedom is also at the base of the social and political problems. But in the order of temporal life, it is not a divine freedom which is the object of our desires, but rather a freedom proportionate to the human condition and to the natural possibilities of our earthly existence.[21]

Now, it seems to be precisely to the requirements of this proportion to the human condition that the newer articulation of social philosophy in regard to development seems to base itself, together with a rejection of the kind of liberalism that seems to claim the possibility of removing all kinds of suffering.

From this background, then, perhaps the kind of intellectual analysis that is called generally "conservative," though in a new and more precise sense, ought to merit some consideration. Conservatism will mean "keeping" of valuable and worthwhile things, to be sure, but since much of the most modern political and economic institutions have been formed by liberal and socialist thought, conservatism will mean in practice a newness and experimentation over against the tried and found wanting institutions that are presently in existence. Development of the Third World will not be seen mainly in terms of aid due in "justice," but in terms of fostering and encouraging those personalist realities and moral values arising out of freedom and nature.

The Economist noted the dimensions of what is at stake:

It once seemed possible to argue that aid held the key to development. Today, that optimism seems misplaced. Development is a much more complex business than was once imagined; and aid's contribution to it essentially marginal.

The rich countries have anyway not produced enough aid of the right kind, and the lesser-developed countries have tapped other sources of funds. "Trade, not aid" has become the favorite slogan and with some justification. The ldc's received nearly $300 billion in foreign currency for their exports in 1977, while aid from all sources was barely $20 billion.[22]

With this background, a new analysis of conservative thought has been gaining intellectual ascendancy, particularly in the United States. Into this change are the reconsidered views of a Frederick von Hayek and, especially, the newer views of Irving Kristol, Paul Johnson, Wilfred Beckermann, P.T. Bauer, Peter Drucker, and Norman Macrae.[23]

In a recent appreciation of von Hayek, *The New York Times* recalled the sense of von Hayek's appeal:

I believe that people will discover that the most widely held ideas which dominated the 20th Century, those of a planned economy with a just distribution, of freeing ourselves from repression and conventional morals, of permissive education as a way to freedom, and the replacement of the market by a rational arrangement of a body with corporate powers, were all based on a superstition in the strict sense of the word....

> The current drive toward a welfare state to create a 'just economy'...is nonsense. Only individual action can be just. As the distribution of health or strength or beauty in the world cannot be a matter of justice, so the distribution of things....[24]

The detailed attacks on the distributionist and socialist hypothesis of a John Rawls and other apologists of a collective society have begun to make their marks along with the ever increasing evidence that over-government is the major cause of underdevelopment.

"Liberals sometimes say that poor countries need a higher proportion of government control," Norman Macrae wrote. "The worst thing we human beings have been doing since Auschwitz is to make politics a more power-grabbing and profitable occupation than is moneymaking in the poor majority of the world. A main result has been to pass on the poorest of human beings from odious dictatorship to odious dictatorship."[25] This means that more and more economic liberty must be located not in governmental plans and bureaucracies, but in the individual persons and in smaller groups.

Irving Kristol has suggested the historical dimensions of this view:

> The 20th Century widened this break between capitalist apologetics and the Judaeo-Christian tradition, as the defense of capitalism came to be expressed more boldly in terms of a

hedonistic, 'libertarian' ethic…. There is a secular faith here in the capacity of the 'autonomous' individual to create his own moral order, to perfect his humanity by a process of original 'creativity.' In the eyes of the Judaeo-Christian tradition, of course, this vision is as utopian as socialism itself—and, in many respects, far less admirable.

…Adam Smith had nothing flattering to say about the 'profit motive' per se—or even about businessmen as a class. The virtues he celebrated were those familiar to the Judaeo-Christian tradition: sympathy, compassion, generosity, public-spiritedness.

His great and original contribution, however, was to point out how the sum of self-interested economic actions, in themselves nonmoral, resulted in an institution—the market economy—that *was* moral, because it permitted everyone to better his condition even though each participant sought only his own particular good.

A market economy, by promoting economic growth and the most effective allocation of resources, helped render the human estate more habitable. Moreover, it did so in such a way as to encourage the self-reliance and spirit of responsibility of the individual, therewith shaping characters capable of self-government and, ultimately, of constituting a self-governing polity of free men.[26]

In other words, both at the level of societal theory and at the level of economic progress, the Judaeo-Christian worldview is the backdrop for a secure sense of scientific and economic progress. Profit can be used well or badly, but it does represent the possibility of locating the impulse for society at the personal level, something that is most dubiously accomplished without its possibility.

It is in this context that the neo-conservative trend takes shape. Historically, of course, England has been considered the classic home of conservative political philosophy. Edmund Burke is still the greatest writer in the field; English common law is still the representative of the wisdom of the common man. Cardinal Newman, Walter Bagehot, and Michael Oakeshott remain vital stimuli for anyone who thinks seriously about political ideas from this point of view.[27] Futhermore, the British have a political party that has sought over the years to give concrete expression to conservative ideas and institutions.

By contrast, in the United States, the Republican Party could never have been called exactly "conservative" in theory. In origin, it was closer to the continental idea of "liberal." The legacy of a John Calhoun and the South, which in many ways came closer to conservatism, was by historical accident associated with the Democratic Party. Yet, the arrangement was always uncomfortable, especially as the United States never had a truly "revolutionary" tradition.

Scope and Sources

However, for the past several decades, there has been quietly growing a solid and forceful intellectual movement that now, as Peter Steinfels has remarked, may be the most academic, articulate, and forceful phenomenon in the United States.[28] The older conservative thought—that of Russell Kirk, Peter Viereck, William Buckley, *The National Review, The Modern Age, The Intercollegiate Review*—were mostly libertarian or Christian in original cultural background. More recently, however, the basic vanguard of conservative thinking has added a very strong Jewish component, itself a major event in Jewish intellectual history. Irving Kristol, as was noted, has been very forceful. *The Public Interest* and *Commentary* have become basic reading. There are some Catholic names in this newer influx, especially Senator Daniel Patrick Moynihan, in many ways the most articulate of them all.[29] Even *The New Republic*, formerly a sort of liberal bible, has taken a much more conservative line since it was purchased by a Jewish sociology professor, formerly at Harvard.[30]

Jimmy Carter, no doubt, came to the White House on an ostensibly conservative Southern wave. But, as Professor Samuel Beer wrote of him: "Jimmy Carter is both a romantic and a technocrat. By upbringing he is a Southern Baptist, who, although given to quoting Reinhold Niebuhr, professes a faith in the goodness of human nature that is Wordsworthian in its innocence."[31] In general, in recent times, the Democratic Party in the United States remains the party of the bureaucracy, big labor, centralized state, and social engineering—many of the basic ideas that have come to dominate Third World thinking. Until the election of 1980, the conservative movement had found its source of strength in the journals, in the American Enterprise Institute, in the general force of its argumentation about the policies of the liberals that have apparently been failing.

There is little doubt in the United States, at least, that the Jewish shift to more classical conservative interests—family, national and military defense, the normalcy of social inequalities, subsidiarity—is related to the exigencies of the existence of Israel and the special relationship this implies. Today, for instance, 60% of US foreign aid (4.3 billion dollars) goes to Egypt and Israel, with Israel getting 2/3 of this. Thus, in terms of actual money and time, Israel is probably the number one US concern.

However, the neoconservative movement is also profoundly intellectual in its origin and in its own right. The first principles of this new interest among conservatives are the result of a hard, analytic, factual look at what actually goes on in socialist states, the same kind of concern

Jean-François Revel manifested earlier in France regarding the policies of *Nouvel Observateur*.[32] It is not surprising, as Professor Jeffrey Hart at Dartmouth University pointed out, that so many conservative thinkers today are former socialists.[33] The Jewish conservative intellectual in particular has come more and more to drop that brand of ideological thought now typified rather by the Catholic intellectual, flirting with marxism.

The evidence from Iran and other Middle Eastern areas of a strong revival of fundamentalist Islam, the terrible facts of Cambodia and Vietnam, the realization that the latter was an imperial power in its area, along with the testimony of Russian Christians, have forced our attention on the need to recognize the existence of religion as a political reality and on the need to distinguish it from fanaticism and from mere political and economic categories.[34] Professor John T. Smith at Yale University wrote in this connection:

> Our highly secularized society, regarding religion as merely a 'primitive' and passing stage in human development that is now superseded, has created a dangerous spiritual vacuum. Young people who reject the American gospel of wealth and power, which conceals this vacuum for their parents, are sensitive to the emptiness surrounding them; the despair it engenders readily leads to their acceptance of the charismatic fanatic

because they believe he can deliver them from the nihilism of our time. The religious concern is a permanent one....

Critical evaluation is essential, but it will have to be made in terms appropriate to the nature of moral and religious belief.[35]

The historic concern of conservative philosophy, as opposed to most modern liberal or marxist theory, has been to take religion seriously, not to try to explain it away or to reduce it to sociological categories as has been the tendency of the Enlightenment heritage.[36] The most disarmed intellectuals and politicians in the modern world, thus the most dangerous ones, are precisely those who think they can explain religion in terms of power or economic activity. Growing realization of this latter inadequacy supports the conservative mood.

In this connection, it is worthwhile to note the inability of *The New York Times* Editorial on Puebla (January 30, 1979) to comprehend John Paul II's insistence on the central importance of faith and religion in any terms other than the premises of the liberal concern exclusively with this world. By contrast, Leopold Tyrmand wrote in *The Wall Street Journal:* "Pope John Paul II knows that the Christian weapon—faith—is useless today without a philosophical dimension and that Catholic personalism, the belief that humans transcend sociopolitical conditioning, is the center of the global struggle."[37] Tyrmand noted with bitterness that "Any investigation of the Soviet eradication of religion is out of the question in many Western institutions of Catholic learning." In this area, it has been the Jews, not the Catholics, who have made the issue of religious freedom before the state to be a major public issue.

Perhaps the most profound source of change is, then, the reintroduction of the idea of original sin, whatever it may be called. Irving Kristol's remarks illustrate how this appears:

> When a slum population wrecks a brand new housing project, it is the designers of the project who are blamed, never the inhabitants. Those inhabitants are promptly relocated in other housing—which they will also wreck, since there are no rewards or punishments attached to existing motivations. There is thought to be no need for such rewards or punishments, since officials at HEW (Department of Housing, Education, and Welfare) and our liberal social scientists know that poor people have only good motivations.

> They know this as matter of faith—by liberal revelation, as it were. To question this principle of the original goodness of human nature—and its corollary: the ease of improvement of human nature—would also set limits to that most profound of liberal passions, the passion of self-righteous compassion. It is this passion that defines the very essence of modern liberalism and which—not so incidently—legitimates the liberal exercise of the intrusive authority in social and economic life. So it is not surprising that,

> with such a secure anchor in both secular faith and self-interest, the liberal motivation is, of all motivations, the least responsive to messages from the real world.[38]

Original sin as an element in political thought from Augustine has been a basic factor in this conservative sense of "messages from the real world," an account of how men do act, even the poor.[39] The strength of conservatism today largely stems, in this sense, from the belief that utopian and liberal politics have somehow led to absolutism, to the evidence that there is something intrinsically corrupting about theories that seek to improve men by social engineering or purely political institutions. That Lord Acton's famous principle about the corrupting nature of absolute power has been forgotten by so many clerical, liberal, and socialist thinkers is the basis of a reaction towards conservative realism.

The consequence of this is a long overdue, thorough reexamination of capitalism in the light of the vast failures of socialist practices, especially in their specific contributions to the underdevelopment of the Third World which, by its own testimony, chose socialism in the first place as the fastest way to development. In this sense, paradoxically, the conservative has become the political optimist, the practical man of our time, the one who can figure out what really needs to be done. Herman Kahn's remarks on educational incapacity in the educated are to the point:

Educated incapacity often refers to an ac-
quired or learned inability to understand or even
perceive a problem, much less a solution....
Educated incapacity in the United States today
seems to derive from the general educational and
intellectual milieu rather than from a specific
education. This milieu is found in clearest form at
leading universities in the United States—particularly in the departments of psychology,
sociology, and history, and to a degree in the
humanities generally. Individuals raised in this
milieu often have difficulty with relatively simple
degrees of reality testing—eg., about the attitudes
of the lower middle classes, national security
issues, national prestige, welfare, and race.[40]

Thus, the socialist or liberationist seems to deal
mostly in abstractions and promises, the hopes of
a very narrow class and not the realities of the
whole human experience.

The Christian Context

In a remarkable series of books and essays,
then, the case for a democratic, moral, and responsible "capitalism," if that term is still to be
maintained, is being hammered out.[41] This was,
of course, the burden of Catholic social thought
of several decades ago, as anyone will understand who takes the time to reread Jacques Maritain's still remarkable *Reflections on America*, the
book that more than any other set the European
and Catholic political left against him. The cur-

rent Christian concern for the Third World is deeply affected by what Irving Kristol called "compassion" or guilt, but backward in appreciating what really develops, what really alleviates poverty. The failure to account for this newer intellectual climate makes Christian thought seem more and more isolated, merely a follower of current ideology.

Theodore White, in his recent book on history, remarked that he has now returned to the view that ideas are the most important determinants of the public order. Christopher Dawson used to insist rather that behind ideas were also the movements of the spirit, of selection and judgment.[42] No one in year 29 AD, Dawson said, realized that the most important event in the world was taking place on a Cross in far-off Judea. Contemporary Christianity has been marked by an almost tragic inattention to ideas and metaphysics.[43] In an era when most of the deepest problems are considered in terms of politics and ideologies, Christians have not noted the force of newer ideas that are, in fact, in many ways, rooted in classic Catholic social thought and the intellectual background that supported it.

Thus, no more striking contrast in these remarks on Christianity and the cures of poverty can be found than that evidenced by the differences between Michael Harrington's *The Vast Majority: A Journey to the World's Poor* and Ed-

ward Norman's *Christianity and the World Order.*
Harrington, as he recounts in his book, is an ex-
Catholic, a socialist intellectual, who lost his
faith, it would seem, because of the Christian
theology of suffering.[44] This was, as Professor
Minogue remarked earlier, the sign of the liberal
in the modern world, the rejection of suffering
by a political alternative.[45] Rejecting the deeper
Christian meanings, Harrington then must explain the world's poverty in terms of a morality
of exploitation as the cause of suffering, in man's
injustice to man.[46] Meaning thus is to be defined
in relation to a social restructuring:

> America is at the center of a complex, struc-
> tured and interdependent system, historically and
> presently suffused with capitalist values and
> priorities, which massively reproduces the in-
> justices of a world partitioned among the fat and
> the starving. In the not-so-long run, there is no
> practical political philosophy of making a pro-
> gressive change in this basic injustice. Fundamen-
> tally, mechanisms must be transformed to do
> that. There must be...not merely a world political
> government, but a world government that would
> allocate the goods and resources of the earth on
> something like a fair basis.[47]

The danger and even impossibility of this
proposal lies at the basis of much of the newer
thinking about the real way to aid the poor. The
locking of the world into a universal political
distribution system seems a proposal for a tyranny of gigantic proportions.

Reaction to such socialist oriented proposals and liberal ones of similar import seeks to diffuse and provide an alternative for this concentration of power in a single allocating authority at a world level. It also seeks to underscore the futility of Christianity in allying itself in such a project. E. R. Norman's remarks are the most well-known and trenchant:

> Christianity has an extraordinary propensity to regard its own replacement with benign approval.... The politicization of Christianity (is) a symptom of its decay as an authentic religion. It is losing sight of its own rootedness in a spiritual tradition.... The present decline of Christianity in the developed world, furthermore, is not a consequence of successful assault by its enemies. It is due to the surrender of its unique claims to an understanding of the nature of men made by its own leaders.[48]

This again emphasizes the dangers of the division of the elite and the normal faithful in both faith and society, how religion can seem to be widespread and declining at the same time.

But this would mean, however, in the face of the movements to identify religion with social philosophy, a reemphasis on a transcendent reality as the basis to free men to look at the poor and their social order with non-ideologically conditioned eyes. Norman continued:

> What Christians most need in our day, therefore, is to see that the complicated mixture

of the Infinite in the structures of time is explicable according to the spiritual interpretations of religious tradition—and does not require them to turn, instead, to the inappropriate explanations of secular culture. Both in daily life and in the worship of the church, the prevailing emphasis upon the transformation of the material world has robbed men of their bridge to eternity.

Around them, as in every age, they hear the clatter of disintegrating structures and the shouts of outraged humanity. But the priest in the sanctuary no longer speaks to them of the evidences of the unseen world, discovered amidst the rubble of this present one. He refers them, instead, to intellectualized interpretations of the wrong social practices and political principles which have, in the view of conventional wisdom, brought suffering to the society of man.[49]

This Anglican view would have much similarity with John Paul II's like concern about the primacy of religious reality in any social ethic.[50] However, as Professor John Finnis has wisely suggested, there is in the specifically Catholic tradition, perhaps, more willingness to find order in nature and society due to its Aristotelian and Thomist backgrounds.[51]

The effect of this, then, is a return to the primacy of the person, even to a reconsideration of natural law as we shall see in the following chapter, as the origin and center of thought about poverty and development as well as about the meaning of man in the world. Even Professor

Karl Popper has begun to suggest an episte-
mological and moral theory that bears striking
resemblance to where Aquinas began his considerations on the uniqueness of the human person, though Popper still seems overly enamored
by a self-made or man-made world.[52] Social
theories about the poor, in other words, remain
dependent on metaphysical and religious theories about the structure and meaning of the
human person.[53]

The "cures" of poverty are not only religious
and metaphysical, of course, but without careful
attention to these realities, there will be
necessary political consequences approaching
totalitarianism. The alleviation of the poor, their
suffering, as the great secular project has become
a substitute for the metaphysical reflections on
the nature and being of man. This is why the
newer critical theories generally called "conservative" are of such potential long-range importance in the area of development, because they
begin with a critical analysis of these absolute
systems already in being to seek a return to the
real sources of human action and good. The real
task, then, is not the "conservation" of what
exists, for that is already largely living ideology,
but rather an authentic freeing of the powers and
dignities of the human person, poor or rich, as
the origin of the new and the keeper of the values
of the old. We can, therefore, in this way begin
to cure some of the poverty, without at the

same time locking ourselves into an ideology that undermines the dignity of our kind.

Footnotes:

[1] *The Tablet,* London, April 28, 1979, p. 418.

[2] *Church Alert,* Geneva, January-March, 1979, p. 15.

[3] Cf. below, Footnote # 23.

[4] Herman Kahn, *World Economic Development,* New York, Morrow, 1979, p. 64. Cf. also Norman Macrae, "Must Japan Slow?" Survey, *The Economist,* London, February 23, 1980.

[5] Cf. E. F. Schumacher, *Small Is Beautiful,* New York, Harper Perennial, 1973; Norman Macrae, "The Brusque Recessional," Survey, *The Economist,* December 23, 1978. Cf. also the author's "Rethinking the Nature of Government," *The Modern Age,* Spring, 1979, pp. 158-67.

[6] Cf. Macrae, "Must Japan Slow?", *ibid.;* P. T. Bauer, "Western Guilt and Third World Poverty," *Commentary,* January, 1976, pp. 31-38.

[7] Arthur Schlesinger, Jr., "Human Rights and the American Tradition," *Foreign Affairs,* # 3, 1979, p. 503.

[8] Cf. the author's "Intellectual World Shifts to the Right," *National Catholic Register,* Los Angeles, March 25 and April 1, 1979.

[9] *The Economist,* London, April 21, 1979, p. 79.

[10] *L'Express,* Paris, May 5, 1979, p. 75.

[11] Cf. Jeanne Kirkpatrick, "Democracies and Dictatorships," *Commentary,* November, 1979.

[12] P. Y. Bauer, "Breaking the Grip of Poverty," *The Wall Street Journal,* April 18, 1979.

[13] Kenneth Minogue, *The Liberal Mind,* New York, Vintage, 1968, p. 6. Cf. Glenn Tinder, *Political Thinking,* Boston, Little, Brown, 1974.

[14] Minogue, *ibid.,* p. 7. Cf. also Willard Gaylin, *"Doing Good": The Limits of Benevolence,* New York, Seabury, 1978. Cf. also the author's "Conservatism and Development," *Cultures et Développement,* Louvain, #2, 1977, pp. 315-34.

[15] Minogue, *ibid.,* p. 8.

[16] *90th Anniversary of Rerum Novarum,* Rome, Pontifical Commission on Justice and Peace, 1979, Juspax, # 9.

"Finally, it must be stressed, and stressed again, that it is social democracy, not capitalism, that is hurting the less developed countries. Guaranteeing workers jobs in specific industrial and geographic locales, regional subsidies, an ever growing government share of national income...are not what capitalism and free markets are about. The LDC's should be clear on this." Melvyn Krauss, "Social Democracies and Foreign Aid," *The Wall Street Journal*, September 12, 1979.

[17] Minogue, *ibid.*, pp. 129-30.

[18] Cf. Professor Sardar, *Nature*, 273, 176, 1978; Professor Riggs, *Physics Bulletin*, 29, 295, 1978; S. Jaki, *Science and Creation*, Edinburg, Scottish Academic Press, 1974.

[19] P. E. Hodgson, "Third World Science," *The Tablet*, London, January 6, 1979, p. 6.

[20] Cf. Hannah Arendt, *The Human Condition*, Garden City, Doubleday Anchor, 1959, Chapter V. The centrality of the person has been the basic theme of all papal social thought in modern times. Cf. John Paul II, Address of April 25, 1979.

[21] Jacques Maritain, "Confession of Faith," in *The Social and Political Philosophy of Jacques Maritain*, Notre Dame, University of Notre Dame Press, 1976, p. 336.

[22] "Aid for Development," *The Economist*, April 28, 1979, p. 46.

[23] Cf. the following materials: N. Macrae, "The Brusque Recessional," *The Economist*, December 23, 1978; W. Beckermann, *Two Cheers for the Affluent Society*, New York, St. Martin's, 1974; Ben Wattenberg, *The Real America*, New York, Capricorn, 1976; Edward Banfield, *The Unheavenly City Revisited*, Boston, Little, Brown, 1974; Irving Kristol, *Two Cheers for Capitalism*, New York, Basic, 1978; Herman Kahn, *The Next 200 Years*, New York, Morrow, 1976; Herman Kahn, *World Economic Development*, New York, Morrow, 1979; Peter Drucker, *The Age of Discontinuity*, New York, Harper Colophon, 1969; Michael Novak, *The American Vision: An Essay on the Future of Democratic Capitalism*, Washington, American Enterprise Institute, 1978; *Will Capitalism Survive? A Challenge by Paul Johnson*, Washington, Ethics and Public Policy Center, 1979; *Challenges to a Liberal International Economic Order*, R. Amacher, Editor, Washington, American Enterprise Institute, 1979; W. Beckmann, *What Attracts Intellectuals to Socialism?* Boulder, Golem, 1978; William Pfaff, "Economic Development," *The New Yorker*, December 24, 1978; Paul Johnson, "Has Capitalism a Future?" *The Wall Street Journal*, September 29, 1978; P. T. Bauer, "Foreign Aid: An Instrument for Progress?" London, IES, 1966. Almost the only comparable formally Catholic sources would be R. Heckel's *Self-*

Reliance, Rome, Commission on Justice and Peace, 1978; B. Sorge, *Capitalismo, Scelta di Classe, Socialismo*, Roma, Coines, 1973; J. O'Donohue, "Socialist Ideology," *The Tablet*, London, 27 January-10 February, 1979.

24 *The New York Times*, May 7, 1979.

25 Norman Macrae, "Brusque...," *ibid.*, p. 50.

26 Irving Kristol, "No Cheers for the Profit Motive," *The Wall Street Journal*, February 20, 1979.

27 Cf. Russell Kirk, *The Conservative Mind*, Chicago, Gateway, 1953; G. Niemeyer, "Conservatism and the New Political Theory," *The Modern Age*, Spring, 1979; Lord Denning, *The Discipline of Law*, London, Butterworth, 1979.

28 Peter Steinfels, "Neoconservatism: An Idea Whose Time Is Now," *Esquire*, February 13, 1979, pp. 23-42.

29 Daniel Moynihan, "The United States in Opposition," *Commentary*, March, 1975, pp. 31-44.

30 S. Rattner, *The New York Times*, January 29, 1979.

31 *The New Republic*, January 27, 1979.

32 Cf. above, Footnote # 10.

33 *The National Review*, April 28, 1978.

34 Cf. "American Religion," *The Economist*, April 5, 1980, pp. 12-20.

35 *The New York Times*, December 4, 1978.

36 Cf. Kirk, *ibid.*, p. 29.

37 Leopold Tyrmand, "Poland, Marxism and John Paul II," *The Wall Street Journal*, December 6, 1978.

38 Irving Kristol, "Human Nature and Social Reform," *The Wall Street Journal*, September 18, 1978. Cf. also Lloyd Cohen, "Traditional and Modern Views of Crime and Punishment," *The Intercollegiate Review*, Fall, 1978, pp. 33-36.

39 Cf. Henry Fairlie, *The Deadly Sins Today*, Washington, New Republic, 1978.

40 Kahn, World, *ibid.*, pp. 483-84.

41 Cf. Footnote # 23.

42 Cf. Christopher Dawson, *Religion and the Rise of Western Culture*, Garden City, Doubleday Image, 1958; "St. Augustine and His Age," *St. Augustine*, New York, Meridian, 1957, pp. 11-78.

43 Cf. John Senior, *The Death of Christian Culture*, New Rochelle, Arlington House, 1978; E. F. Schumacher, *A Guide for the Perplexed*, New York, Harper Colophon, 1977; Christopher Der-

rick, *Escape from Skepticism: Liberal Education as if the Truth Really Mattered*, La Salle, Illinois, Sherwood Sudgen, 1978; Andrew Woznicki, *Karol Wojtyla's Existential Humanism*, New Britain, Mariel, 1980; Harry Blamires, *The Christian Mind*, Ann Arbor, Servant, 1978.

[44] Michael Harrington, *The Vast Majority*, New York, Simon and Schuster, 1977, p. 253. Cf. p. 95.

[45] Cf. Footnote # 13.

[46] Cf. above, Chapter III.

[47] Harrington, *ibid.*, p. 253.

[48] E. R. Norman, *Christianity and the World Order*, New York, Oxford, 1979, pp. 12-13.

[49] *Ibid.*, pp. 84-85.

[50] Cf. John Paul II, *Redemptor Hominis*, Rome, Vatican Press, 1979.

[51] Cf. John Finnis, "Catholic Faith and the World Order: Reflections on the Reith Lectures," *The Clergy Review*, London, September, 1979, pp. 309-17.

[52] Karl Popper, *Unended Quest*, London, Fontana, 1976, p. 187ff.

[53] "That he (Jesus) is unique or outstanding in any way that is more than accidental and empirical, if indeed in any way at all, inevitably appears doubtful if he is in no way different metaphysically from other men." Eric Mascall, *Theology and the Gospel of Christ*, London, SPCK, 1977, p. 205. Cf. also, especially p. 153ff.

CHAPTER VIII

On the Christian Statement of the Natural Law

It is, I submit, an absurd academic situation that students have to go to the professors of theology, to universities run by churches, to some Union Theological Seminary, or to holiday sermons, in order to engage in a discussion— sometimes shallow, but at other times profound and absorbing—of the alternative of God's reality and of the light it might shed on political events, while our schools or social sciences deal only with the other alternative.

The great natural scientists of our time are more readily inclined to take account of the divine alternative than are social scientists, who seem to be duped by their own methodological conventions and thereby bereave themselves and their students of some of the great adventures of ideas.

> —*Arnold Brecht,* Political Theory: The Foundations of Twentieth Century Thought, *Princeton, Princeton University Press, 1959, p. 475.*

A theory of natural law claims to be able to identify conditions and principles of practical right-mindedness, of good and proper order among men and in individual conduct. Unless some such claim is justified, analytical jurisprudence in particular and (at least the major part of) all social sciences in general can have no critically justified criteria for the formulation of general concepts, and must be content to be no more than manifestations of the various concepts peculiar to particular peoples and/or to the particular theorists who concern themselves with those people.

> —*John Finnis,* Natural Law and Natural Rights, *Oxford, Clarendon, 1980, p. 18.*

Notions of common obligation, duties to the poor, right and wrong ways of doing things keep coming up in all contemporary discussions. Indeed, we suggested earlier, the existence of moral passion, the belief that the reason why things do not go well in politics or economics has to do with the notion that things ought to go better, that there ought to be a locus for responsibility and blame when things are wrong. In recent times, questions of human rights and duties in foreign and domestic policy lie at the heart of contemporary events. And such questions cannot adequately be confronted without some sense of the older tradition, called natural law, and how it relates to contemporary thought. Professor E. B. F. Midgley's remarks were to the issue:

> What is urgently required is an analysis of the vicissitudes of the natural law tradition—including its philosophical and even theological ramifications—in order to determine how that tradition came to appear untenable and how it needs to be restored and developed as the basis for a modern normative theory of international relations.[1]

Undoubtedly, of course, it is also safe to add that no subject in political theory is more likely to be ignored or misunderstood in the modern university of public forum than the natural law, this in spite of its honored place in the history of political, religious, legal, and philosophical thought.[2]

And yet, there is a methodological reason for this inattention, or, more commonly, opposition to the natural law, since the natural law stands at the threshold of contemporary political and social theory's most sacred doctrine, the distinction between *is* and *ought*, between *facts* and *values*. For if we argue, with Josef Pieper in his remarkable *Reality and the Good*, for the philosophical unity of this distinction, that value is rooted precisely in being, we necessarily undermine much of the self-established authenticity of much academic social theory.[3] On the other hand, Alexander Passerin d'Entreves' point must surely be constantly repeated: "There is really not one tradition of natural law, but many. The medieval and modern conceptions of the natural law are two different doctrines; the continuity between them is mainly a question of words."[4]

This would mean, then, that logically we must be quite careful to identify the precise natural law we accept or reject. Moreover, when we speak of a "Christian" natural law, we may seem to be close to a contradiction in terms. We must not be surprised, consequently, to find many statements of its content, some veering into the modern doctrines of which d'Entreves spoke, appearing in Christian guise. In fact, a fideist tradition might bluntly deny any natural law at all. Some pessimistic views of original sin would also deny any validity to reason. And many have thought that Vatican II implied that the natural law was to be downplayed.

On the other hand, there is an increased scholarly interest in this topic. The studies of Professor Finnis and Professor Midgley are most valuable. Thus, there is a view that if we cannot exactly "prove" the natural law, we need quickly, if yet quietly, to produce something rather like it, both for ethical and for what are called scientific purposes. In their recent survey, "A Discipline in Search of Its Paradigm: Reflections on the Post-Behavioral Era in Political Science," Professors Kushner and de Miro did not even bring up the subject of natural law. Nonetheless, in its effort to be "scientific," political thought has come up with ideas that sound suspiciously like it:

> Two fundamental assumptions of the new political economy are central to formal theory: rationality and methodological individualism. Rationality...is conceived as purpose or goal-oriented—that is, people behave *as if* they order their alternative courses of action and choose that which is most preferred....

> For formal theorists, the individualistic postulate merely assumes that there is no social choice wholly apart from individual preferences. Collective choice must be considered in the context of individual decision making.[5]

For anyone familiar with natural law theory, with its notions of natural ends and prudential, individual choice in accordance with them, this presentation of the two alternatives of contemporary political science in terms of choice and goal will seem ironic, especially when the "as if" must evidently be added for contemporary intellectual purposes. Thus, for the student of Aristotle, Cicero, Augustine, and Aquinas, what is revealed by omission under the guise of "scientific paradigm" is the need to account for human choice in terms of the goals of natural reason.

Professor Paul Sigmund has, in a similar context, however, suggested why natural law must deal with choice but likewise with what must be called "right choice," for it is clear that political life must account for wrong choice, for bad forms of rule and the personal characters related to them, as Plato and Aristotle clearly understood. Professor Sigmund wrote in his *Natural Law in Political Thought*:

> Furthermore, when a case is made for the use of natural law today, it usually turns out to be so ambiguous, misleading, and controversial, as to be merely useless as a meaningful way of discussing ethics and politics. Too much time is spent on indicating what is not meant by natural law (ie., John Courtney Murray's *We Hold These Truths*), and in tracing its history (ie, Scott Buchanan's *Rediscovering Natural Law*), or denouncing its opponents (ie, Leo Strauss' *Natural Law and History*), rather than showing how it can be applied today. Natural law currently seems to have become more of a barrier than an aid to communication on moral and political problems.
>
> But what is there that can replace the appeal to natural law as a source of norms to evaluate and criticize existing institutions and practices?[6]

This latter pressing question emphasizes the almost desperate efforts of Professor Brecht and, indeed, many of the political science profession to escape the consequences of the intellectual position into which it has argued itself either by rejecting or misunderstanding natural law.[7]

We cannot, perhaps, understand the importance of this latter trend to discover that which will do for contemporary theory what natural law did for classical thought until we clearly recognize that, in a real sense, there is an implicit rediscovery of natural law principles which is, at the same time, a *rejection* of precisely *Christian* natural law.[8] Indeed, as Professor Wilhelmsen argued in his recent *Christianity and Political Philosophy,* the current silence about Christianity in academic political theory is the main thing most in need of intellectual explanation. For this is itself the result of the very kinds of arbitrary "options" that contemporary positivists most warn us about.[9]

Questions for Political Theory

Without doubt, the locus classicus of this effort to reclaim natural law from the Christians is at first sight at least found in Professor Strauss' *Natural Right and History,* even though in *The City and Man,* he seems rather closer to the Christian view of this subject. The real context of this issue, as Professor Strauss recognized, is the possibility of revelation. Strauss, to be sure, did not disagree with the classical Christians on the basic point of whether political theory necessarily closed itself off from revelation as a principle. He recognized that the possibility of revelation—Jewish, Christian, Muslim—must be considered. He rather argued that the concrete content of natural law—which Professor Sigmund worried was not specific enough—was in Aquinas much too specific, too much conditioned by the divine law. This meant that "the ultimate consequence of the Thomistic view of natural law is that natural law is practically inseparable not only from natural theology—ie, from a natural theology which is, in fact, based on belief on biblical revelation—but even from revealed theology."[10]

For Strauss, then, modern natural law has reacted against this tendency to rely on revelation so that, as was also the case in the Greek classics, moral truths have greater natural evidence than natural theology. Secondly, the position of Catholics in particular on the issues of "the indissolubility of marriage and birth control" is a further reason to embrace the classics by rejecting the Christian view, which sees these positions as precisions of natural law.[11] In this sense, at least, Professor Strauss did recognize what political theory is reluctant to face, that the moral and political questions arising out of the "human life" issues of contemporary politics are rooted ultimately in political philosophy itself.

Furthermore, in the context of John Paul II's reaffirmation of the very issues used by Professor Strauss to separate himself from the Catholic natural law positions, it is doubly valuable to re-emphasize the pertinence of

Strauss to the issue at hand, namely, that of the nature and content of Christian natural law over against that aspect of Strauss' thought that seeks a natural law apart from any revelation, though not necessarily opposed to it. Professor Strauss, in this latter sense, remained Thomist to the extent that he did not close off the theoretical possibility that natural law might in fact include what revelation discovered in it.

Moreover, it is noteworthy that those contemporary theologians and critics from within the Church especially, who dissent, on the very issues Strauss suggested, from the content of the natural law, usually have felt it necessary also to reject natural law itself or to erect a counter-magisterium over against the papacy. This new quasi-magisterium then does not find in the natural law what Professor Strauss did not find in it, either. These latter critics would either return to a pre-Christian natural law which, with Strauss, did not find the precisions evidently indicated from revelational authority or, conversely, they argue that faith cannot contradict "reason" so that these additions are simply wrong. Reason then becomes the statistical account of what men in fact do as the norm of ethical possibility. They return, in other words, from the viewpoint of the history of political theory, to the philosophical position of Machiavelli, a position from which Strauss himself was at pains to distinguish himself.[12]

Here, however, it is well to pay attention to the reason why some effort to rehabilitate something that looks very much like natural law seems valid in contemporary political theory. Anyone familiar with the Thomistic tradition might legitimately wonder whether this reconsideration is not, at bottom, an implicit admission of the obvious fact of a stable human essence, which involves freedom but likewise acknowledges even as a principle of the practical order, to use Aristotle's term, a criterion which reason discovers but does not make.[13] To include freedom in essence suggests the possibility of rejecting reason itself and, therefore, human essence or nature in any act of affirming a natural law. And this happens by calling good, by doing deeds that are in fact against natural law as it exists in human beings. In other words, that men act against natural law criteria is proof not of its non-existence, but of its existence and validity.

The conclusion of Professor Brecht's study on *Political Theory,* then, was this: "Inescapable, universal elements in human thinking and feeling, such as the interrelation between justice and truth or veracity, are important accretions to the area of intersubjectively transmissible knowledge."[14] Even though each of these words of Professor Brecht was carefully chosen and highly nuanced, still his observations provided much of the impetus to construct 'purely' human theories of justice, such as those of Professor Rawls or Professor Nozick, theories which have sought chastely to have established justice and its content without any aid of revelation.[15]

Yet, if we compare such projects with statements of competent Christian thinkers in the same areas, we cannot be quite so sure that "natural law" may not still be the correct word or, if not, at least the idea that is most in need to confront what remains the basic issue of political philosophy, namely, "Why are not *all* actions and thoughts of rulers and citizens equally good and true?" Professor Heinrich Rommen, in a work Strauss admired, wrote:

> The conservation of the natural law was possible in the *philosophia perennis* because natural law was not considered a polemic weapon or a rationalist system of all civil and penal law, of minute rules of procedure, of specific forms of constitutional and international law. Rather, it formulated only a few general principles. All human law—that is, the positive law, statute law and customary law of the state, the Church, the international community, and the rules of autonomous bodies within the state—is a determination or consequence of these principles.... Natural law thus remains the paramount measure and the superior critical norm of judgment for the justice of human law. But human law itself is necessary.[16]

If we compare this passage from Professor Rommen with the two caveats registered by Professor

Sigmund, we realize that Rommen saw natural law's generality to be a virtue, whereas Sigmund saw it as a defect. Yet, it was this very quality of generality that enabled it to perform the tasks of "evaluating" and criticizing existing institutions and practices for which Professor Sigmund felt we had to turn elsewhere.

Likewise, Professor Brecht's desire to establish justice and truth as "intersubjectively transmissible knowledge" is aware of the danger to which positivist denials of universal, binding values can lead. Classical natural law theory was quite aware of this so that truth and justice were considered to be transcendent to particular laws or non-rationally chosen ends. This very transcendence—the Platonic idea of justice itself —still needed embodiment in particular constitutions or acts. Peter Drucker made this point particularly well in his discussion of the requirements for the American presidency and hence, presumably, for any rationally elected official:

> To be effective, our next President must, however, kindle in this generation...the excitement of politics. He must convince it that politics deals with great issues, that it is concerned with right and wrong rather than with procedures, with the nature and destiny of man rather than with 'who gets what.'[17]

Such a program, of course, is a direct challenge to the very nature of modern political science in comparison with earlier natural law orientations establishing the theoretical and practical need to begin with right and wrong and to continue this judgment in each particular political act so that justice is a reality and not merely an ideal, a reality that admits, consequently, its own limits.

Standards

The temptation to reduce all argument about what is good or right to questions of custom or opinion is, historically, sophist, even when the sophist position is itself argued philosophically. This is done when the very existence of any "absolute" is conceived to be itself a threat to "freedom," which is taken as a higher norm than truth. The Roman historian Tacitus recounted perhaps the classic scene in which philosophical diversity is reduced not to the category of truth or error, but to mere amusement, because neither truth nor error much mattered. Thus, the truth factor of varying opinions and its consequences become a mere matter of a pleasantry. Of the Court of the Emperor Nero in 59 AD, then, Tacitus bitingly wrote: "(Nero) would also bestow some leisure after his banquets on the teachers of philosophy, for he enjoyed the wrangles of opposing dogmatists. And some there were who liked to exhibit their gloomy faces and looks, as one of the amusements of the Court."[18]

No one who would hold that moral and political truths do in fact "exist," that they are not merely bantering opinions, then, can ever escape for long the charge that all ethical opinions are only subjective, that they are little better than a diversion of pretentious and gloomy philosophers. Yet, that such was not the case was the very enterprise with which Plato began political philosophy in the first place.

Consequently, as Professor Reo Christenson suggested in his essay, "Natural Law: Maybe the Fathers Were Right," few are willing to admit that Auschwitz, as an example of something clearly wrong, was merely another "opinion," that rejection of ancient and contemporary crimes is just a culturally conditioned option which may someday become acceptable. No doubt, various holocausts are still being perpetrated and justified by our various 20th Century ideologies. Nonetheless, the philosophical point is well taken that if there are no general ethical or political truths which also bear on particular events and acts, then the objections to a Nero or a Hitler must lose their force. In this sense, therefore, the service a Hitler or a Nero rendered to political philosophy is incalculable, for almost single-handedly, it demands a reconsideration of the "scientific" and "value-free" hypothesis upon which modern social sciences have been justifying themselves.

Professor Christenson, then, rightly wondered why Auschwitz or any similar horror was wrong if values really were culturally relative, as much of contemporary social science has argued.[19] Interestingly enough, a good number of the reflective studies made after World War II by Ernest Cassirer, Jacques Maritain, A. D. Lindsay, Walter Lippmann, Eric Voegelin, and Leo Strauss were based upon the idea that there was indeed something objectively unnatural, something definitely "wrong," beyond our own preferences and "as ifs" in the Hitler experience, an experience—unfortunately, history has told us—not confined exclusively to the Nazis. Thus, in liberal theory, a Hitler may perhaps have been entitled to his "opinions," but the human race is quite certain that his position was absolutely wrong. And this latter can only be upheld on something that sounds like natural law, whether based on the testimony of general consensus, as Professor Christenson himself suspected, or on the theory of classic Christian natural law.

This latter position, however, runs into a view common to many segments of political theory that all theory of right and wrong in human action is itself "absolutist" and consequently the "cause" of holocaust, even though the contradictory of this view reveals signs of the original positivist position, which, as we have seen, we also have good reasons to avoid for the same reasons. Behind the question of natural law in its philosophical formulation, then, was the question of an abiding "human nature," of what it is throughout the ages that identifies and distinguishes each member of the human species so that he is neither "beast or god," as Aristotle pointed out. Even though the specious principle of Hume that the contrary of every matter of fact is possible was evidently, if rather uncritically, held to have destroyed any common essence grounded in particular human reality but not placed there by itself, the fact is that a standard of human value remained which enabled us to condemn what was in fact held to be wrong, and this not merely by virtue of some Kantian postulate of the mind.

This conflict between positivist theory and contemporary political judgment can be seen in several ways. On a practical side, The National Town Meeting in the Kennedy Center in Washington held a discussion on "Lying: Moral Choice in Public and Private Life." No doubt, the problem of the legitimacy of "lying" already appeared in *The Republic* of Plato, where there seemed some justification for it. However, as this particular Town Meeting brought out in a striking way, we live in a time of rather strict standards about lying. This may be one of Richard Nixon's legacies to public morality, for he forced the general public to acknowledge, if they were to condemn him, that "lying was wrong." Without this latter general principle operative in Nixon's particular case, without a holding that "lying was wrong" to be more than opinion, those who condemned Mr. Nixon were only hypocritical to have charged him by the standard of truth against lying. In this sense, we may in fact be closer to the strict standards of Cicero's *De Officiis* than to Plato.

In the course of the discussion on lying, which curiously sounded much like treatises in the old moral theology textbooks, two points pertinent to absolute standards were made: The first was by Senator Mark Hatfield of Oregon:

> I think as one who makes a commitment or attempts to live within the Judaeo-Christian ethic and its teachings, one must always seek to make the highest moral choice within a world which is imperfect, dealing with institutions and individuals who are fallen in nature because of their imperfections and sins.[20]

And when asked whether communists do not lie as a matter of public policy, Senator Hatfield continued:

> ...In a communist country, it has as one of its theses atheism. Obviously, their whole measurement is mankind, humankind. I think in a country like ours, in the Judaeo-Christian faith, we believe in the perfection, at least most of us believe in a perfection of God that becomes our point of reference, that becomes our model, that becomes something to measure ourselves against. If we are solely measuring against each other, then we come to the lowest denominator in our society, rather than the highest possible fulfillment of our kind.[21]

Readers of Plato will recognize here a similarity to the famous passage in *The Laws* in which Protagoras was corrected. God, not man, Plato said, is the measure of all things (# 716). Thus, even the imperfect world needs a standard other than what men do in fact do, something to measure themselves *against*, so they will what they can be, what in fact they ought sometimes to be, even if they are not so.

A further point relative to absolute standards was brought up by Professor Sissela Bok, the wife of the President of Harvard and herself a writer on the subject of lying. When asked about the causes of lying, Dr. Bok replied:

> I would say also that in the last few generations, Americans have been deprived of something they always had in the past in their higher education. All through the 18th and 19th Centuries, Americans have had courses in ethics. That was the crowning course in their curriculum designed to pull everything together and to put before them problems they might face later on.
>
> Somehow in the last few generations, that has dried up and now we are finding that people are asking once again to be allowed to take these questions seriously in their education.[22]

Such are remarkable words, and not just for Americans, for they mean nothing less than that we cannot really avoid the problem, either in education or politics, of whether there is an ethical and an unethical.

Rational and Religious

Western civilization has been unique because it has both a rational and a religious response to ethical questions. Indeed, in the central tradition, the two relate to the same problem, that of what the human person ought to do to be as good, as perfect as he can, and this even granting that he may not actually succeed in being good. And when we know what a person ought to do, we likewise know what he ought not to do. Neither the natural law nor the Decalogue thought the two, what we ought to do and what we ought not to do, were the same. Lying, consequently, to continue this example, was in fact a wrong and justified the impassioned outbursts against public figures caught in acts of lying.

A second way the conflict between positivist theory and particular political judgment can be understood is from the side of theory itself. The very effort to reject absolutism by specifically rejecting human essence, and therefore a norm of natural law, in practice looks very problematic. In Professor Vernon van Dyke's *Political Science: A Philosophical Analysis,* for example, Plato was held to be the cause of "absolutist" aberrations. This was because "forms" were said to have been confused with things, abstractions like justice or the good were "reified." Such a confusion, in Professor van Dyke's view, encouraged those who wanted to establish good and make evil disappear. As a result, "repressive and bloody dictatorships" were justified in order to establish this absolutely existing justice or good.

Beginning already with Aristotle, no doubt, philosophers have suspected some problem with the exact understanding of platonic forms.[23] Professor van Dyke, however, compounded the error by the tenor of his rejection of platonic theory:

> ...Those who thought they were defining a thing were, instead, simply stipulating the meaning of a word. The essence of justice was what the defining person declared it to be. Confusion on the point has cost untold years of wasted intellectual effort. More seriously, it has undoubtedly affected the course of political events, for people seem to be able to devote themselves more wholeheartedly to a foreordained essence than to a man-made meaning. The feeling that they are fighting on the side of the Lord gives them courage and strength. Moreover, the notion of essences reinforces authoritarianism especially, for it implies Truth that exists independently of the majority will.[24]

The notion that truth somehow does "not" exist independently of the majority will, however, seems by far the more dangerous position. The rejection of essence leads directly to a relativism finding its own "truth" in nothing more stable than majority will. Unless there is a criterion to subject and judge the majority will itself, the tyranny of the majority becomes the final norm.

Professor van Dyke, thus, rejected "essentialism" by embracing an emotional, relativist thesis, one that placed truth in no firm foundation. Paradoxically, it was precisely to avoid the totalitarian dangers of a position such as this that gave rise to natural law in the first place. If Auschwitz or any other similar crime was merely consensus, opinion, or emotion, then in some eventual circumstance, it could become *true*, as it were. The absolute, the "essence" of natural law, which, as Aristotle explained to Plato, was not to be understood merely as a reification, must rather be seen as a real principle of being and its ontological diversity.[25]

Clifford Kossel has suggested how the principles of the natural law are derived:

> Are there some...natural affective judgments? There are, but they are difficult to determine and formulate. St. Thomas has best described these in an article in which he asks whether the natural contains one or many principles (I-II, 94, 2).
>
> The goods to which we are naturally inclined and which are naturally known as goods to be accomplished by men are found at three levels.
>
> Like all substances, we tend to be, and we know that it is good to preserve and develop our being; like all animals, we tend to the preservation of the species and know that this is good; finally, we tend to the specifically human good, to know the truth about ourselves, the universe, and

God, and to communicate with our peers through societal life. There is no moral precept which is not a determination of one of these essential goods; they contain in principle the totality of the human good.[26]

The thrust of this position is not from ought to fact, but rather from fact to ought, wherein the intellect serves as the illumination of what does exist in each person.[27] This is why natural law begins with an exercise of truth, with the classical function of all intellect to know that which is, beginning with what is most immediate to us, with ourselves as things we did not make.[28]

The "Christian" statement of the natural law, then, cannot and does not present itself as inventing new additions to the content of natural law. If something "new" is learned in the course of history or reflection, it is learned, as Maritain once wrote, because it is already there to be learned.[29] Christianity does accept that there is revelation, that the divine mind does communicate to and with human minds, however much such intellects may be dissimilar. But the truths which are properly speaking "revealed" are likewise intended to result in and increase precisely thought, truth. Consequently, since one can think better because of revelation, because of the challenge and insights of this revealed order, because of what one has learned about himself and his kind, this does not mean that what men now discover under its influence, as Strauss implied, *ipso facto* is beyond reason. If we see by a borrowed light, we still see, and indeed we may come to see without this added light.

Current Trends

Currently, two things may be said to be happening with regard to natural law. The first is, as Professor Henry Veatch has suggested, that the philosophical objections to it in the modern era are themselves breaking down.[30] The second is that the alternatives to natural law, which have necessarily been invented or resorted to as substitutes for it, still leave a great deal of uncertainty, so that we have never more lacked a common basis within which to communicate and live with one another in truth. Both of these factors are, undoubtedly, evidence for what Aquinas called the natural "necessity" of divine law, of what is usually called revelation (I-II, 91, 4). That is, he held that, in fact, most men would not be able in practice to follow or live the natural law by themselves, let alone know what its more delicate points might be. An indirect result of revelation, however, which would not have this as its direct or proper purpose, would be the clarification of what is to be thought about those general principles we do discover by reflection to be operative in ourselves.

What we have in our time is, therefore, a growing list of verifiable "consequences" of *not* accepting the so-called secondary or tertiary principles of the natural law—which Aquinas said only the very wise could reach by themselves—and a likewise growing determination of what is in fact "right," arising from Christian religious sources as well as from the general consensus of mankind about particular cases, like the lying of public figures. Plato, in *The Republic*, did not want to hear justice praised for rewards or punishments that might result from its practice. With perhaps more realism, Christianity has not hesitated to employ rewards and punishments as a motive for learning to do good even if we may not understand fully why the good is good. This was something Plato also came to in *The Laws*. With Aristotle, Christianity has argued that the only way to become good is to do good things. And the only way to do what is good is to know what things are good to do.

Thus, we have a growing list of "oughts" and a growing list of "consequences" for violating the oughts. Strauss was noble to strive to know all one could by his own reason, so that the men who needed it most would not be alienated by the fact that most men learned by faith. He suspected that some men would be scandalized when they began to suspect that reasonable things might indeed be in conformity with revelation. In this context, then, Christianity has seemed especially maddening to many, since it is not primarily concerned with the best polity in which all the oughts were to be realized and none of the ought-nots permitted, a society of no rewards and punishments, a society of only justice, the dream from Plato to Rawls—or better, from Platonists to Rawls. Augustine, in this sense, as Hannah Arendt wrote, is still the first Christian political philosopher, since he saved us from rigid platonic logic by discovering the existence of *The City of God,* wherein Plato's valid hopes might indeed be realized. This left us living in something considerably less than perfection. Indeed, as Burke saw, when we tried to inaugurate perfection, we usually created the worst of states.

And so we have produced among us the worst of states, often by our very idealism, as in perhaps the Cambodia of today. We are more and more hesitant to suggest that this worst state did not itself result from our opinions about the status of right and wrong. A Hitler or a Nero or a Cambodian marxist, consequently, had opinions, and we are loathe theoretically to condemn them because we fear the right almost as much as the wrong, when we acknowledge even a difference not based on majority will. As Francis Canavan recently wrote, J. S. Mill never told us what he would have done if his theory of liberty led to Auschwitz.[31] A Gandhi, however, did tell us. He said that those who live in such a society should voluntarily suffer.[32] Gandhi is cited last not to advocate or even encourage complete pacifism, but to suggest that even when we arrive at the necessity of absolute principles because of our experience with relative ones, we still may not know precisely what to do. Natural reason may not always tell us this in particular, even though it may well suggest something must be done. We may rage over what is wrong without knowing how to correct it, or to prevent our corrections, as in Vietnam-Cambodia, from making bad things worse. We cannot be at all sure that Gandhi gave the best answer in 1938, however much we may suspect Neville Chamberlain gave the wrong advice in about the same year.

A Christian statement of the natural law, consequently, ought indeed to enable us to *reason* better; but at the same time, it will be a statement addressed mostly to the ordinary and the "fallen," to use ancient theological realism which teaches us to beware of trusting too much in ourselves. Christianity is a theory of personal redemption and salvation, not directly a theory of human nobility. Men are not in Christianity encouraged to become Greek gods to stand against the ages in perfect form, but they are urged to save their souls, as it is put, in whatever society they might find themselves, worst as well as best. When it analyzes things of the world, of politics, Christianity proceeds from nature to grace, as if the proper way to reach the latter is to begin with the former.

Yet, in the order of actual living, Christianity begins with grace, with faith to do the actually taught, revealed commands. In doing this, it learns about reason. This is why the unity of reason and revelation—usually stated as 'faith cannot contradict reason'—remains the central operative thesis of any specifically Christian reflection on natural law. Failing to understand this, most of modern political theory has not known how to take account of "Christian natural law." But positively, this also must mean that revelation has its proper effect in thought as well as action, when things are seen by everyone which were, perhaps, only obscure to the wise, if then.[33]

Furthermore, this is why it is crucial, as an intellectual endeavor, for opponents of Christianity to separate pure reason from reason reflected on by faith. For if the latter is indeed more "reasonable," as Christian tradition has positively argued—a point to which we will turn in the following chapter—then its "revelation" cannot properly be considered as totally "irrational" or a product of mere emotion, as much of modern philosophy would have it. In fact, it can be seen as a positive asset.[34] This is the ultimate reason that Christianity in the structure of the Christian Church has asserted that intelligence is an essential aspect of faith itself.

The Christian statement of the natural law, then, still stands at the frontier of the ultimate question of political theory, the question, as Professor Strauss put it, that arrives with philosophy at "quid sit Deus," at the question of the essence of God in its relation to our own personal essences.[35] The "divine alternative," as Professor Brecht put it, ought to be a normal part of our education, especially when we study politics. Sissela Bok was right; education ought to end with ethics "to pull everything together and to put before (us) problems (we) might face" in actual public life. The natural law presumes ethics. Ethics presumes metaphysics. Metaphysics does not presume, but it does not exclude revelation. And revelation is primarily a thing of intelligence, so that it might reach human life in individual persons, in John, Paul, and Mary. In the end, to avoid Christian natural law is, ironically, to avoid natural law altogether, if not in theory, at least in practice.

Footnotes:

[1] E. B. F. Midgley, *The Natural Law Tradition and the Theory of International Relations,* London, Elek, 1975, p. xviii.

[2] Cf. Heinrich Rommen, *The Natural Law,* St. Louis, B. Herder, 1947; Michael B. Crowe, *The Changing Profile of the Natural Law,* The Hague, Martinus Nijhoff, 1977; Henry Veatch, "The Natural Law," *Literature of Liberty,* October-December, 1978. The latter two contain extensive bibliographies of natural law literature. Cf. also the author's "Generalization and Concrete Activity in Natural Law Theory," *Archiv für Rechts-und Sozialphilosophie,* Mai, 1959; "Culture and Human Rights," *America,* January 14, 1978, pp. 14-17.

[3] Cf. Josef Pieper, *Reality and the Good,* Trans. S. Lange, Chicago, Regnery, 1967.

[4] Alexander Passerin d'Entreves, *Natural Law: An Historical Survey,* New York, Harper Torchbooks, 1965, p. 11.

⁵ Harvey W. Kushner and Gerald de Maio, "A Discipline in Search of its Paradigm: Reflections on the Post-Behavioral Era in Political Science," *The Centennial Review*, June, 1979, p. 277.

⁶ Paul Sigmund, *Natural Law in Political Thought*, Cambridge, Mass., Winthrop, 1971, p. 208.

⁷ Christian Bay went so far as to suggest that if contemporary political scientists had no "values," then logically they could support the left in modern politics without scruple. Cf. C. Bay, "A Critical Evaluation of Behavioral Literature," in *Contemporary Political Thought*, Ed. J. Gould, New York, Holt, 1969, pp. 137-60; C. Bay, "Thoughts and Purposes of Political Education," in *The Post-Behavioral Era*, Ed. G. Carey, New York, McKay, 1973, pp. 88-102.

⁸ Cf. Midgley, *ibid.* Cf. also John Finnis, *Natural Law and Natural Right*, Oxford, Clarendon, 1980.

⁹ Frederick D. Wilhelmsen, *Christianity and Political Philosophy*, Athens, University of Georgia Press, 1978. Cf. also the author's "Political Theory: The Place of Christianity," *Modern Age*, Winter, 1981, pp. 26-33.

¹⁰ Leo Strauss, *Natural Right and History*, Chicago, University of Georgia Press, 1953, p. 164.

¹¹ *Ibid.*

¹² Cf. Leo Strauss, *Thoughts on Machiavelli*, Glencoe, Illinois, The Free Press, 1958. Cf. also Charles N. R. McCoy, *The Structure of Political Thought*, New York, McGraw-Hill, 1963, Chapter VI.

¹³ Cf. J. M. Bochenski, *Philosophy—an Introduction*, New York, Harper Torchbooks, 1972, pp. 63-92. Cf. also Stanley Jaki, "Religion and Science: The Cosmic Connection," in *Belief, Faith and Reason*, J. A. Howard, Editor, Belfast, Christian Journals, 1981, pp. 11-28.

¹⁴ Arnold Brecht, *Political Theory: The Foundations of Twentieth Century Thought*, Princeton, Princeton University Press, 1959, p. 497.

¹⁵ Cf. the author's "From Catholic 'Social Doctrine' to the 'Kingdom of God on Earth'," *Communio*, Winter, 1976, pp. 284-300; "Apocalypse as a Secular Enterprise," *The Scottish Journal of Theology*, # 4, 1976, pp. 357-73; "The Christian Guardians," *The Downside Review*, January, 1979, pp. 1-9.

¹⁶ Heinrich Rommen, *The State in Catholic Thought*, St. Louis, B. Herder, 1945, "Natural Law and Positive Law in the Philosophia Perennis," p. 205. Cf. the Review of Rommen's book by Leo Strauss in *What Is Political Philosophy?*, Westport, The Greenwood Press, 1976, pp. 281-84.

17 Peter Drucker, *Men, Ideas, and Politics*, New York, Harper Colophon, 1969, p. 149.

18 Tacitus, *Annals*, 14, 16.

19 Reo Christenson, *Heresies: Right and Left, Some Political Assumptions Re-examined*, New York, Harper, 1973, pp. 1-17. Cf. also William Blackstone, *Political Philosophy*, New York, Crowell, 1973, Part II and Chapter 13.

20 National Town Meeting, *Lying: Moral Choices in Public and Private Life*, Washington, Hoover Reporting Company, 1979, p. 36.

21 *Ibid.*, p. 41.

22 *Ibid.*, p. 37.

23 Cf. Bochenski, *ibid.*, pp. 31-41.

24 Vernon van Dyke, *Political Science: A Philosophical Analysis*, Stanford, University Press, 1960, p. 68.

25 Cf. Bochenski, *ibid.*

26 Clifford Kossel, *Some Problems of Truth in Ethics*, 19th Jesuit Philosophical Association Proceedings, 1957.

27 Pieper, *ibid.*

28 Cf. E. Gilson, "The Future of Augustinian Metaphysics," *St. Augustine*, New York, Meridian, 1957, pp. 287-316.

29 Cf. Jacques Maritain, *Man and the State*, Chicago, University of Chicago Press, 1951, "The First Element (Ontological) in Natural Law, The Second Element (Gnoseological) in Natural Law," pp. 84-95.

30 Henry Veatch, *ibid.*, pp. 7-28.

31 Francis Canavan, "J. S. Mill on Freedom of Expression," *The Modern Age*, Fall, 1979, pp. 362-69.

32 Mahatma Gandhi, "The Jews," in *Social and Political Philosophy*, Ed. J. Somerville, Garden City, Doubleday Anchor, 1963, p. 535.

33 Cf. F. Wilhelmsen, "Faith and Reason," *The Modern Age*, Winter, 1979, pp. 25-32. Cf. also James Steintrager, "Political Philosophy, Political Theology, and Morality," *The Thomist*, July, 1968, pp. 307-32.

34 Cf. the author's "The Recovery of Metaphysics," *Divinitas*, Rome, # 2, 1979, pp. 200-19.

35 Leo Strauss, *The City and Man*, Chicago, University of Chicago Press, 1978, p. 241.

CHAPTER IX

Political Philosophy and Catholicism

The Thomists remain to remind their contemporaries that whatever evils there may be in modern, as in earlier, political life, there is no necessity to ignore the truth about the ends of political life or to despair of it or to revolt against it. So long as it is feasible, the good man in politics will continue to do what can be done in furtherance of the common good. Sometimes he may have to resign; sometimes he may have to suffer persecution and even, in extreme cases, martyrdom— but, whatever the outcome, the truth remains.

—E. B. F. Midgley, University of Aberdeen, "Concerning the Modernist Subversion of Political Philosophy," The New Scholasticism, *Spring, 1979, p. 190.*

Where Christianity in general and Catholicism in particular fits into political theory has been the general topic of reflection in these considerations. This naturally concerns the whole area of poverty, political reform, tyranny, together with the improvements that might in fact be expected in this world. In this sense, an enthusiasm for change and improvement may well be the most dangerous and unimproving approach one could take. Indeed, we have argued that the improvement that might legitimately be expected is largely jeopardized by notions of reform and improvement that will result in fact in anything but a betterment of the human condition. This latter realism has been traditionally part of political thought associated with Christianity, though it is much less in evidence today, unfortunately. There is, furthermore, a problem more peculiar to Catholicism, one that arose, as we saw in the previous chapter, over the natural law as it was criticized by Professor Leo Strauss, surely one of the very greatest political philosophers of this century. It is to this question that we must now turn in any complete accounting for our subject of Christianity and Politics.

At first sight, to approach this subject through an obscure controversy at Yale University over the refusal to grant tenure to a young political science professor might seem to be of little interest to the specifically Catholic investment in intelligence. Yet, in its own way, this will lead us to the very heart of the central issue of our time, the decline of Catholicism as a specific intellectual force in the contemporary world.[1] This occurs at a time when people like Father Stanislaus Jaki in science and Professor John Senior in philosophy are arguing with great force that classical Christianity does possess the intellectual structure to answer the very questions that modern thought and experience have been unable to handle.[2]

This is not to say, of course, that Catholics may not individually count, but rather that they do not count because of what they hold *qua* Catholic. The person who is usually called a Catholic "intellectual" in the media today is most often apt to be someone whose intellectual formation is modernist or ideological, someone who openly or implicitly sees his role as saving the Church by reinterpreting its dogma or mission in the light of secular or ideological thought. John Senior is quite blunt on this point:

> To say that freedom of religion excludes the right to teach what you believe is a contradiction in terms. It is a bitter joke to think of the university as the last refuge of religious bigotry. I have used the term *medieval* and not *Catholic* because the words are not coterminous. I wish they were. But, on the one hand, there are many Catholics moving away from the monastic center of their Church in the name of an untried spirit they falsely identify with the Second Vatican Council; and, on the other hand, there are some outside the visible Church who very well may be part of an invisible monastic tradition. So there is no question here at all of a religious establishment but,

quite the reverse, of an inquisitorial Liberalism ruthlessly exterminating everything that disagrees with it—in the name of freedom.[3]

Behind this is the assumption that an orthodox Christian proves his intellectuality only by disagreeing with the creedal structure of the faith. Malcolm Muggeridge put the situation humorously well: "A convert is perhaps a sated sensualist, or ga-ga, or terrified of dying, anything except overwhelmed by the sheer beauty and truth of the Incarnation and our Lord's birth, ministry, death and resurrection as recorded in the Gospels."[4] That faith leads to a deeper intelligence is a proposition that is dogmatically rejected, even though, as we saw in the previous chapter, this may be the real fear of any theory of faith and reason in the classic sense.

In any case, both *The Wall Street Journal* and *The Washington Star* thought the Yale incident worthy of comment. Professor Thomas Pangle, it seems, ran into difficulty with Yale's Political Science Department's prevailing behaviorist orthodoxy because of his association "with a school of thought emphasizing the classical writings and denigrating modern social science."[5] Moreover, Edwin Yoder pointed out that Pangle was a student of Professor Leo Strauss who, almost single-handedly, along with Hannah Arendt and Eric Voegelin, has reestablished the serious consideration of classical political philosophy in the United States and

Europe. Strauss died in 1973. He insisted that politics cannot fully or properly be studied without attention to philosophic questions whose origins lie in Greek thought. Yoder remarked, perhaps a bit ironically, "One would like to know more about this apparently heretical school of thought fostered by Professor Strauss, the factionalism it seems to generate in political science departments."[6] No one in professional political science, of course, can avoid knowing of Professor Strauss, but it is probably true that the meaning of his thought is not generally recognized in particularly Christian circles.

Underneath the departmental infighting, then, and not merely confined to Yale, lies a whole world of intellectual controversy of great moment to the present disarray evident in the particularly Catholic mind. For Leo Strauss was undoubtedly the key thinker who has succeeded in forcing us to reconsider the validity of revelation with its relation to thought and politics as such. Professor Frederick Wilhemsen, in his important study *Christianity and Political Philosophy*, to which we have previously referred, has held that especially the Straussian school of thought in American political science departments has so rarified both reason and revelation that they can have no relationship to each other. This minute Straussian study of the classics and the moderns in political thought has resulted in a persistent neglect of Christianity, particularly Christian philosophy itself.[7]

And there is little doubt that Strauss, following his own methodology, his dogged belief that the prejudice of modern thinkers is so great against revelation that it is best not to mention it much, but rather to keep it in secret writing, held that the preliminary fight of our time is to reestablish philosophy as such on grounds that do not presuppose revelation. Once the theoretical bias of the whole structure of modern thought, particularly its historicist and anti-value bias, is unearthed, then perhaps an attention to revelation will again be possible. The first task, then, in this view, is philosophical.

Faith and Reason Reconsidered

Professor E. B. F. Migdley has taken a much less sympathetic view towards the Straussian enterprise because, in his view, Strauss himself betrayed certain modernist attitudes which had origins, as Father Charles N. R. McCoy pointed out in his important *The Structure of Political Thought,* in Greek thought, especially in post-Aristotelian theory itself.[8] Thus, a return to the classics might result in a return to the very problems Christian philosophy tried to correct in ancient times.

> After all, Strauss writes not merely of the non-traditional origin of the philosophical genius

of Plato but also implies that the highest philosophy is not susceptible of being upheld in a tradition even when it has been discovered. Strauss tells us that the classical political philosophy 'has never been equalled' in the pre-classical period and he expresses doubt about the feasibility of a return to classical philosophy in modern times. Yet, all this does not involve a definitive rejection of traditionalism. It does involve a view of the eternal order as something so elusive and uncertain that it is not susceptible of *being really* known at all.[9]

That philosophy could be known and kept, even more so with faith, was precisely the thesis to which Gilson and Maritain most addressed themselves. It may be true, however, that the present state of philosophical attitude in Christianity may be proving Strauss more correct than we could have expected. Strauss was, at least in his political writings, rather inclined to separate rigidly philosophy and revelation so that the unity of the human personality was itself in doubt. Strauss did not hold revelation, particularly Jewish revelation, was impossible. But he did often seem to doubt that any philosophical reflection on revelation, or any question or insight originally presented to the mind by faith, could still be called philosophy.[10]

Pertinence of Pure Philosophy

In his last book, Jacques Maritain put down a statement about philosophy and theology that is pertinent to the context of Strauss' analysis of political philosophy:

> ...The light of Christian philosophy is not, like that of theology, the light of Faith illuminating Reason in order to enable it to acquire some understanding of revealed mysteries, but the light of Reason comforted by Faith in order to do better its own work of intellectual investigation: that which authorizes Christian philosophy, at the summit of its possibilities, to concern itself according to its proper mode with matters which pertain to theology; it remains, then, subordinated to theology, but it is undoubtedly—on condition of being instructed by it—more open to a work of research and of investigation; at this moment the ancilla becomes research worker.

> The last word will belong naturally to the theologian. But it is the philosopher—the Christian philosopher in the state in which the concrete situation of human nature, fallen and redeemed, *requires that he be,*—it is the philosopher who in such a case will have presented to the theologian the hypothesis of research.[11]

For Strauss, however, any "ancilla" notion meant, *ipso facto,* a corruption of the purity of philosophy, or at least the suspicion of such corruption.

Strauss, moreover, was a careful reader of Plato and recognized that the opposition between man and the city was indeed most basic. Politics was the realm of "opinion"; philosophy was the realm of truth, even if the city would not receive it. This led to paradoxical results for Strauss, since he held that the whole enterprise of modern thought in politics was seriously distorted against man from Machiavelli on. Thus, modern politics has not been controlled by those natural limits which were founded in the classics, especially in Aristotle. Politics have turned, therefore, on the kind of being man has received. In this context, then, Strauss at times admitted a special place for particularly Catholic theory.

At a Lecture at the Jesuit-run University of Detroit in the early 1960's, Strauss remarked:

> When you look around yourself, not at the University of Detroit, not at other Catholic institutions, but at non-Catholic institutions, I think you can say that with very few exceptions, political philosophy has disappeared. Political philosophy, the decay of political philosophy into ideology, reveals itself today most obviously in the fact that in both research and teaching political philosophy has been replaced by the history of political philosophy.[12]

In this context, then, I wish here to suggest that Strauss' then favorable opinion of the condition of political philosophy in the Catholic tradition of around two decades ago has now been rendered largely obsolete by the widespread appearance of precisely "ideology" in Catholic universities, presses, and social action centers as substitutes for genuine Christian political theory.[13]

Strauss, moreover, made a further valuable reflection concerning the nature of his precise problem with Catholic intelligence. In the same lecture series, Professor Strauss went on:

> Political philosophy is an activity in the West today only in Thomism. This creates a difficulty, however, even for the Thomists, because it gives rise to the suspicion that it is the Christian Catholic faith, and not human reason, which supports this political philosophy. Therefore, it is necessary even for the Thomists to show that the Aristotelian conception of political philosophy... has not been rejected by modern thought.[14]

Thomism at its best, of course, has always understood something of this, but it has likewise refused to accept the Straussian implication that reason under the light of faith is somehow unreasonable.

We live in a period, however, when Catholic Christians have mostly ceased requiring much Thomism or even philosophy of their clerics, religious or lay.[15] This was the very foundation of Catholic Christian strength, as Strauss suggested. Seminary and university curricula no longer require much, if any, of it. This, in my opinion, is undoubtedly the origin of the influx of ideology into Christian circles, such that they are not, from a Straussian view, as immune from ideology as he might have hoped.[16]

Yet, if Thomism begins again to make considerably more sense, precisely as an authentic foundation to political and scientific philosophy —something Stanislaus Jaki's recent Gifford Lectures suggest—then, of course, we are back where Leo XIII put us a century ago. However, this time, the pursuit of Aquinas will come from exigencies precisely in the secular order and from political philosophy itself.[17] Philosophy has its own exigencies. In this sense, Professor Strauss was right in reminding Catholic Christians of their own tradition as precisely one that relates to the intellectual structure of the problems modern man is facing.

The significance of this, then, can further be approached from a peculiar concern of John Paul II. On June 5, 1979, he remarked to the Polish Bishops:

> In conformity with the tradition of European thought, which goes back to the greatest works of antiquity and which found its full confirmation and deeper development in the Gospel and in Christianity, *political activity* also—indeed, especially—finds its proper meaning in solicitude for God's people, which is a good of an ethical nature. From here, that whole social teaching of the Church derives its deepest meanings, a teaching that, especially in our time, beginning from the end of the nineteenth century, has been enormously enriched by all the problems of the present day.

> This does not mean that the Church's social teaching appeared only at the turn of the century; in fact, it existed from the beginning, as a conse-

quence of the Gospel and of the vision of man the Gospel brought into relationships with other people, and especially in community and social life.[18]

Both in Mexico and in Poland, then, John Paul II specifically addressed himself to the question of whether Christians had their own sources and content of social thought or whether they were rather brokers, dependent upon outside sources for the content of thought itself. The *great works of antiquity*, it is to be noted, were included within the confines of Christian thought.[19]

Popes do not speak in such a manner, no doubt, unless there are Christians who wish to maintain the opposite of what they affirm.[20] For some time, it has been clear that Catholics in particular no longer think exclusively within their own independent tradition.[21] The thesis is proposed that there is no such thing as Catholic social thought with its own sources and therefore no relation to the classics. What follows is a "pluralism," a freedom to choose from among the various ideological "options," as it is put. The root cause of this is a refusal to consider both the actual design and content of scripture itself except in a priori ideological categories. Marxist oriented presentations in some Christian publications are only the most glaring examples of this. Alongside of this is a misunderstanding of the intrinsic nature of political and economic philosophy as such. This is why Strauss, in a way, is so significant for Christian thought, for his very project is to attack the roots of precisely the ideological structure of modern thought over against faith and reason. The observation of Etienne Gilson is not out of sympathy with the Straussian premises: "The fourteen centuries of history...were dominated by two distinct influences: Greek philosophy and Christianity. Every time educated Christians came in contact with Greek philosophical sources, there was a blossoming of theological and philosophical speculation."[22]

Disciplinary and Intellectual Integrity

What is at stake, of course, is the disciplinary and intellectual integrity of Catholicism itself. Social action then takes on forms and patterns unrelated to its norms and experienced values.[23] Professor Frederick Wilhelmsen, in his essay on "Faith and Reason," has stated the situation quite well:

> ...This supposed opposition (between faith and reason) has returned to the American academy where it occupies the very highest posts of power in the most prestigious as well as in the more moderate institutions of higher learning in the nation. Theology is becoming mindless and philosophy is becoming incorporeal. The vacant mindlessness of the former and the insubstantiality of the latter are breeding theological idiocy

and philosophical irrelevance. The study of theology has been radically divorced from the great tradition of scholastic philosophy and the reading of scripture substitutes for the middle term in a simple piece of reasoning.

Much Greek and no logic mark the vast majority of our seminaries today. In the very moment in which theology departments divide the time of their students into pondering biblical texts and espousing the social gospel, philosophy departments increasingly teach their discipline as though Christianity had never happened.[24]

These are frank words, rather accurately descriptive of too much of the actual situation.[25]

It is not without interest in this context to note that while the resurgence of neo-conservative theory in the United States, which we touched on in Chapter VII, is largely Jewish or orthodox Christian in the classical sense, in France conservatism has often, as *The Economist* noted, taken on an anti-Christian orientation.

Even Europe's old pagan gods have a place in the new right's thinking. By their diversity, they are seen as having made a more positive contribution to European culture than Christianity, which gets a low rating from new right intellectuals.

The movement's recently published handbook, ''Ten Years of Cultural Combat for a Renaissance,'' argues that Christianity is no help in the European identity crisis, since it was born outside Europe and has become the sort of blanket totalitarian world order which hinders the development of the individual personality. Condemning Christianity as a subversive, it charges: "The greatest reproach that can be made against Christianity is that it launched an egalitarian cycle that led to democracy, then to socialism and marxism." By contrast, ancient Europe judged men by their qualities and faults, on merit....[26]

What is interesting here is that the French new right has accepted the Christian left at its own face value, as nothing but a social activism based upon an ideology rooted in the specific reaction of modern thought to classical and Christian thought. Strauss also, as did medieval Christianity itself, recognized the very dubious nature of much egalitarian theory and its relation to modern ideology.[27]

It is precisely here, in any case, that Christianity is most glaringly in need of its own tradition of political philosophy. We have seen, without it, the very concept of "rights" become so politicized and controverted that they now mean mostly the opposite of what they meant in classical natural law theory.[28] Abortion and homosexuality are now the leading examples of "human rights," so unclear are we about what the normalcy of mankind is without the structures of faith. No doubt, rights still serve, especially for the Jews—Christians have made little effective use of them, even when their own interests were at stake—as instruments of political power. This is especially true in the case of the efforts to aid Russian Jews escape. But in the Third World—a term of perhaps little unified meaning—"human rights" have more and more become, often thanks to Christian confusions, subsumed into structural, marxist analysis so that the individual and the City of God are both lost in a discussion of political forms, forms often recognized as totalitarian by most critics at least since classical political thought.

In a recent Address to the American Catholic Historical Association, Professor Philip Gleason recounted how relatively late and volatile was the appearance of theological studies in Catholic universities. Religion passed from catechism to apologetics, to college theology, to the latest religious studies, which contain no longer a specifically Catholic presupposition. There was, some forty years or so ago, a general confidence that "the body of Catholic doctrine would stand forever." But it did not so last.

Thus, Professor Gleason reflected:

...The predominant impression I can recall feeling during the midst of the Catholic upheaval of the 1960's was the impression of disintegration. This word inevitably carries evaluative connotations, but I mean it more as a descriptive term. That is, the strongest sense I had was of a church, a religious tradition, that was coming undone, breaking apart, losing its coherence....[29]

In this context, it is interesting to speculate that the one traditionally Catholic country which did not appear to fall into the heresy of social activism and dogmatic chaos during this period was Poland. There are several reasons for this, not the least of which was that that ideology towards which most western and Third World theories tended was already the established doctrine in Poland. It did not take a Solzhenitsyn or a Polish Pope to tell the ordinary Pole the perils of such an option. But beyond this, as Leopold Tyrmand incisively remarked, what saved the Church in Poland was precisely its attention to its forgotten weapon, its "intellectual riches."

> Karol Wojtyla was one of the architects of the intellectualization strategy. He is a neo-Thomist scholar.... St. Thomas lived in a period when new scientific revelations were seen to be challenging the laws of God. Now, when the totalitarian ideas and social concepts deem themselves scientific, Aquinas' arguments seem to many more valid than ever. Simply put, Thomism leads to a theory of human liberty that is entitled to distinguish between the absolute and the dogmatic in matters of faith, and firmly rejects determinist philosophies such as Marxism.[30]

This is precisely the issue. The validity of Christian philosophy *is* the issue today. Without this philosophy, the faith is easily, as the Christian left again and again demonstrates, subverted into an essentially this-worldly doctrine.[31]

Signs of Change

There are slight signs, however, that a general change in intellectual atmosphere is in the air. Seminary students are wondering why so little and such non-traditional philosophy is the steady substance of their curriculum. Professor Bruce Haywood wrote:

> Slavery takes many forms. It isn't always chains and the lash upon the back. Huxley's brave new world of instant gratification is as horrible a prison as Big Brother's police state. The processes of education, corrupted, can deceive us with the illusion of our growth or make us the captive of a label. Genuinely liberal, they can still set us free.
>
> It is time for our colleges and universities to talk again about the worth of a free lifetime while we are still able to distinguish between the *training* of young people and their *education*. It is time to restore the priority of being over doing.[32]

This is, of course, the classical priority.

Professor Strauss himself was most perceptive when he wrote:

> Here, we are touching on what, from the point of view of the sociology of philosophy, is the most important difference between Christianity on the one hand, and Islam as well as Judaism on the other. For Christianity, the sacred doctrine is revealed theology; for the Jew and the Muslim, sacred doctrine is, at least primarily, the legal interpretation of the Divine Law. The sacred doc-

trine in the latter sense has, to say the least, much less in common with philosophy than sacred doctrine in the former sense.

It is ultimately for this reason that the status of philosophy was, as a matter of principle, much more precarious in Judaism and in Islam than in Christianity; in Christianity, philosophy became part of the officially recognized and even required training of the student of sacred doctrine. This difference explains partly the eventual collapse of philosophical inquiry in the Islamic and Jewish world, a collapse which has no parallel in the western world.[33]

This collapse, which did not occur in medieval times or even up until the 1960's, as Professor Gleason suggested, was something Professor Strauss could not have anticipated. But its root cause was the one Strauss had insisted before the academic world to be the most crucial one—the validity of reason before revelation.

In allowing theology and social science to become reasonless, however, Catholicism in particular has paid a great contemporary price, that of its intellectual plausibility. Before the tendencies of the powerful Straussian tradition, which would separate the two realms if only to save revelation, Christianity repeats with Gilson:

How can a speculation be rational and philosophical if it is tied up with religious beliefs? Here again, history as such has no competence to answer the question. It knows, however, that far from sterilizing philosophical speculation, this alliance of two distinct orders of thought has given philosophy a new life and brought about positive philosophical results. The history of the influence of Christianity on the development of modern philosophy, quite independently of scholasticism and sometimes even in reaction against its methods, would be another field of investigation.

From what little is already known of it, it appears that objectivity in judgment and freedom from settled intellectual prejudices are not the exclusive property of pagan philosophers, that reason is not always found at its best on the side of what is commonly called rationalism, and that, at any rate, *the range of intelligibility is incomparably wider than that of reason.* This is the lesson which only the frequentation of the true philosophical masterminds can teach us. Why should we feel afraid to be living in their company?[34]

Why indeed?

Before the counter tendency of Christians towards the very ideology of which Strauss warned continues much farther, we should recall with Aquinas, as Professor Heinrich Rommen used to say, what we have learned in political philosophy because we were forced to think about this faith.

Political life belongs to the realm of nature which is not absorbed by the new order of grace, but, on the contrary, is blessed and perfected. The great changes in meaning and import lay far more in the presuppositions in the theology, and in the moral and legal philosophy of the new spiritual power. From this viewpoint the following principles and premises emerge:

First, the idea of the Christian person; then the Christian idea that not earthly happiness in intellectual life alone, but the salvation of the soul and the glory of God for and in the life beyond are the last end of man and of ethics; and thirdly, that by the side of the only perfect society, the city of men of the ancients, the Church takes her place as a perfect society, the City of God, free and beyond the power and sovereignty of the state. From now on the idea of man no longer finds its absolute fulfillment in the citizen. Man's end transcends the state....[35]

These are precisely the considerations that are most missing when ideology becomes the heart of Christian activism.

Gary Wills and John East, then, were undoubtedly correct. In addition to the Thomism we so desperately need, we also need an Augustine to remind us what the City of God is about.[36] Leo Strauss, in spite of his caution about revelation, was right to insist that we cannot avoid classical political philosophy. But Professors Midgley and Wilhelmsen were likewise right in stressing that with revelation, we do not reason against reason, but with it. It is precisely the "reason" without revelation that is becoming unreasonable as the controversies over ecology, human rights, and the development of the so-called Third World reveal. We can, finally, be grateful to John Paul II, the Pole who understood

that the intellectual riches of the faith are its first
defense, when he reminded us that we have our
own independent sources of social philosophy.
These are the ancients *and* the Gospels in the
light of which we can think sanely about political
things.

Footnotes:

¹ Cf. the author's "Catholicism and Intelligence: The Reconciliation of the World and Truth," *The Clergy Review*, London, July,
1977; "The Condition of Catholic Intelligence," *The New Oxford
Review*, September, 1979; "The Recovery of Metaphysics,"
Divinitas, Rome, # 2, 1979.

² Cf. S. Jaki, *The Road of Science and the Ways of God*, Chicago,
University of Chicago Press, 1978.

³ John Senior, *The Death of Christian Culture*, New Rochelle,
Arlington House, 1978, pp. 176-77.

⁴ Malcolm Muggeridge, "Divine Laughter," *The National
Catholic Register*, August 5, 1979.

⁵ *The Wall Street Journal*, August 31, 1979.

⁶ *The Washington Star*, September 6, 1979.

⁷ Frederick D. Wilhelmsen, *Christianity and Political Theory*,
Athens, University of Georgia Press, 1978, Chapter 8.

⁸ Charles N. R. McCoy, The Structure of Political Thought,
New York, McGraw-Hill, 1963, Chapter 3; E. B. F. Midgley, "Concerning the Modernist Subversion of Political Philosophy," *The
New Scholasticism*, Spring, 1979. Cf. also McCoy's "On the Revival
of Classical Political Philosophy," *The Review of Politics*, April,
1973.

⁹ Midgley, *ibid.*, p. 177.

¹⁰ Cf. especially, Leo Strauss, *Natural Law and History*, Chicago,
University of Chicago Press, 1953, pp. 163-64.

¹¹ Jacques Maritain, *On the Grace and Humanity of Jesus*, New
York, Herder and Herder, 1969, pp. 11-12.

¹² Strauss, "The Crisis of Our Time," *The Predicament of
Modern Politics*, Ed. H. Spaeth, Detroit, University of Detroit Press,
1964, p. 51.

[13] Cf. Chapter I. Cf. also the author's "On the Non-Catholic Revival of Catholic Social Thought," *The Month,* March, 1977.

[14] Strauss, "The Crisis of Political Philosophy," *Predicament, ibid.,* p. 92.

[15] Cf. the work of Eric Mascall, an Anglican Theologian, who has done so very much to keep Thomism up to date and vital. Cf. also the author's "Some Unsolicited Advice to Wary Seminarians," *The Priest,* April, 1980, pp. 37-40.

[16] Cf. Jaki, *ibid.*

[17] Cf. Midgley, *ibid.*

[18] John Paul II, "To the Polish Episcopate," June 5, 1979, *L'Osservatore Romano,* English, July 2, 1979, p. 8. Cf. also R. Heckel, Editor, *The Human Person and Social Structures,* Rome, Pontifical Commission on Justice and Peace, 1980; R. Heckel, *The Use of the Expression 'Social Doctrine' of the Church,* Rome, Pontifical Commission on Justice and Peace, 1980.

[19] Cf. John Paul II, "Address to Latin American Bishops," January 29, 1979, III. 7, in *Puebla: A Pilgrimage of Faith,* Documents of John Paul II's Mexican Trip, Boston, Daughters of St. Paul, 1979.

[20] Cf. the author's "From Catholic 'Social Doctrine' to the 'Kingdom of God on Earth'," *Communio,* Winter, 1976.

[21] For a similar analysis of conditions within Protestant social thought, Cf. E. Lefever, *Amsterdam to Nairobi:* The World Council of Churches and the Third World, Washington, Ethics and Public Policy Center, 1979; Paul Seabury, "Trendier than Thou, the Episcopal Church and the Secular World," *Harper's,* December, 1979; E. R. Norman, *Christianity and the World Order,* New York, Oxford, 1979.

[22] Etienne Gilson, *History of Christian Philosophy in the Middle Ages,* New York, Random House, 1955; p. 540.

[23] Cf. in this regard, John Paul II's Address to a group of United States Bishops on the importance of doctrine and discipline, November 9, 1979, in *The Pope Speaks,* # 1, 1979.

[24] Frederick D. Wilhelmsen, "Faith and Reason," *The Modern Age,* Winter, 1979, p. 25.

[25] The Apostolic Constitution on Education, *Sapientia Christiana,* of April 29, 1979, in *L'Osservatore Romano,* English, June 4, 1979, is also pertinent here.

[26] "France's New Right in Search of Old European Roots," *The Economist,* September 1, 1979, p. 33.

[27] Cf. Irving Kristol, "About Equality," *Two Cheers for Capitalism,* New York, Basic, 1978, pp. 171-87.

[28] Cf. the author's "Second Thoughts on Human Rights," *Faith and Reason,* Winter, 1975-76, pp. 44-59.

[29] Philip Gleason, University of Notre Dame, Presidential Address to the 59th Annual Convention of the American Catholic Historical Association, San Francisco, December 29, 1978, p. 17.

[30] Leopold Tyrmand, "Poland, Marxism, and John Paul II," *The Wall Street Journal,* December 6, 1978.

Cf. also, Francis Lescoe, *Philosophy Serving the Contemporary Needs of the Church,* New Britain, Conn., Mariel, 1979; Andrew Woznicki, *A Christian Humanism: Karol Wojtyla's Existentialism,* New Britain, Conn., Mariel, 1980.

[31] Cf. footnote # 1.

[32] Bruce Haywood, "The Dehumanization of Higher Education," *The Chronicle of Higher Education,* January 8, 1979.

[33] Leo Strauss, *Persecution and the Art of Writing,* Westport, Conn., Greenwood, 1973, pp. 18-19.

[34] Gilson, *ibid.,* p. 545.

[35] Heinrich Rommen, *The State in Catholic Thought,* St. Louis, B. Herder, 1945, p. 29.

[36] Cf. Gary Wills, *Confessions of a Conservative,* Garden City, Doubleday, 1979, Part 4; John East, "The Political Relevance of St. Augustine," *The Modern Age,* Spring, 1972.

CHAPTER X

America in Recent Catholic Social Theory

In actual fact, it is in America that I have had a real experience of concrete, existential democracy: not as a set of abstract slogans, or as a lofty ideal, but as an actual, human, working, perpetually tested and repeatedly readjusted way of life. Here I met democracy as a living reality.

—*Jacques Maritain,* Reflections on America, *1958.*

Political philosophy in general and Christian political thought in particular have never quite known what to make of the United States. Michael Novak, with some justice, has recently argued that the present Vatican does not have a good appreciation for the genius of the American economic system, so that Christianity does not know how the country can work to aid the whole range of problems in the world.[1] Furthermore, with serious changes in American moral values, particularly in the area of life and its value, the positive sides of the American contribution are less able to be appreciated in isolation. Nonetheless, the inability to understand the place of American tradition in Christian social thought has itself been a main problem for both America and Christian thought.

In his essay on America's "Third Century," Norman Macrae cited a well-known passage from G. K. Chesterton's *What I Saw in America,* a book still worth reading in the light of what will be suggested about America, Catholic social thought, and the possibilities available to us on the Earth and in the cosmos.[2] Chesterton said: "There is nothing the matter with Americans except their ideals. The real American is all right; it is the ideal American who is all wrong." This is a sentiment also found in Ben Wattenberg's *The Real America.* What it suggests is that there are many theoretical things wrong with the way America attempts to aid the poor, especially on the question of human life. On the other hand, it is also true that the ability of revolutionary thought to convince much of the world that the American experience has nothing to offer to them is the major reason for underdevelopment, or at least for a development that does not understand either human sized or human directed institutions in their concrete forms, yet in new and inventive ways. The countries that did understand this, the so-called "neo-confucian countries," are well on their way to outpacing their inspirations. This is an unpopular view. Yet, it too should be argued and stated within the tradition of Christianity and politics.

Several scholars and critics have wondered of late whether Catholic social reflection, at least in its most vociferous centers, has not definitely taken on an anti-American turn.[3] Curiously, this bias is perhaps most clearly enunciated by American Catholics. Indeed, there is an anti-American school of Christian social thought which reduces most of the social ills of the world to the West in general and to the United States in particular. We have already seen much of this. And this is not an exclusively Catholic phenomenon. Protestant literature often has much the same spirit if we judge from, for example, Robert McAfee Brown's heavy-handed discourse, "Who Is This Jesus Christ Who Frees and Unites?"[4] However, we propose here to deal mostly with the Catholic aspect of the problem.

Anti-American Christian Social Thought

All of this anti-American Christian social thought is in a way most paradoxical. Historically, Catholic social thought in America, while often critical of given institutions or practices, always saw its major task as accepting and reconciling the truly unique American political and economic institutions with the Christian faith as understood by Catholics.[5] The laymen of the Baltimore Catholic Congress of 1889 stated roundly: "We repudiate with equal earnestness the assertion that we need to lay aside any of our devotedness to our Church to be true Americans; the insinuation that we need to abate any of our country's principles and institutions to be faithful Catholics."[6] In fact, there were many scholars who suspected that the American political genius owed much more to the earlier scholastic and Christian traditions than it was ever willing to acknowledge.[7] The ease with which Catholic immigrants became Americans tends to substantiate this in a way. American ethnic immigrants, in fact, lived in as bad housing, social and discriminatory conditions as existed anywhere in the world before or since. Yet, they advanced almost without benefit of any of the vast social, economic, or recompensatory structures which many today are claiming to be required for a more just society. Moreover, they generally have not been bitter over their past in spite of its pains, but have seen America as a way to fulfill hope, even religious hope, or at least the opportunity to worship God as they choose.

Elsewhere in this connection, I have argued that there is some ultimate philosophical relation between "America" as a problem in political theory and the peculiar locus of Christianity within this same political theory, such that Christianity freed politics. It allowed politics to be only politics, and not ideology or a substitute religion.[8] It is precisely this freedom from ideology that has made American experience so different and productive in the world. This is why, also, America in recent years has been seen to be the major enemy by social ideologues. Even Christians are accepting ideology as a guideline for meaning and are attempting to effect political and economic goals through its instrumentality, as we have already seen.

In any case, American Catholics were often most critical of European economic and social ideas and institutions that did not conform to American practice, since they believed their own system was in fact nearer to the ideals of Christian social thought. The famous insistence of Cardinal Gibbons that American labor unions were *not* European labor unions (and still are not) is perhaps the most celebrated example of this. Further, the economic and political ideas of European Christians—the distributism of Belloc and Gill, the Christian Democratic Parties and Unions of the Continent, the somewhat mystical personalism of Mounier, the diplomatic structure of the Holy See, the Corporate State, or Christians for Socialism—did not seem particularly welcome among American Catholics. They felt that they had escaped from many of the old world ills into a more realistic and dynamic economic and political life, even one superior for the faith itself. The separation of Church and

State, which centuries of European Catholics deplored, was often seen by Americans as contributing to Catholic well-being.

It would be foolish to argue that Catholic Americans in the past never misplaced their trust. In recent years, however, it has become something of a fad to take a stance against the main line of American political and economic experience. The Vietnam War was one important occasion of this, but not the only one or, as its aftermath has clearly shown, the most important one.[9] The stance against much of American policy and worth has affected Catholic intellectuals and activists in a rather peculiar way. It has made them oblivious to the real connection between American experience and Catholic social thought. Indeed, it would seem, the professed goals of Catholic social thought are in jeopardy throughout the world today largely because of a failure to understand and elaborate on American experience, with all its admitted deficiencies.[10]

This failure to develop their own traditions has led many Catholics and Christian thinkers into idealist, quasi-marxist expressions of various sorts. Although not always conscious, their net effect will still be to prevent men from achieving sanely and reasonably rapidly the articulated goals of this same Christian social thought. And the figure of many Christians in the rest of the world escaping from contemporary absolutist systems will come to haunt the kind of Christian social thought that is so often preached today. Somewhere today, we can rest assured, there is a new Rolf Hochhuth preparing to accuse dramatically the Christian social gospel of betraying the very premises for which it ought to have stood. If we read, say, *Gulag* carefully, we can already sense this new attention to the roots of Christianity's true meaning in confrontation with the ideologies of our time.[11]

In understanding this crucial issue, Maritain's book, *Reflections on America,* is a kind of watershed, though some of its points were found some thirty years earlier in the previously mentioned book of Chesterton, *What I Saw in America.* Indeed, there is not a little of it in de Tocqueville himself. In retrospect, Maritain's book is significant because its very existence came to be viewed as a kind of unforgivable sin by the European and Latin American Left. And its scandal has only grown more glaringly as the years have passed. Maritain represented a kind of challenge through which specifically Christian democratic philosophy was finally legitimized.[12] But as the Catholic left has proceeded unabashedly on a road of socialism, so contemptuously viewed by those Christians who actually live in such socialisms, Maritain's book on America really undermined the very propositions of this radical trend which has persistently sought to overcome the limits placed on the left by formal papal social thought. So much is this so today that there are many Catholics who profess to identify Christian social thought with getting rid of "capitalism," by which they mean not the 19th Century variety of the early encyclicals, but the late 20th Century species embodied in anything American.

The Problem of Capitalism in Avoiding Ideology

Joseph Comblin often has spoken of capitalism in this vein of a whole system that needs to be removed.[13] Father L. Lebret, who had so much influence on Catholic social thinking for a time, was noticeably one-sided in his pejorative analysis of America.[14] Denys Turner, as we indicated earlier, wrote in *The New Blackfriars*, itself often a spokesman for the Christian left, that getting rid of capitalism is the great mission common to Catholics and marxists.[15] Giulio Girardi, something of a high priest of it all, was so carried away in a Christmas sermon a couple of years ago that he preached:

> Capitalism today has the historical role of being the destruction of hope. Capitalism is the process of suffocating at all levels the expectations of the people, the expectations of men. It renders their future impossible. From the beginning, it condemns so many children to death. It is an enormous abortion.[16]

One is tempted, in such a context, to wonder if the author ever has condemned real abortion with the same zeal and to point out that the most common accusation against capitalism is that it arouses "expectations," rather than suffocates them.

What is important in this context of Maritain's book, however, is that such apocalyptic visions of capitalism have little to do with the American system as it actually exists. Maritain had stood for the existence of an authentic, independent social philosophy—the existence of which is rejected in many European Catholic journals of a socialist tendency—and he found this system corresponding in many ways, though not all, with what went on in America.[17] He suggested this experience was quite unknown to most Europeans, a thesis that Jean Servan-Schreiber was to take up in another way in *The American Challenge*. This must also be seen in a context in which Japan and the neo-Confucian cultures as well as much of Europe have learned to do the things American enterprise did even better than the Americans.

One of Maritain's political followers, Eduardo Frei, the former Chilean Christian Democratic leader, still retains the theoretical essence of Maritain, which derives from the common Christian outlook:

> Christian Democrats do not live on anti-communism. They live on their own affirmation;

they live on their own faith in man, in his destiny, in his rights, in his immortal essence. They have faith in justice and liberty. They have other interpretations of history and other concepts of the methods and ends which they should follow to realize a truly human society.[18]

But the frank recognition of an outlook, an authentic, independent source of precisely Catholic social thought is, until very recently with John Paul II's interventions, becoming rarer, as many seek to see in the *praxis* of various marxisms the way to reach Christian goals.

What, then, explains the tendency of Catholic social thinkers ideologically to locate all the world's evils in America, while such perceptive voices as Macrae and Solzhenitsyn are maintaining that if we really want human abundance and freedom in the Christian tradition, then we had better look to certain key (though not all) features of the American system as it works itself out in practice? This is not an easy question to answer, to be sure. It does not require denying admitted American failures, nor does it require denying that much American propaganda in the areas of population and ecology is highly dubious from a Christian point of view.[19] One line of thought would be to suggest that some of the essential elements of Catholic social thought, of distributism in particular, are now returning into vogue. *Small Is Beautiful* is rather unabashedly similiar to *The Outline of Sanity* of Chesterton or the principle of subsidiarity of *Quadragesimo Anno* of Pius XI, while many anti-pollution experts, like René duBois, are busily rediscovering the wonders of the self-sufficient Benedictine monastery.[20] Vladimir Maximov stated:

> The destruction of the historical memory is the sense and substance of totalitarianism, of totalitarian doctrine. This is the scope and means of marxist doctrine. It is to deprive man of his historical memory, of moral roots, of the basis of historical tradition, which is to constrain him to forget his divine origins.[21]

It is this historical forgetfulness that has enabled Catholic social spokesmen too often to lose contact with their own intellectual tradition, made up, as it is, from the very fabric and experience of real men and women.

A second approach that would explain this difficulty of finding a social thought fully distinguished from the ideologies lies in the American Catholic's inability to define accurately the political situation before him in the world. This is why strong voices of Catholic sensibility like that of Daniel Moynihan are brushed aside so easily. Moynihan calls bluntly for a return to real political description, accurate political reporting and definition.[22] He insists on calling forms of government what they are, on not equivocating about them. If they are tyrannies, they should be called such. If they are oligarchies, they should receive this label too. There is no longer any sense in claiming that we have some 150 "democracies" in the world simply because most have this word in their titles and are recognized as such by the United Nations. It is, as John Bunzel said, anti-democratic to deny real differences and to allow our words to deny facts.[23]

Peter Berger also has insisted that we recognize that there are degrees of evil in politics, a theme we touched on in Chapter III. We must reject identifying, say, oligarchy with tyranny.[24] Needless to say, the long and harsh dealings with and interpretations of Spain, Portugal, Greece, Korea, Vietnam, Brazil, and Chile comprise one long history of confusion on this point. Where the error lies is not in claiming that such authoritarian regimes have or have had something wrong, but in using this as a justification for the neglect of the far more serious and threatening aspects of the really totalitarian regimes. Prudence remains a prime political virtue. Catholic social thinkers have generally failed to make such distinctions in recent years, often allying themselves with interests of a suspiciously anti-human cast. Perhaps this is because they have forgotten that Augustine is also one of their authentic predecessors in how Christians think about politics.[25]

A third, perhaps key reason for this disaffection with America has been the belief that the world's condition was America's "fault," a belief based on the untested assumption that no one could be rich unless he had exploited somebody else.[26] This may well be the single most dangerous and false idea in all of contemporary political and social thought. Thus, in this view, since America is relatively rich, it *must* be so unjustly. No space is to be allowed for differences in attitude to work, to freedom, to genius, to energy, to good will. The dubiousness of this exploitation approach is clear. Not only does it go against the very ameliorative instincts and practices of American political and economic traditions, but it puts sole blame for the condition of the world's poor on precisely those who are most successful in improving the lot of the same poor.

Too often both social and missionary theology have given up on those practical efforts that actually do things for people. Rather, it goes off into radical political and revolutionary reforms which in fact result in a greater disorientation, which reach no concrete person, and which are usually pale rehashings of some ideological, usually marxist, position. The ultimate difficulty with this viewpoint, as we have suggested earlier, lies in its confusion between sin and finiteness. Many of the things wrong with and in the world are not the results of actual sin or evil. The exploitation approach reduces all to somebody else's sin or bias, so that moral anger is the only response. Not only does this remove much of the adventure inherent in the world, but it also makes what is really wrong into an abstraction.[27] This same confusion exists also in connection with the rise of envy among nations and peoples as a primary political determinant, with a corresponding decline of any formal attention to the second kind of justice that Aristotle warned was an essential part of human nature, the kind that insists equality is a proportionate thing.[28] Or perhaps, since distributive justice is receiving enormous attention in many areas, as we have seen in the case of Professor Rawls, it is better to say that the good of diversity is itself what is little appreciated in contemporary social reflections.[29]

The Purely Human Solution

The variations of these themes are endless: the poor are poor because the rich are not helping them. The fact that the so-called Third World countries that have developed—Korea, Taiwan, Japan, Brazil, Singapore—did so by imitating fairly closely American and western European economic norms, with their own initiatives, is invariably seen as mere proof of exploitation or fascism. Every effort is made to see such nations in unfavorable circumstances, so that they cannot act as judgments on the failures of the left. But more is at issue. The belief that somehow all answers are known is implicit in the frenetic criticism that adequate help is not given. Too, there is an implicit passing over of the freedom of the receiver, a failure to account for cultures or values or religions or ideologies or intelligences that do not want to change in a given way or with a given outlook. The belief that the West or America is somehow totally responsible for poverty or exploitation bears a kind of contempt for other people's faults and weaknesses and indeed sins, all of which are also essential parts of the problem.

Thus, the Third World's problems—poverty, productivity, liberty, population, distribution, stable order—are not merely individual problems. They are usually the direct result of the choice of ideology on the part of those new and old nations, a choice that neatly seeks to avoid the issue of one's own finitude and sinfulness, of the quality of one's own choices. As nations increasingly choose (or have chosen for them) a brand of socialism as a model, they in all likelihood also assure themselves of a very slow and low-level rate of development and a necessity for widespread social coercion. The next step for the admirers of this choice is usually to explain how necessary such a choice was, given the local situation. However, even this approach is having its rapid crisis of conscience. For today the discussions about Third World development that we find in Christian social thought are no longer dialogues between the West and the individual countries. The dialogue has another partner. It is beginning to look like the voice of Christian conscience about the Third World must be read in Solzhenitsyn's *Letter to the Soviet Leaders* and in why Cubans try to escape, not in our own revolutionary theories which find African, Asian, or Latin American socialism to be "independent" or "indigenous" waves of the future.[30] All hypotheses up until even a couple of years ago are now less pertinent. The powerful white men that the African will have to deal with from now on will more likely be coming from Havana or Odessa or Warsaw than from Kansas City or even Pretoria. Indeed, it will be interesting to see how long even the Chinese last in Africa.

In any case, a kind of socialist ideal which exists no place on Earth is proposed as a solution, in Christian terms, for the very real problems of the world for which we ought to have some sympathy. I have, of course, read Michael Harrington, Jacques Ellul, and J. K. Galbraith about the American experience and the socialist one either coalescing or growing into one another. Development theorists, moreover, have often looked upon ecumenism as a way to avoid an impasse between marxism and Christianity. The political and economic forms that might indeed develop have come to be looked upon as "capitalism," as a kind of evil that cannot be tried. The result, however, is that in practice because of this lack of development, the future becomes a hopeless bout with dictatorships and social control presented as if these were necessary conclusions from Christian social principles. When it deviates from its own traditions, Christian social thought is thus coming ever nearer to assisting men to be locked up in systems that can only be anti-human.

The upshot is that we must cooperate, the argument goes, in Christian terms with an ideological system, since it does have the power. We should do this, it is said, in the name of justice, since this is what the ideological systems claim they are achieving. No doubt, Christians cannot wholly avoid the realities of totalitarian or authoritarian systems. Christians have lived in every kind of society, no matter how corrupt, and will evidently have to continue to do so. But one of the faults of recent Christain social theory lies precisely in the failure to face the harsh realities of what is produced in socialist systems. We can hope for and work for better systems, but they do not always come. And if Christians identify faith too much with ideal social conditions, they may well end up making religion so esoteric that it will have nothing to tell real men and women. Of course, Catholic social thought can never be afraid to ask the very hard questions about performance. And such questions should be asked of all regimes within a comparative framework that recognizes a better and a worse, even in corruption and evil. As Theodore Mulder observed:

I believe it is clear what I intend to say when I affirm that today the social doctrine of the Church is not static but dynamic. We are not possessed of a closed system which gives the impression of guaranteeing the just solution for every possible case. The first thing is to ask ourselves what are today the vital social problems and by what avenues ought we to seek a just and equitable solution.[31]

If there is anything that can save Catholic social thought from some of its temptations today, it is probably a very careful reading of the various Russian and Jewish exiles, of the performance records of the various marxist states.[32]

The argument, of course, is often put forth that the developed countries ought to help the underdeveloped ones, that the terms of trade are unbalanced, that capitalism is different in Latin America or Africa, that that difference is due not to local law or force or custom, but to greed outside western political control, something intrinsic to the system. The assumption is always that the difference is due to the so-called capitalists and not to the local situation or moral climate of the country or to ideological causes. No one would deny that capitalism has its sins. But one of its virtues is its capacity to acknowledge false starts and change ways, something socialist systems have shown great difficulties in doing. Since there is a sense of gradualism and correctability in their outlook, capitalist and

American type systems can be changed and improved, whereas socialism's defects are most often blamed on somebody else. Interestingly, the "pacifism" of Solzhenitsyn is based precisely on forcing communism to live with and acknowledge its own errors.[33] Christian social thought should not, further, neglect the spiritual principle behind this social problem, for a deterministic view of the world and man makes him out to be quite different from a view which admits the possibility of repentance and change and growth based on man's inner freedom.

Confronting socialism's own existential failures and its tendencies to lapse into coercion, its most serious proponents—Christian, marxist, or utopian—are forced into defending a kind of pure socialism that never existed. Actual socialisms are either bureaucratized or severely restrictive of basic freedoms and of dubious efficiency. The French marxist, Jean Ellenstein, even maintained the curious thesis that the reason we could trust the French Communists to be democratic did not lie in marxism but in the French democratic tradition, that antedated socialism and which would prevent the abuses manifested in all existing forms of communism.[34]

Finding a Christian Solution

But Christian social thought, if it is really serious about helping the Third World to help itself, must return to those pre-socialist and non-socialist institutions and traditions—not the least of which, as Norman Macrae pointed out, is the transnational corporation—which can do the job of transferring knowhow, management, and capital quickly and freely to places where the demand and need most exist.[35] In this we encounter the whole problem of the adequacy of the national state, with which Catholic social thought in particular has had great difficulty since its origin. This political form has been universally chosen, and socialism, which itself was originally against the national state, has now argued most of its virtues within the national frame of reference.

Thinkers limited by the concept of the State fail to consider seriously those institutions such as the corporation whose very reality is related to an international existence which transcends the competence and scope of the national state. Catholic social thought, even in its early modern origins in Suarez and Vittoria, has been aware of this broader level. The present demand that the national state or institutions directly controlled by it be the ultimate arbiters at the international level of all economic and social policy—this neo-mercantilism of the left—will merely ruin the institutions that might just succeed in meeting most of man's basic problems of housing, food production, transportation, and education. One of the things that is characteristic of recent leftist

Christian social thought is the idea that government will save us. No one denies any more, except some anarchists, that government is necessary. But much more attention needs to be paid to its performance and capacity to do actually the things that are required. It is no longer true that most of the things performed by government are best performed by government or its vast numbers of employees. It is here that present Catholic criticism most often fails.

Catholic social thought, especially in the United States, has made two serious mistakes in recent years: 1) It has failed to understand the positive international implications of American experience for the achievement of the true goals of its own thought, such as the example of the Morrill Act or the Homestead Act. And 2) it has begun to see its main function as protest, such that much time is spent on what is wrong, very little on what is right. A rereading of Maritain's book, though no panacea, would be a beginning to right this imbalance. Catholics have not been able to recognize what is right in their own traditions, nor have they often perceived where the basic Christian values are in fact already being realized or being denied.

Furthermore, there is an even more fundamental issue which can be pointed out either by maintaining that the social reality and function of charity have been deliberately downplayed, or by reaffirming that there is no justice in this world in any ultimate sense. It is an illusion to pretend that there is or will be such perfect justice, even when man and the world are remade through some successful ideology. That function of charity which consists in overcoming, repairing and forgiving the necessary deficiencies of justice, its harshness, its indifference to particular situations, is precisely one of the central contributions of Catholic social thought which barely receives adequate attention.[36] Aquinas' remark on the necessity of divine law over against human law must remain an active, essential element within Christian social teaching, the idea that law cannot punish all wrongs or mandate all virtue.

In a sense, perhaps, we have misread the idea of Aquinas, which found echo in *Rerum Novarum,* about the need to have a sufficiency of goods to expect most men to practice virtue. Catholic social thought often has interpreted this to mean that first we build a good society, then we will have charity and goodness. Undoubtedly, it is the other way around. And this is why scripture begins with a change of heart and not a program of political or economic reform. We need to rediscover the primacy of friendship and charity as both our goal and our mode of operation even in the worst of conditions. Indeed, it would seem that the use of hate, envy, and anger in so much of contemporary ideology and political practice, all justified in the name of the people who will come to be just when the evils of property division and oppression are demolished, is the antithesis of how Christians ought to conceive their own ideals. Leo XIII's insistence that men are not necessarily opposed to one another is much closer to the truth than those Christian social philosophers who are trying to reconcile, as they call it, violence with love.

Christian social philosophy has claimed that it did have its own articulated view of man, society, and the world, a view that recognized the freedom of the varieties of concrete, incarnate entities to find their own ways. A few thinkers, at least, have attempted to pinpoint the ideas central to any wise thinking about the place of Christians in the public order and their impact on it. Stanley Hauerwas has spoken of the dangers of making man's will the source of all values. "Defining man as maker," he wrote, "has...made contemporary ethics unable to come to terms with the human condition."[37] Indeed, we need to recall clearly that what we are as men is already given to us, and that the "measure of moral goodness ultimately lies outside of ourselves."[38] Oswald von Nell-Bruening recently reminded us that Karl Marx is the great opponent of Catholic social theory, and that Catholics must give "clearer and blunter meaning (to) the not-to-be-abrogated opposition between the last end of the belief in God and Atheism."[39] It is, then, absolutely necessary that we recognize the opponents of the Christian spirit and spirituality, to which we will turn in the following chapter. Finally, John Hallowell identified Christianity's main social function as providing principles to better accomplish the task of reform without abrogating the need for such reform. Christianity also saves men, he said, "from the illusion that we can establish a system which is perfect or make a reform which is final."[40]

Christians need to see the limits of the social order itself, both as a political and as a spiritual reality. Indeed, one of the most essential things we need is an authentic spirituality that does recognize the importance of a transcendent, Triune God, and our personal relation to Him, no matter what our political or economic state. Politics cannot be itself until worship finds its proper locus and object.[41] Contemporary Catholic thought has often confused us on these issues because it has lost contact with its own roots and with the real needs of others. Should the net result of contemporary Christian social attitudes be to lock many more men and women up in new ideological tyrannies, it will be indeed a new opium of the people precisely by attempting to avoid the idea that Christianity has no political point.

Catholic social thought has been concerned, rightly, with the lot of men in the world during this life. There is an authentic spirituality and wisdom in approaching this reality that is also Christian. Yet, if Christianity means anything, it means that salvation does not lie here, nor is it a product of the public order as such. "Only if we are concerned about the salvation of our souls," John Hallowell concluded, "shall we be of much use in saving the world; only if our eyes are focused on the Kingdom of God shall we see with clearer vision what needs to be done here and now...."[42] In a certain sense, then, it is precisely because the American economic-political system does allow men space beyond themselves and itself that it comes closest to allowing the right development of the world.

Catholic social thought, indeed, is being forced by events to return to the American experience in working out some basic problems. The alternative is the neo-Caesaro-papism of the left which identifies religion with politics in the creation of a new holy order in the world, which sees religion as a tool to cement what are essentially finite limits to man's ultimate meaning. When these two visions are in contact and in conflict, Christianity will, if it be authentic, also return to its own roots and ask this time in a very specifically political sense, what it profits a man to gain the whole world and lose his soul. Man does have a transcendent destiny which cannot end by identifying it with the well-being of some or even all people, the ultimate abstraction. Whenever Christian social thought does not keep this fact clearly before men, it has betrayed not only religion but politics itself.

Footnotes:

¹ Cf. Michael Novak, "The Politics of John Paul II," *Commentary*, December, 1979.

² *The Economist*, October 25, 1975, Survey, p. 8.

³ James Finn, "On the Way to the Bicentennial," *Worldview*, April, 1975, pp. 7-8.

⁴ "And lastly I am a citizen of the United States of America in a world where both small and large nations are struggling to become free from the political, economic, and military domination of the United States of America." R. M. Brown, *The Ecumenical Review*, Geneva, January, 1976, pp. 11-12.

⁵ Cf. A. I. Abell, *American Catholic Thought on Social Questions*, Indianapolis, Bobbs-Merril, 1968.

⁶ Cf. John Tracey Ellis, *Documents on American Catholic Church History*, Milwaukee, Bruce, 1956, pp. 167ff. Cf. also Philip Gleason, "Mass and Maypole Revisited: American Catholics and the Middle Ages," *The Catholic Historical Review*, July, 1971.

⁷ Father Morehouse F. X. Millar, SJ used to write well in *Thought* during the 1920's and 1930's on this subject as does today Professor Ellis Sandoz, from another point of view.

⁸ Cf. the author's "Theory in American Politics," *The Modern Age*, Spring, 1960, pp. 150-59; "The Theory and Practice of American Politics," *Communio*, Spring, 1980, pp. 72-89.

⁹ The replacing of the Vietnam War in proper political perspective is undoubtedly the great task of this age of historians.

¹⁰ Cf. the author's "Bicentennial," *Christian Order*, London, July, 1976, pp. 405-18.

¹¹ Solzhenitsyn's Addresses of June 30, 1975 and July 9, 1975, in which he praises the American attitude and record but worries about the American innocence. This should be compared with his devastating analysis of the British of April 2, 1976. It might be noted, however, that Solzhenitsyn was invited to speak on the BBC, but at this stage American media fundamentally ignored him.

¹² Jacques Maritain, *Reflections on America*, New York, Scribner's, 1958. Cf. also E. A. Goerner, "Aristocracy and Natural Right," *The American Journal of Jurisprudence*, 1972, pp. 1-13.

¹³ Cf. J. Comblin, "Il significato della participazione politica dei cattolici alla rivoluzione in America Latina," in *Coscienza Cristiana e Impegny Politico*, Milano, Mondadori, 1971, pp. 107-32; "Développement ou Revolution?" *Cultures et Développement*, Louvain, # 1, 1972, pp. 3-34; Cf. also R. North, "Theology of Revolution," *Theology Digest*, Winter, 1975.

14 Cf. L. Lebret, *Suicide ou suivire de l'Occident?* Paris, Ouvrières, 1958.

15 Denys Turner, *New Blackfriars,* June, 1975.

16 *Il Tetto,* Aprile, 1975, p. 127.

17 Cf. Roger Heckel, *The Use of the Expression 'Social Doctrine' of the Church,* Rome, Pontifical Commission on Justice and Peace, 1980, #1.

18 Eduardo Frei, "Democrazia, mezzo insostituibile di governo," *Il Popolo,* Roma, Aprile 4, 1976.

19 Cf. the author's *Human Dignity and Human Numbers,* Staten Island, Alba House, 1971; "Some Intellectual Origins of Population-Environment Theories," in *Population in Perspective,* Dunedin, New Zealand, The Tablet, 1973, pp. 128-43: *Welcome Number 4,000,000,000,* Canfield, Ohio, Alba House, 1977.

20 R. duBois, "Conservation, Stewardship, and the Heart of Man," *Audubon,* September, 1972; E. F. Schumacher, *Small Is Beautiful,* New York, Perennial, 1973.

21 *Il Popolo,* Roma, Maggio 1, 1976.

22 D. Moynihan, "The Caged Revolution," *Harper's,* January, 1976.

23 John Bunzel, "An Elitist Badge Worn With Honor," *San Jose Mercury,* 1977.

24 Peter Berger, "The Classification of Tyrannies," *Worldview,* June, 1975, pp. 8-9; Jeane Kirkpatrick, "Democracies and Dictatorships," *Commentary,* November, 1979.

25 Cf. the author's "The Missing Element in Christian Social Thought," *Social Survey,* Melbourne, July, 1975, pp. 165-71.

26 Cf. P. T. Bauer, "Commentary," in *Challenges to a Liberal Economic Order,* R. Amacher, Editor, Washington, American Enterprise Institute, 1979, pp. 462-66; Wilfred Beckerman, "The Fallacy of Finite Resources," *Social Survey,* June, 1957, pp. 140-47.

27 Cf. Chapter III.

28 Cf. Aristotle, *The Ethics,* Chapter V.

29 Cf. John Rawls, *A Theory of Justice,* Cambridge, Harvard University Press, 1971. For a discussion of the social and theological nature of otherness, cf. G. Meilaender, *The Taste for the Other,* Grand Rapids, Eerdmans, 1978.

30 Cf. A. Solzhenitzyn, *Letter to the Soviet Leaders,* New York, Harper's, 1974; "A Revolution Not for Copying," *The Economist,* May 10, 1980, pp. 11-12.

[31] Theodore Mulder, "L'insegnamento sociale della Chiesa nel Concilio Vaticano II e dopo," *Vita e Pensiero,* Milano, Marzo-Aprile, 1975, p. 233.

[32] *Russia Cristiana,* Luglio-Agosto, 1973, pp. 3-16. Cf. also Solzhenitsyn, "Da Sotto I Massi," *Russia Cristiana,* Gennaio-Febbraio, 1975.

[33] Cf. Footnote # 12.

[34] "Entretien avec Jean Ellenstein sur le phénomène stalinien, la démocratie et le socialisme," *Esprit,* Paris, Février, 1976, p. 241ff.
"La proprieté de l'etat n'est pas socialisme. L'autosuffisance n'est pas socialisme. Ces politiques sont peut-être des choix intelligents, les mouvements socialistes peuvent les soutenir. Mais une gouvernment socialiste, quand viendra ne ressemblera pas à celui de L'URSS, dé la China, du Chile d'Allende, ou de la Tanzania d'aujourd'hui...." I. Wallerstein, "Sous-développement et dépendance," *Esprit,* Paris, Fevrier, 1974, p. 211ff.

[35] Cf. N. Macrae, "The Future of International Business," *The Economist,* London, January 20, 1972; "The People We Have Become," *The Economist,* April 28, 1973; "America's Third Century," *The Economist,* October 25, 1975; "The Brusque Recessional," *The Economist,* December 24, 1978.

[36] Cf. the author's "The Re-Discovery of Charity," *Spiritual Life,* Winter, 1979, pp. 195-203. Cf. also John Paul II's Encyclical *Dives in Misericordia, 1980.*

[37] S. Hauerwas, "The Significance of Vision," *Sciences Religieuses,* Montreal, # 1, 1972, p. 36.

[38] *Ibid.*

[39] O. von Nell-Bruening, "Auseinandersetzung mit Marx und Seiner Lehre," *Stimmen der Zeit,* Marz, 1976, p. 182. Cf. also "Fede cristiana e Marxismo," *La Civiltá* Cattolica, Roma, Gennaio, 1976, pp. 105-15.

[40] John Hallowell, *Main Currents in Modern Political Thought,* New York, Holt, 1950, p. 692.

[41] Cf. Chapter I. Cf. also the author's "Interior and Exterior Spirituality," *The American Ecclesiastical Review,* September, 1975, pp. 490-503.

[42] Hallowell, *ibid.,* p. 695.

CHAPTER XI

On Remaking Man and the World

I believe in the tragic element of history. I believe there is a tragedy of the man who works very hard and never gets what he wants. And then there is the even more bitter tragedy of the man who gets what he wants and then finds he does not want it.

—Henry Kissinger

...Vladimir Maximov is the man who has pointed out the most important cultural phenomenon of the 1970's: the surprising rebirth of Christian spirituality which paradoxically is coming from the atheist East and now is diffusing its seed in western Europe with the testimony of the new dissidents from the East.

—Fausto Ginfranceschi

Our God is none other than the masses of the Chinese people.

—Mao Tse-tung

What, in the light of the place of America in Christian social thought, in the tendency of this thought to expect a practical meeting of the human problems at hand, yet a skepticism about the eventual reaching of human perfection in this world, can we expect of the spiritual outlook of Christians? This is a much more important question than we realize if we grant that indeed the newer concerns of people are not for politics but for an authentic political limitation that allows religion a proper place in human life, a place that is not merely a substitute for or extension of politics.

If the question of the orientation of Christian spirituality lies at the very heart of the divisions of social thought and theology, it is well perhaps to attempt a restatement of the central Christian sensibilities before the social order. No intellectual or spiritual issue is more pressing than that of the human condition itself, its acceptability, its origins, what can and cannot be expected of it. Man cannot be promised happiness, secular or religious, and even then be expected really to be content when he does not achieve it. And if we insist further that we must achieve this happiness *before* we die, then our dogmatic belief that this life is all that there is available will make even our limited happiness an agony. Indeed, it might be argued, as Aristotle already did in *The Ethics,* that unless we first straighten out our thoughts and expectations about what happiness is, we shall inevitably spend the rest of our days seeking it where it is not. That is, we shall very likely get what we search for only to discover that such is not really the happiness we desire.

In this sense, then, the pursuit of happiness, that noble Jeffersonian phrase, is the promoter of all revolutionary change and spirituality. The real possibility of false happiness is the great tragedy of our lot precisely because it can be ultimately traced to a decision to achieve something we did not want. Modern spiritual and social thought is largely a search to escape this consequence and rather to assign happiness to be unattainable because of some defect or fault not located in the human will. And to be a "social animal" means precisely not to be isolated from the effects of the wills of others, for better or for worse. Suffering, then, is necessarily a factor in the lot of the good. And the desire to eliminate suffering, personal or social, can become the exact locus of all disorder when it proposes that the creation of a being who can suffer is itself the original fault. Men as we know them in life and history, in other words, ought not to exist in this perspective.

Optimists and Pessimists

There are, then, as we have seen, optimists and pessimists about in great abundance, men who are in agreement about only one doctrine, that the present life of man on this green Earth is intolerable, that consequently it must be changed either by a total economic reconstruction, as in socialist theories, or in a laboratory induced genetic conception or mutation, or a moral rearmament, or a psychological or educational transformation. The search is one for *the new man,* because for many it is now accepted as common dogma that the kind of man who has been and who now is must be indefensible and unendurable. This belief is what lies behind the "christianization" of someone like the late Mao Tse-tung, who proposed a new man on Earth exempt significantly from the moral defects of imperfect men.[1] As the ultimate root of our defects is traced in Christian theology to original sin and to its tangible signs in giving birth in pain, working in sweat, division of property, and coercive government, nothing less is proposed than the elimination of the root scar. Will, then, men be like gods?

Jacques Lecarrière concluded his study on the monks of the ancient desert in this fashion:

"Why asceticism?" was the question asked at the beginning of this book. A new reply can now be given: not only because asceticism is the rejection of the material world and a repudiation of the state in which man finds himself, but also because it leads towards the 'new man,' capable of overcoming the problem of space, of treating suffering with contempt and of passing through centuries of time—a man, in fact, having the substance and the power of the angels.[2]

The difference between a Mao Tse-tung and the anchorites, stylites, and dendrites of eastern desert is not, in some basic sense, very great. What the monk sought for himself or his small community, Mao sought for his vast society and the world. All men were finally to escape from humanhood itself. Sin and evil used to be symbolically and actually found in the cities and the world, in the public world, from which the few fled to the desert wastes, empty, except for the human heart, of the prevailing corruption.

Now the corrupt human condition is only found in the few—called no longer sinners but bourgeoise, capitalists, imperialists—from whom the ninety-nine percent of humanity are fleeing as the causes of their evils, evils which can even infect the minds and habits of convinced socialists.[3] Continual purging and cultural revolution in this system took the place of days of recollection and penance. The monks escaped to live with God. The modern mass ascetics—and they are that—escape to find "man." The ancient theology held that the point of contact between the two, man and God, was the Incarnation and the Cross. The modern world is rather terrified at this conclusion, so that its elan falls back on the desperate belief that there must be an alternative. Our public world is the living out of these alternatives being tried, tested, rejected, one by one.

All public controversy originates at the deepest level, then, in the proposition that man is not as he ought to be, a theme as old as man himself, a theme of Scripture, Old and New. And since man "ought" somehow to be different, then it naturally follows that there ought to be a way to change man, a way not subject to the classical Christian limits which place man's ultimate happiness beyond this life, a way to remove what is keeping man from his higher state of perfection to which all schools of optimistic thought feel he is called. Technology, education, analysis, nutrition, grace, revolution, will, politics, economics, genetics, even the discovery of other cosmic inhabitants, who have learned how to cope with these faults we humans still manifest, are all candidates to supply the magic means to effect the desired change in the human situation. The optimists are those who claim that the scars can be remodeled or removed. They are secular humanists if this removal is subject to the efforts of man alone in this life. They are Christian humanists, usually also socialists, if they believe that combined with human effort, divine grace will assist in removing these evils from man on this Earth. The older evolutionary optimistic view, which was sure of a cosmic plan but dubious of a planner, is probably less in evidence today.

The pessimists, on the other hand, of which there is an increasing number especially in scientific circles, the same circles which but a few decades ago were rigorously optimistic, are beginning to argue that there is some irremediable defect in the human make-up that cannot be cured. This means that the happiness of mankind must be conceived largely in terms of the species and in terms of "cutting necessary losses." Certain popular schools of demography are fond of this grim approach, concluding *a priori* that the Earth must not be expected to provide for everyone, especially for the men who do now exist and who act in the way they do. Salvation, which has now become often a this-worldly concept, demands the establishment of a strong restrainer—if not exactly a Leviathan, at least a Caesar. The initial commands of *Genesis* are reversed. The Earth is more important than man. Animals are not man's servants.[4]

Therefore, only a few men, a few billions at a time at most are to be allowed to share the Earth's fragile surpluses for as long a time as possible. Thus, to imagine human welfare to be defined principally in terms of stretching out an existing life of man for as long as possible, to believe that this will satisfy the individual's drive for meaning and significance as the only future believed available, this dream must be protected from the actually existing men themselves, who are now seen as causing the one really definable fault in this world, that is, the very desires and structures of present, common men. We, therefore, must define our numbers and wants to enable generations down the ages to survive. Immortality has again become circular length of ages.

Other forms of pessimism argue rather from the instability of the human condition. Sooner or later, some madman, some mad society, now endowed with the modern means of destruction, will eliminate the rest of men, probably for a pique, a slight of some sort. We are all on a jumbo jet with a mad scientist in control who does not care about death, nor about anyone else. The jet is the Earth. This theme is either nuclear or biological. The scientist, the former symbol of rational progress, has become a new Faust, the guilty one because his knowledge made this destructive eventuality possible, while statistics now make probabilities certainties. The irreformability of men, the fact that they cannot all be changed in time, leads to this pessimism. The "last things" leave only an incinerated planet floating in "the silent spaces," which no longer frighten because no one is about to be frightened. We are a long way here from the relation of Christianity and the universe which we touched on previously.

A Rereading of Thomas à Kempis

In the Southern Italian city of Bari several years ago, I had a chance to reread Thomas à

Kempis, his famous *The Imitation of Christ.* The spiritual individualism, the unconcern with the fate of the world in this classic work are simply astonishing. And in the light of the moods and themes we have been following, this particular book somehow seems enormously refreshing in a way. How seldomly do we hear these famous words of à Kempis! "O quam breves, quam falsae, quam inordinatae et turpes omnes sunt!"[5] "Non enim omne desiderium est a Spiritu Sancto; etiam si homini videatur rectum et bonum."[6] "Vanum est et breve omne humanum solatium."[7]

At first sight, of course, *The Imitation of Christ* can outdo even the most despondent contemporary pessimist. Indeed, à Kempis made one wonder about the direct spiritual origin of the desire to change man radically, since this most Christian book is simply filled with the same despair about the present world and the same drives for a new man that we discover today everywhere under secular forms. It should not be overlooked either that the human effort to remake man and the world has a long history. In its modern origins, Machiavelli and Hobbes said that man was evil and corrupt. Rousseau said he was good, but his institutions were evil. Hegel knew the history of man and of the world were somehow of the spirit. But what a rereading of à Kempis makes absolutely clear—rereading Augustine would have much the same effect—is that the Christian does not even attempt to claim that his own happiness and his destiny are of his own tragic making, except in the sense of a freedom to choose the one salvation "too good to be true," the participation in the life of the Triune God through the Cross, through the world wherein it once stood. If there is a sort of ruthlessness in Christianity, I suspect it lies in its stubborn refusal to acknowledge any other way. "Ambula ubi vis, quaere quodcumque volueris: et non invenies altiorem vitam supra, nec securiorem viam infra: nisi viam sanctae Crucis."[8] This is from the famous, always unsettling Chapter in Book Two, "De Regia Via Sanctae Crucis"—"On the Royal Road of the Holy Cross."

Here, then, it seems clear that there is no alternative to the Christian contemplative view which concentrates man's spiritual focus on the individual person's relation to God. This relationship transcends every public, political form. Most of the basic evils connected with man and the world may not be eliminated except through the mitigating effects of the Christian spiritual life. Any promise of a perfectly complete and happy human life in this world, now or down the ages, is necessarily against the destiny man has been offered. We can tidy things up a bit, of course, and it is a spiritual thing to do so, but in the best of our efforts, most of our faults will shift or reappear. The spiritual meaning of our era is the empirical, public testing of the proposed alternatives which somehow seem inevitably to end up deforming man. The contemplative vocation must retain its presence in Christianity, as à Kempis saw, precisely in order to keep men open to a divine beyond their expectations. But it is as man, not someone else, that we are saved. "Homo es, et non Deus: caro es, non Angelus." [9]

What Is To Be Contemplated?

Otto of Hapsburg wrote a penetrating essay in *La Revue des Deux Mondes* entitled, "La contemplation dans le monde d'aujourd'hui." In the context of what is being suggested here, this is an invaluable reflection. First of all, Otto of Hapsburg pointed out that the occasions and places for contemplating God in our homes, cities, schools, and businesses are ever less in this century. Feast days, fast days, times of prayer and silences, symbols of the divine have been progressively secularized. Further, the object of contemplation in modern times has shifted deliberately from God to what man could do with and by himself in this world. The think-tank has replaced the monastery as the place of reflection.[10]

> In the midst of their anxieties, doubts, and sufferings, men formerly had the possibility of finding refuge for themselves in meditation or contemplation. With the beginning of our era, that richness of religious life is progressively lost.

It has been even knowingly destroyed. In the Enlightenment it was declared a superstition.[11]

This is why, as Carl Becker also remarked, this world became the object of men's spiritual drives because of the insistence that the reality of God did not exist as a proper or adequate object of persons or even societies.[12]

In the beginning, then, it was simply assumed that the loss of God and the fears that His existence evidently invoked would remove anxiety from the human realm. Instead, it has increased it. "The spiritual agony of men supposedly freed from God surpasses by far the fear of former generations at the mention of the devil or hell."[13] This can be confirmed, as we can examine for ourselves, in almost any newspaper or journal today. The loss of contemplation is resulting in the loss of man. The conclusion of Otto of Hapsburg's remarks is striking:

> At the dawn of the Third Millennium, we cannot close our eyes to mounting recourse to drugs, to the increasing negation of all moral principles, to the rapid fall into anarchy. There are only two responses to this: the totalitarianism of communism transforming man into a member of an anthill or a return to the creator God and the Christian doctrine of salvation.[14]

The one thing a Christian view of history might well add to this is that a totalitarian system may be the grave out of which an authentic Christianity might appear. In any case, especially in the past decade, that the other alternatives seem less and less serious contenders seems more and more clear.

Anyone attentive to marxist literature today cannot escape the feeling that the official marxists, at least, of all varieties believe that they are on the winning side, that the course of history is in their favor. One principle Christian response to this is, as we noted earlier often, the effort to baptize communism by largely accepting its worldly asceticism and objectives as valid, lacking only a vague Christian atmosphere. Christianity thus becomes a supporter of those world transforming regimes in power. Religion is no longer opium but fertilizer. The Moscow Patriarch Pimen, for example, sent a Letter to a Conference of European Churches in which he stated, as spiritual, Christian objectives, supported by proper scripture citations, the precise current objectives Soviet foreign policy had been striving to achieve.[15]

Why this is of interest is because several years ago, Solzhenitsyn wrote an Open Letter to this same Patriarch accusing him of keeping the substance of Christianity from the Russian people. The Russian spiritual movements argue rather that communism is a failure and must simply be abandoned. Consequently, the religious estimation of the relation of communism to the very possibility of a Christian spirituality must continually be kept in the foreground.

The Religious Question

We are wrong if we think that religion is not a forceful reality in the world.[16] What we refuse to recognize is the degree to which political regimes—marxist, liberal, even Hindu and Muslim—directly deny Christianity the liberty to preach and freely to influence men. John Paul II's address to the United Nations was directly concerned with this problem.[17] Robert Nisbet's remarks were perceptive, when he noted that there is a growth of fundamentalist religions and that this would be stronger were it not for political force used against it.[18] The question is why the gates against religions must be closed by force. Is it to keep man from knowing any vision of his lot other than the official one?

The reflections of Vladimir Maximov are significant in this regard:

> For Maximov, there is a great division between the horizontal and the vertical dimension. Closing himself in the first, in the immanent, man obscures his divine vision and condemns himself to all the errors and to all the horrors. The other, the transcendent, brings the individual back to his interiority and pushes him to liberate himself from materialist pride to conquer the Kingdom of God. And the providential plane is such that so much the greater are the evils, lies, presumptions, and vilenesses of man, so much the closer is salvation that arises from suffering....

Thus, it is admirable to solidify two elements apparently so contradictory: On the one hand, the Christian capacity to comprehend charitably evil and, on the other, the firmness, likewise Christian, which responds to an evangelical invitation not to use ambiguous words, not to welcome compromises, to recognize always the adversary however he masks himself and however strong he might be. This is a firmament of special value because it arises in the very context of the most threatening and merciless enemy of the West.[19]

Christian spirituality, therefore, must fearlessly remain what it is in order to allow to men a real alternative in this world and to this world, even while learning what this world really is in the vision of creation.

"Regnum Dei intra vos est (Lc., 17:20-21), dicit Dominus. Converte te ex toto corde ad Dominum: et relinque hunc miserum mundum, et inveniet anima tua requiem."[20] These are hard doctrines in a world in which we are told that there are too many hungry, starving, sick, exploited, oppressed, and sad. Christian spirituality does not consist in doing nothing about such things. Indeed, it gives a primary spiritual motivation why one should even worry about such things. But it does insist that the doing of these things can be done in a way that degrades man further if we are not careful. It also begins by locating the happiness men ultimately search for outside the limits of the world as we know it. Christianity cannot promise a new man, in the foreseeable future, from whom the perils of existence and freedom will be completely eliminated. Christian spirituality, in other words, believes in the absoluteness of each human person whose spiritual reach to God transcends worldly existence, even though God so loved the world....

"Si talia sunt opera Dei, ut facile ea humana ratione caperentur: non essent mirabilia nec ineffabilia dicenda."[21] Such are the moving last lines of à Kempis. The tragedy of the world is that most often it does get what it "wants." The essence of Christian spirituality, all the content of prayer and meditation, is to show to us that we do not know what we really want for ourselves or our fellows. This is what is wonderful and ineffable, and why ultimately the Cross is not a "tragedy." We are given what we do not want because that is the only way we can receive it as men. And ultimately, what we do not "want" ends up to be the repair of the scar of our condition—not its removal, but its being put in place. The alternatives to Christianity, in other words, are wrong because they are right. There *is* something wrong with the human condition. But when we boldly choose to set it aright, we claim a divine power that is not ours.

In the Last Discourse of John, it says, "I am the Way, the Truth, and the Life." Spirituality and politics today are ever more converging about this very statement. They are both learning that there is no other alternative which somehow keeps man to be man in its reforms. By allowing him his weaknesses and foibles and sufferings, he is exempt from the impossible task of totally remaking himself and his world. He then can discover that the world he is given is a passing home, changeable somewhat, hauntingly beautiful at times, a place somehow best fit for what man is to become before the Lord.

And men and women are persons who are to rise again. This is what Christianity has always believed. And it is why, too, Christian spirituality is not a worldly movement, why each of us can transcend the world itself. Professor Cameron put the issue rather directly:

> I am simply suggesting that what (the Gospels) are designed to convey to the reader is that in some way the bodily life of the dead Jesus was renewed and that the presupposition that Jesus' bones rest in Palestine is incompatible with what the evangelists wished to convey. That this was the drift of the Gospels was never doubted, by believers or unbelievers, until the 19th Century.
>
> Now it is common to argue that the evangelists are subtle writers who really intended to convey that Jesus "lives on," is raised from the dead, only in some extended Pickwickean sense. Why this should be so is in part to be explained by a general feeling that accounts of miracles are always either impostures or dressings-up for symbolic purposes of ordinary happenings, but in

part, too, by a belief that whatever the victory over death of any man may be, it cannot be a bodily victory.[22]

That it is a "bodily victory" is the Christian doctrine, the one that grounds again the whole of authentic hope and salvation, the one that forbids any mere political solution to ultimate personal problems of individual destiny.

The absolute personhood of man, then, turns out to be what was intended in creation and redemption. It can never be repeated enough. *It is all right to be merely a man.* Human history seems to reveal curiously that it is man, not God, who is most slow to accept the joys and sorrows and conditions of this given Earth.

The great prayer remains: "Lord, give me what I do not want."

Homo es, et non Deus: caro es, non Angelus.

A man you are, not God. Flesh you are, not an Angel.

Such is he who is to be born, redeemed, resurrected in and from this cosmos, before the Lord, Creator of Heaven and Earth. Of such is still the Christian belief, the basis of its sanity and sanctity.

Footnotes:

[1] For a long and rather curiously one-sided view of this, cf. Leon Triviere, "L'homme nouvelle en Chine," *Etudes,* Paris, Mars, 1975.

[2] Jacques Lecarrière, *Men Possessed by God,* Garden City, Doubleday, 1964, p. 204.

[3] "What is this dictatorship for? Its first function is to suppress the reactionary classes and elements and those exploiters in the country who range themselves against the socialist revolution, to suppress all those who try to wreck our socialist construction; that is to say, to solve the contradictions between ourselves and the enemy within the country. For instance, to arrest, try and sentence certain counter-revolutionaries, and for a specified period of time to deprive landlords and bureaucrat-capitalists of their right to vote and freedom of speech—all this comes within the scope of our dictatorship. To maintain law and order and safeguard the interests of the people, it is likewise necessary to exercise dictatorship over robbers, swindlers, murderers, arsonists, hooligans, and other scoundrels who seriously disrupt social order." Mao Tse-tung, "On the Handling of Contradictions among the People," January, 1940, in *China in Revolution*, Ed. V. Simone, New York, 1968, p. 469.

[4] Cf. the author's "On the Christian Love of Animals," *Vital Speeches*, November 15, 1976, pp. 81-86; "On Animals and Men," *Social Survey*, Melbourne, December, 1976, pp. 325-32; "The Animal Rights Movement and Christianity," *Doctrine and Life*, Dublin, December, 1979, pp. 656-73.

[5] "Oh, how short, how false, how inordinate and vile all men are!" *De Imitatione Christi*, Ratisbonae, Pustet, 1937, III, 12, 16. Author's translations.

[6] "Not every desire is from the Holy Spirit even if it seems right and good to man." III, 18, 5.

[7] "It is brief and vain, all human consolation." III, 16, 10.

[8] "Walk wherever you wish, seek whatever you desire; you will not find a higher way above nor a more secure way below except the way of the Holy Cross." II, 12, 13.

[9] "You are a man, not a God; you are flesh, not an Angel." III, 51, 15.

[10] Otto of Hapsburg, "La contemplation dans le monde d'aujourd'hui," *Révue des Deux Mondes*, Janvier, 1975, p. 50.

[11] *Ibid.*

[12] Carl Becker, *The Heavenly City of the Eighteenth Century Philosophers*, New Haven, Yale, 1932; Robert Nisbet, *History of the Idea of Progress*, New York, Basic, 1980.

[13] Otto of Hapsburg, *ibid.*, p. 52.

[14] *Ibid.*, p. 54.

[15] "Botschaft des hochheiligen Patriarchen Pimen an die Vollversammlung der Konferenz Europaischer Kirchen, 'Nyborb VII,'" *Stimme der Orthodoxie*, Berlin, # 12, 1974, pp. 2-4.

[16] Cf. "American Religion," *The Economist*, April 5, 1980, pp. 15-19.

[17] Address of October 2, 1979.

[18] R. Nisbet, "The Quest for Community," *Dialogue*, no. 4, 1973, pp. 17-18.

[19] In Fausto Gianfranceschi, "Colloquio a Roma con lo scrittore Russo...," *Il Tempo*, Roma, March 29, 1975.

[20] "The Kingdom of God is among you (Lk. 17:20-21), says the Lord. Be converted with your whole heart to the Lord. And leave this miserable world and you will find rest in your soul." II, 1. 1.

[21] "If such are the works of God that such things could be easily comprehended by the human reason, then there would be no way for calling them marvelous or ineffable." IV, 18, 23. These are in fact the last lines of the book.

[22] J. M. Cameron, "Body and Person: Sexuality and Death," *The Catholic Mind*, September, 1977, pp. 19-20.

CONCLUSION

Christianity and Politics

There is no peace in this life.... In the world to come hath been promised that which in this world we are seeking.

—*Augustine*, On Psalm 48, *Second Sermon.*

The myth—so apparent in our time—that there is only one last enemy of civilization to be fought, and this one the greatest of all (so that its defeat will make the world 'safe for democracy'), can be made to wear the mask of religion, but it is opposed to the very essentials of Christian doctrine.

—*Herbert Butterfield, "Christianity and Politics," in* Herbert Butterfield: Writings on Christianity and History, *New York, Oxford, 1979, p. 52.*

The arguments of all of these reflections on atheism, spirituality, natural law, political philosophy, revolution and the universe have

315

turned on some basic aspect of the relation of Christianity and Politics. This does not mean that the relation of the two determines everything else. But it does mean that much of the controversy in our time on issues that do not appear at first sight related to this general topic turn out, on reflection, to be quite intimately connected. I have suggested that a deviation from the central orthodoxy of the Christian faith, that which was contained in and meant by the scriptures, creeds, councils, and traditions can and has resulted in a confusion in the area of public life and practice.[1] Moreover, I have maintained that the balance and fruitfulness of Christianity are by far the richest means we have to account for both what is right and what is wrong among us. I further think that this approach accounts for what we need to account for, whether it be poverty, leisure, the universe, our spiritual happiness, or our position in the world.

Thus, I have not been primarily concerned with what might normally be called "social problems," because I think that, before these can be discussed, we must be clear on the nature of Christianity and politics. What I must call the principal enthusiasms of our era, revolutionary socialism and ecology, cannot be thought of in isolation from their own goals and views of man. For all their good intentions and visions, we must know why they have problems with their ends, their views of men and reality. Unless we realize such directions in them, our practical politics can never be clear and settled. Theories, as John XXIII implied, can be better than they sound when put in practice through history. They can also be, by the same token, worse. But in any case, it is well to know what they are and how they are related to Christian thought and practice. This is what I have tried to do in these chapters, to see the sanity and fruitfulness of Christianity both by following where its denial leads and where its affirmation supports the kind of being we have been given.

To conclude, I want to put the relation of politics and Christianity in historic perspective, but only briefly. I wish to do this in order to reaffirm, once again, that the primacy of God, the doctrine that the modern era especially has not been able to come to terms with, is precisely the thing that can keep politics to be politics, and not a pseudo-religion, the fate of most of the ideologies that we have had to deal with in recent years. It is a temptation of Christians, I realize, to see their mission in domesticating the errors of any age. There is nothing wrong with this. Indeed, it is quite the right thing to do. But a more rigorous intellectual approach would have to attempt something further, something more difficult. And that would be to see just wherein ideological movements lead, how they are related to answers and doctrines already found in the Christian tradition. I have been concerned with Catholic social theories and tendencies, though I quite agree with Dale Vree that today orthodoxy and heresy are usually not co-terminous with the old Catholic-Protestant division.[2] What I have believed and assumed is that there is a case to be made for the central Christián positions, a case that more than anything illumines the intellectual structure of the contemporary world. Politics and Christianity are what keep before us both the validity of the projects we do have in this world and the reason why the world is not enough.

Happiness as an ethical-political project has had Greek origins. Political speculation practically began by asking what human happiness was. Needless to say, the question is still being asked. Aristotle had made happiness the final cause of why men act. His analysis provided really two kinds of happiness, a practical or political one and a contemplative one. The two were related but not the same. Indeed, for Aristotle, the higher form of happiness was a result of first establishing an economic and political order with abundance and leisure. Happiness was the activity of the highest faculties on the highest objects in a full life, as Aristotle put it in *The Ethics*. Both the political common good and the order of the universe fulfilled this definition, except that the latter obviously had limitations because of man's mortality.

Death, then, seemed to cut off the individual, and the group was not precisely a proper subject of "happiness," even though it could last longer than the individual life. This tension was to be a consistent problem throughout political history. How do we reconcile the kind of imperfect happiness that is attainable in some degree in this life with the kind of perfect happiness that man seeks? Aristotle had insisted on our legitimate political happiness by saying that a man who lived by himself was either a beast or a god; hence the recurrence of both of these elements throughout history—a politics that tended to beastiality, politics that tended to angelism. But Aristotle warned that if we confuse political and contemplative happiness, we could very easily end up by destroying the kind of finite political happiness achievable by man on Earth.

Plato, of course, had already set the stage for these reflections in the Last Book of *The Republic*. Plato wanted to know if the good man could live in any existing state. He concluded that he could only live in the kind of ideal state he designed, which had no real corresponding ground in any existing state, each of which bore the marks of human pride and avarice. But even at the end of *The Republic*, Plato posed the necessity of immortality of the soul as a *political* necessity, because justice will never be fully rewarded in this life, nor injustice sufficiently punished. This unresolvable aspect of worldly justice cannot last intellectually, so that immortality is concluded as a necessary consequence of the conditions of life in this world in imperfect societies, the only kind there are.

Those philosophies that followed Plato and Aristotle sought to achieve the perfection of man by withdrawing him from society and by rejecting political life. The sole function of politics was to let man live in peace. Stoicism in particular was the direct antithesis of Plato and Aristotle because it elevated *autarkia,* self-sufficiency, to the highest virtue of the individual *(autarkia* was a property of the *polis* to the Greeks), while seeking law and reason apart from any particular society. This set politics at odds with the kind of home men were used to living in.

Christianity transformed this notion of universal law and brotherhood to refer to the concrete, existing neighbor, not some generalized abstraction. The meaning of Christianity in politics, then, came to be that it enabled politics to disassociate itself from man's quest for ultimate happiness, while at the same time giving him something valid to do during his life. Politics was only politics. Salvation was to be found elsewhere. This meant not only that politics was not holiness but that its end was not salvation, either, since salvation is a gift that transcends all worldly orders. Thus, the world could have a purpose, and man within it, neither of which need be identified with the ultimate kind of goal for which man was created. The Christian idea of Incarnation and Resurrection served to limit and define the kind of goals pure politics could have and expect. In this sense, Christianity freed politics to be politics and did not let it be some other religion which attempted to explain or create all reality and happiness by political methods.

Needless to say, mankind has not been always happy with the solution, never less so than today, as I have tried to suggest. Augustine, of course, became the spokesman for the view that politics could not attain God. Politics were given as remedies for sin. Men in all societies would be proud, spiteful, greedy, and grasping. There was no institutional cure to this situation. Nothing could eradicate its reality from men. If men were virtuous and careful, they might some-what limit the scope of evil, but the hope to elim-inate it was illusory and even dangerous. By giving false hopes, politics risks making things considerably worse, since the search for the meaning of all things is the deepest in man. The political realism of Augustine, then, came to the maddening limit to all theories that proposed a political way to salvation.

In confronting this abidingness of sinful man —something Thucydides, Plato, Aristotle, the Old Testament, and Paul took for granted—the newer theories are ever forced to propose a change in the human nature of man as such. In this way, they recognize indirectly the deep-rooted nature of the problem. This change is propounded either as an institutional process, an environmental, or even genetic one, which hopes to get at the roots of what is causing the original difficulty.

Eric Voegelin wrote, in this connection:

> Revolution becomes permanent when the revolutionary posits a goal which *ex definitione* cannot be reached because it requires the transformation of human nature. The unchangeable nature of man constantly places obstacles in the path to the paradisiacal goal....

> For in liberalism (also) there is the irrational element of an eschatological final state, of a society which will produce through its rational methods, without violent disturbances, a condition of lasting peace.... The liberal attack was directed against dogmatism and the authority of religion. If only these influences on thinking and public life would be removed, then the free human being would order society rationally with his autonomous reason. However, if in practice Christianity is successfully driven out of men, they become not rational liberals but ideologues.[3]

Thus, if there is an abiding nature of man, such as that found in the Christian tradition, then all men will expect a much more finite and confined goal to politics which will restore it to tasks that are accomplishable in this world. The removal of all evil, greed, suffering, and disorder is not one such goal. The gradual, careful, imperfect improvement of our condition, through a realistic awareness of sin and envy and greed together with an awareness of the great capacities of reason and technique and experience, is a generally feasible goal. And yet, this is to be always understood in the context of the human will, of the idea that things can get worse.

Undoubtedly, very little in the contemporary scene aids us to distinguish politics and religion. In one sense, this is a good sign, a proof that men will deal with ultimate things, no matter how much they are forbidden or neglected as such. Such problems when suppressed merely appear in other forms. On the other hand, Christianity had argued that we should separate the things of God and those of Caesar. God created the universe to make "more" reality, not less, if we can speak that way. We praise by knowing where things belong. This is a remarkable age in that everything has tended to become politicized. Whether we think the cause of our evils is too many people, too much consumption or technology or government (or all three), the fact remains that no matter how we propose to confront such problems, there is a level of religion that must be retained, no matter how good or bad our politics or economics may be. When Augustine said that "There is no peace in this life," he was speaking for the life in the best *and* worst regimes, both. He was not saying, moreover, that there ought to be peace in this life at any cost, even though he finally defined politics as a kind of temporary peace. He was saying that human persons transcend every political regime, that their main task and dignity in this world were precisely that they were not limited to or exhausted by an earthly task or time.

Thus, our hearts are restless because there is no substitute for "Thee," as Augustine put it. The history of political and social thought is, even today, the desperate search for some substitute that need not admit this fact. And it is because this is so, Christianity, if it remain true to its calling, must not tell men that their main task is an earthly one. But neither must Christianity so explain its principal duty to religion, to God, in such a way that it obscures the fact that that man has a "happiness" in this world, even though it not be the ultimate one. We must know that men can and should improve things, beginning with themselves, still remembering that prosperity is not necessarily a sign of goodness or salvation, at least by itself. But men must not be told that this improvement of the world is what the faith is primarily about. The world in a basic sense is rather unimportant. Voegelin was exactly right. Ideology is what finally replaces devotion when we forget or reject our religious priorities.

Yet, finally, politics is a noble vocation, one "natural" to man, as Aristotle said, provided it is not confused with the worship of God, as it often was in our history. We are social beings, social animals, even in our salvation. But unless we are more than this, even in the best earthly system, then as religious people, we have nothing in particular to tell men about the kind of happiness we persist in searching for. Indeed, in Christianity, happiness, in a sense, is rather something that searches for us.

Some years ago, in the lovely St. Ignatius Church in San Francisco, I heard a Solemn High Mass, full orchestra, the Stanford University Choir, the Archbishop, full, ancient ritual, the Beethoven Mass in C. Major, a glorious occasion. The Entrance Antiphon was from *Revelation:* "Dignus est Agnus, qui occisus est, accipere virtutem et divinitatem et sapientiam et fortitudinem et honorem. Ipsi gloria et imperium in saecula saeculorum" (5:12; 1:6). "How worthy is the Lamb who was slaughtered, to receive Glory and Power and Divinity and Wisdom and Strength and Honor. To Him be glory and rule for ever and ever." Such words, along with the haunting Mozart *Ave Verum Corpus,* are needed at times to make us realize that there is something beyond it all, to which we are being called. Without this reality and without our sense of it, we are merely floundering in despair, however great our worldly ambitions and accomplishments.

In the end, then, there is no worldly cause, no matter how noble it might be, that can hide this fact from us for long. And yet, I suspect, we are very confused on this score precisely by our understanding of the world. We are quite close in our politics to a very old type of idolatry.

This is why we need to know, with Augustine, that "There is no peace in this life.... In the world to come hath been promised that which in this world we are seeking." We seek in this world and we do not find. It is for this that Christianity was finally given to us. This is why our politics are finally limited.

Footnotes:

[1] Dorothy Sayers, *The Whimsical Christian,* New York, Macmillan, 1978. This may well be one of the greatest statements about the importance of the Christian creeds, about Christian intelligence, written in this century.

[2] Dale Vree, *On Synthesizing Marxism and Christianity,* New York, Wiley, 1976, Conclusion.

[3] Eric Voegelin, "Liberalism and Its History," *The Review of Politics,* October, 1974, pp. 519, 517.

BIBLIOGRAPHY

Bibliographies are intended to give a complete and helpful summary of the materials used in the research of a book's subject matter. Here, I will not offer such a bibliography in addition to the footnotes in the text itself. Rather, I believe that an intelligent Christian way of looking at the world is so hard to come by for the average student or interested reader that much groundwork of goodwill and study needs to be undertaken before any reasonable appreciation of the Christian view of politics can be understood.

Consequently, here, I am going to present a few books and essays which either individually or cumulatively would give some beginning to a specifically Catholic and Christian view of the world, which stands behind any Christian notion of politics. I have tried to cite only manageable books. I am going to presume a reader who knows little or nothing of a Christian mentality, even though these books are often of the profoundest nature. I will assume that everyone knows most of the arguments against Christianity, most of the accusations against it. So I will presume to present something for any reasonably honest and curious person who would like to know what Christianity at its best says about itself.

I will list these in no rigid order, neither according to alphabet or size or difficulty. But there will be the personal order of my own preferences, perhaps of my own history, of how I should go about finding out first about Christianity and then about its view of politics. I will not begin by recommending some knowledge of the Old and New Testaments or the Fathers of the Church. Anyone who thinks he can understand something of Christianity without a serious attention to these basic documents that have formed our civilization can hardly be a sympathetic or serious student or reader in the first place. I have made no attempt to list the "latest" or most fashionable, but rather works that come closest to the Christian spirit and its intelligence.

1. J. M. Bochenski, *Philosophy—an Introduction,* New York, Harper Torchbooks, 1972. 112 pp.

2. E. F. Schumacher, *A Guide for the Perplexed,* New York, Harper Colophon, 1977. 147 pp.

3. Dorothy Sayers, *The Whimsical Christian,* New York, Macmillan, 1978. 275 pp.

4. G. K. Chesterton, *Orthodoxy,* Doubleday Image, 1957. 160 pp.

5. C. S. Lewis, *Mere Christianity,* New York, Macmillan, 1952. 190 pp.

6. E. L. Mascall, *The Christian Universe,* London, Darton, 1966. 174 pp.

7. Christopher Dawson, *Religion and the Rise of Western Culture,* Garden City, Doubleday Image, 1957. 252 pp.

8. Oscar Cullmann, *The State in the New Testament,* New York, Scribner's, 1956. 92 pp.

9. Herbert Butterfield, *Christianity and History,* London, Fontana, 1964. 189 pp.

10. Harry Blamires, *The Christian Mind*, Ann Arbor, Servant, 1978. 191 pp.

11. Gilbert Meilaender, *The Taste for the Other: The Social and Ethical Thought of C. S. Lewis*, Grand Rapids, Eerdmans, 1978. 245 pp.

The following works are more specialized and academic, if you will, but still serve as basic background to the themes of Christianity and politics.

1. Jacques Maritain, *Man and the State*, Chicago, University of Chicago Press, 1951.

2. Yves Simon, *The Philosophy of Democratic Government*, Chicago, University of Chicago Press, 1977.

3. Herbert Deane, *The Political and Social Ideas of St. Augustine*, New York, Columbia, 1963.

4. A. P. d'Entreves, *The Natural Law*, New York, Harper Torchbooks, 1951.

5. Josef Pieper, *Scholasticism*, New York, McGraw-Hill, 1968.

6. Etienne Gilson, *Reason and Revelation in the Middle Ages*, New York, Scribner's, 1966.

7. John Henry Newman, *The Idea of a University*, Garden City, Doubleday Image, 1959.

8. Andrew N. Woznicki, *A Christian Humanism: Karol Wojtyla's Existential Personalism*, New Britain, Ct., Mariel, 1980.

9. John Senior, *The Death of Christian Culture*, New Rochelle, Arlington House, 1978.

10. Christopher Dawson, *The Dynamics of World History*, Ed. J. J. Mulloy, La Salle, Ill., Sherwood Sudgen, 1978.

11. Stanislaus Jaki, *The Road of Science and the Ways to God*, Chicago, University of Chicago Press, 1978.

The following is a brief list of Papal Documents worth noting:

1. John XXIII, *Pacem in Terris*, Various Editions.

2. Vatican II, *The Church in the Modern World*, in Documents of Vatican II, New York, Angelus, 1966, pp. 199-308. Also Document on Religious Liberty, same volume, pp. 675-96.

3. Paul VI, *On the 80th Anniversary of Rerum Novarum (Octagesima Adveniens)*, Washington, United States Catholic Conference, 1971.

4. John Paul II, *Redemptor Hominis*, 1979; *Dives in Misericordia*, 1980, Boston, St. Paul Editions.

L'Osservatore Romano publishes an English edition of papal addresses and documents. *The Pope Speaks* does a more selected presentation.

Ronald Lawler's *The Teaching of Christ: A Catholic Catechism for Adults,* Huntington, Indiana, Our Sunday Visitor Press, 1976, is a series of Documents and an orderly presentation of specifically Catholic doctrinal and ritual traditions that is worth knowing about.

The following are some academic works in the area of Christianity and Politics that are worth attention:

1. Frederick D. Wilhelmsen, *Christianity and Political Philosophy,* Athens, University of Georgia Press, 1978.

2. John Courtney Murray, *We Hold These Truths,* Garden City, Doubleday Image, 1965.

3. E. F. Schumacher, *Small Is Beautiful,* New York, Perennial, 1973.

4. E. E. Y. Hales, *The Catholic Church in the Modern World,* Garden City, Doubleday Image, 1960.

5. V. A. Demant, *Theology of Society,* London, Faber and Faber, 1947.

6. Josef Pieper, *The Silence of St. Thomas,* Chicago, Gateway, 1957.

7. *Herbert Butterfield, Writings on Christianity and History,* Ed. C. T. McIntire, New York, Oxford, 1979.

8. *The Social and Political Philosophy of Jacques Maritain,* Ed. J. Evans, Notre Dame, University of Notre Dame Press, 1976.

9. Heinrich Rommen, *The State in Catholic Thought,* St. Louis, B. Herder, 1945. (Recently reissued by The Greenwood Press, Westport, Connecticut.)

10. Richard Bishirjian, *The Development of Political Theory,* Dallas, The Society for the Study of Traditional Culture, 1978.

11. John Finnis, *Natural Law and Natural Right,* Oxford, Clarendon, 1980.

12. Charles N. R. McCoy, *The Structure of Political Thought,* New York, McGraw-Hill, 1963.

13. Ronald Knox, *Enthusiasm,* Oxford, Oxford University Press, 1950.

Finally, I should like to list several of my own books in this general area:

1. *Redeeming the Time*, New York, Sheed and Ward, 1968.

2. *Human Dignity and Human Numbers*, Staten Island, Alba House, 1971.

3. *Far Too Easily Pleased: A Theology of Play, Contemplation, and Festivity*, Los Angeles, Benziger-Macmillan, 1976.

4. *The Praise of 'Sons of Bitches': On the Worship of God by Fallen Men*, Slough, England, St. Paul Publications, 1978.

Acknowledgments

The following chapters are based on previously published essays.

Chapter I. *Worldview*, New York, V. 19, #4, 1976, pp. 26-30.

Chapter II. *The Modern Age*, V. 19, N. 2, Spring, 1975, pp. 157-66.

Chapter III. *World Justice*, Louvain, V. VI, #4, June, 1965, pp. 462-75.

Chapter IV. *Social Survey*, Melbourne, V. 26, #7, July, 1977, pp. 165-72.

Chapter VII. Tentative, *Cultures et Développement*, Louvain.

Chapter VIII. Tentative, *Archiv für Rechts—und Sozialphilosophie*, Darmstadt.

Chapter IX. Forthcoming, *Clergy Review*, London.

Chapter X. *Faith and Reason*, Virginia, V. 3, #1, Spring, 1977, pp. 18-33.

Chapter XI. *Spiritual Life*, Washington, V. 22, #2, Summer, 1976, pp. 106-11.

Conclusion: *Homiletic and Pastoral Review*, New York, V. LXXV, #10, July, 1975, pp. 19-27.

ABOUT THE AUTHOR

Born in Pocahontas, Iowa, January 20, 1928. Educated in Public Schools in Iowa, graduated in 1945 from Knoxville, Iowa High. Attended University of Santa Clara, US Army, 1946-47. Entered California Province, Society of Jesus, 1948. MA Philosophy from Gonzaga University, 1945. PhD in Political Theory from Georgetown University, 1960. MST from University of Santa Clara, 1964. Member of Faculty of Institute of Social Sciences, Gregorian University, Rome, from 1964-77. Member of Government Department, University of San Francisco (Fall Semester in San Francisco, Spring in Rome), from 1968-77. Member of Government Department, Georgetown University, from 1977.

Consultor, Pontifical Commission on Justice and Peace, from 1977. Member, Theological Commission of Archdiocese of Washington from 1977.

Publications: *Redeeming the Time*, New York, Sheed, 1968; *Welcome Number 4,000,000,000*, Canfield, Ohio, Alba Books, 1977; *Human Dignity and Human Numbers,* Staten Island, Alba House, 1971; *Play On: From Games to Celebrations*, Philadelphia, Fortress, 1971; *Far Too Easily Pleased: A Theology of Contemplation, Play, and Leisure,* New York, Benziger-Macmillan, 1976; *The Sixth Paul*, Canfield, Ohio, Alba Books, 1977; *The Praise of 'Sons of Bitches': On the Worship of God by Fallen Men,* Slough, England, St. Paul Publications, 1978.

Written over 100 essays on political, theological, and philosophical issues in such journals as *The Review of Politics*, *Social Survey* (Melbourne), *Studies* (Dublin), *The Thomist*, *Divus Thomas* (Piacenza), *Divinitas* (Rome), *The Commonweal*, *Thought*, *Modern Age*, *Faith and Reason*, *The Way* (London), *The New Oxford Review*, *The Homiletic and Pastoral Review*, *University Bookman*, *Worldview*.

Contributes a bi-monthly column to *The Monitor* San Francisco, *The National Catholic Register*.

INDEX OF NAMES

Abell, A. I., 292

Acts of the Apostles, 42, 173

Adcock, F. E., 60

Adler, Mortimer, 42, 173

á Kempis, Thomas, 302, 303, 305, 311

Anderson, Charles, 30

Angell, Charles, 30

Arendt, Hannah, 10, 14, 51, 63, 146, 148, 210, 237, 246

Aristotle, 38, 42, 48, 49, 50, 52, 55, 59, 62, 104, 106, 119, 122, 139, 171, 217, 218, 228, 232, 233, 236, 248, 251, 293, 296, 318, 319, 320, 321

Arostegui, Luis, 168, 176

Augustine, 26, 60, 66, 89, 105, 134, 137, 202, 217, 278, 315, 323, 324

Ayatollah Khomeini, 17

Bagehot, Walter, 196

Balducci, Ernesto, 160

Banfield, Edward, 210

Bauer, P. T., 185, 193, 209, 293

Bay, Christian, 63, 241

Becker, Carl, 306, 313

Beckerman, Wilfred, 193

Beckman, W. 210

Beer, Samuel, 197

Belloc, Hilaire, 34, 41, 271

Berger, Peter, 278, 293

Berlin, Isaiah, 63

Bigelow, Robert, 48

Bishirjian, Richard, 330

Blackstone, William, 242

Blamires, Harry, 147, 212, 328

Bochenski, J. M., 60, 93, 147, 241, 242, 328

Bok, Sissela, 230, 240

Brecht, Arnold, 214, 218, 222, 240, 241

Brown, Robert McAfee, 269, 292

Buckley, William F., 197

Bunzel, John, 278, 293

Burke, Edmund, 196, 237

Bury, J. B., 93

Butterfield, Herbert, 151, 175, 315, 328, 330

Caesar, 61

Calhoun, John C., 196

Cameron, J. M., 15, 311, 314

Canavan, Francis, 237, 242

Carey, George, 64, 241

Carter, Jimmy, 197

Cassirer, Ernst, 147, 227

Chamberlain, Nevelle, 238

Chesterton, G. K., 14, 268, 273, 276, 328

Christian Science Monitor, 17, 40

Christenson, Reo, 226, 227

Cicero, 59, 217, 229

Clarke, Arthur C., 130, 132, 148

Cobban, Alfred, 63

Cohen, Lloyd, 211

Colozzi, I., 175

Comblin, Joseph, 274, 292

Crombie, A. C., 147

Crowe, Michael, 240
Cullmann, Oscar, 73, 328

Dabney, Dick, 14
Daniel, Jean, 148
d'Asienzi, V., 175
Dawson, Christopher, 60, 63, 204, 211, 328, 329
Deane, Herbert, 92, 329
d'Entreves, Alexander Passerin, 216, 240, 329
deFabrègues, J., 176
DeLubac, Henri, 93
Demant, V. A., 64, 330
Denning, Lord, 211
Derrick, Christopher, 212
Descartes, René, 48, 126
Drucker, Peter, 148, 224, 241
DuBois, Rene, 292
Durand, A., 163, 176

East, John, 40, 263, 266
(The) *Economist* of London, 2, 5, 116, 183, 192, 209, 256, 265, 292, 314
Edelson, Professor, 141
Edson, L., 148
Einstein, Alfred, 135
Ellenstein, Jean, 285, 294
Ellis, John Tracy, 292
Ellul, Jacques, 15, 282
Epistle to the Romans, 56
Evodkimov, Paul, 149

Fairlie, Henry, 56
Ferkiss, Victor, 62
Ferris, Timothy, 144, 148
Feuerbach, Ludwig, 103
Feynman, Richard, 139
Fierro, Alfredo, 14, 40
Finn, James, 292

Finnis, John, 63, 207, 212, 214, 216, 330
Frei, Eduardo, 275, 293
Fuller, Buckminster, 140, 148

Galbraith, J. K., 282
Galilea, Segundo, 150, 163, 175, 176
Gandhi, M., 237, 238, 242
Ganshof, F. L., 60
Gaylin, Willard, 63
Gelo, Fernando, 175
Genesis, 72, 79
Gheddo, Piero, 41, 168, 176
Gibbons, Cardinal, 271
Gill, Eric, 271
Gilson, Etienne, 93, 118, 242, 249, 255, 265, 266
Ginfranceschi, Fausto, 295, 314
Girardi, Giulio, 176, 274
Gleason, Philip, 258, 261, 266, 292
Goerner, E. A., 292
Gould, James and V. Thursby, 62
Gramsci, Antonio, 160
Greaves, A. R. G., 63

Hale, Robert, 164, 165, 176
Hales, E. E. Y., 330
Hallowell, John 290, 291, 294
Hapsburg, Otto of, 305, 306, 313
Harrington, Michael, 204, 205, 212, 282
Hart, Jeffry, 119
Hatfield, Mark, 229
Hauerwas, Stanley, 289, 294
Hazard, Paul, 102, 116
Heckel, Roger, 112, 117, 210, 265, 293

Hegel, 103
Heywood, Bruce, 260, 266
Hick, John, 134, 135, 136, 137, 145, 148
Hitchcock, James, 33
Hitler, Adolf, 226, 227
Hobbes, Thomas, 48, 303
Hobson, J. A., 188
Hochhuth, Rolf, 272
Hodgson, P. E., 189, 190, 210
Holy Cross Quarterly, 29, 40
Huizinga, Jan, 156, 175
Hume, David, 228

Illich, Ivan, 77, 93

Jaki, Stanley, 63, 116, 147, 210, 245, 253, 264, 329
Jefferson, Thomas, 79
Jerrold, Douglas, 3, 14
Joachim of Flora, 22, 27
John XXIII, 98, 317, 329
John of the Cross, 163, 164
John Paul II (Karol Wojtyla), 17, 25, 40, 93, 117, 150, 191, 200, 207, 210, 212, 220, 253, 254, 259, 263, 265, 276, 307, 329
Johnson, Paul, 193, 210
Justin Martyr, 16, 38

Kahn, Herman, 147, 148, 178, 180, 202, 209, 210
Kirk, Russell, 15, 67, 83
Kirkpatrick, Jeane, 14, 209, 293
Kissinger, Henry, 44, 295
Kloppenberg, B., 163, 176
Kolakowski, Lazek, 177
Kossel, Clifford, 233, 242
Krauss, Melvyn, 210

Kristol, Irving, 40, 193, 194, 197, 201, 204, 210, 265
Küng, Hans, 11
Kusher, Harvey and Gerald de Miro, 214, 241

Laski, Herold, 39
Laslett, Peter and W. G. Runciman, 43, 62
Lawlor, Ronald, 330
Lebret, L., 274
Lederberg, Joshua, 148
Lecarrière, Jacques, 312
Lefever, Ernest, 40, 265
Lenin, V., 25
Leo XIII, 40, 162, 253, 289
Lescoe, Francis, 266
Lewis, C. S., 56, 63, 64, 132, 134, 148, 174, 177, 328
Lindsay, A. D., 227
Lippmann, Walter, 227
Locke, John, 48
Luther, Martin, 159
Lyonnet, Stanislaus, 123, 147

Machiavelli, Niccolo, 45, 54, 103
Macrae, Norman, 148, 193, 194, 209, 273, 286, 294
Madariaga, Salvador de, 57, 63
Madison, James, 49
Mao Tse-tung, 25, 29, 37, 96, 295, 299, 313
Marcus Aurelius, 42, 62
Maritain, Jacques, 15, 93, 117, 175, 191, 203, 210, 227, 242, 249, 264, 267, 273, 275, 287, 292, 329, 330
Marsilius of Padua, 30, 36
Marx, Karl, 32, 94, 104, 105, 106, 114, 116, 289

Mascall, Eric A., 65, 93, 117, 127, 147, 148, 212, 265, 328
Maximov, Vladimir, 277, 308
McCoy, Charles N. R., 60, 64, 147, 241, 264, 330
McDonald, Lee Cameron, 60, 64
McNamara, Robert, 19
Midgley, E. B. F., 148, 215, 216, 240, 241, 243, 248, 263, 264, 265
Mill, J. S., 237
Millar, Morehouse F. X., 292
Minogue, Kenneth, 186, 188, 205, 209
Mondin, Battista, 177
Moore, Barrington, 179
Morrell, John, 60
Mounier, Emmanuel, 271
Mount, Ferdinand, 64
Moynihan, Daniel Patrick, 197, 277, 293
Mozart, Wolfgang Amadeus, 325
Muggeridge, Malcolm, 246, 264
Mulder, Theodore, 283, 294
Murray, John Courtney, 218

Nadal, Jerome, 164, 176
New Testament, 59, 116, 164, 175, 200, 328
New York Times, 45, 150, 175, 193, 211
Newman, John Henry, 126, 147, 196, 329
Niebuhr, Reinhold, 92, 198
Niemeyer, Gerhart, 211
Nisbet, Robert, 14, 93, 120, 147, 308, 313, 314
Nixon, Richard, 47, 228
Norman, E. O., 40, 172, 177, 205, 206, 212, 265

North, Robert, 292
Novak, Michael, 210, 267, 292
Nozick, Robert, 223

Oakeshott, Michael, 196
Old Testament, 59, 321, 328
Orlinsky, Harry M., 60

Pangle, Thomas, 246
Pascal, Blaise, 136
Patriarch Pimen, 307
Paul VI, 329
Paul, Saint, 62, 110, 122, 123, 136
Paz, Octavio, 168, 176
Pieper, Josef, 93, 116, 215, 240, 242, 330
Pirenne, Henri, 60
Pius XI, 277
Pius XII, 124, 147
Plato, 37, 45, 48, 49, 50, 52, 59, 62, 154, 171, 218, 226, 228, 229, 230, 233, 236, 237, 249, 250, 319, 320, 321
Pocock, J. G. A., 63
Popper, Karl, 147, 208, 211, 212

Rahner, Karl, 148
Rawls, John, 194, 237, 280, 293
Revel, Jean-François, 184, 199
Rommen, Heinrich A., 25, 40, 223, 240, 241, 262, 266, 330
Rousseau, Jean Jacques, 28, 49, 103, 120, 146, 156, 183, 303

Sabine, George, 60, 64
Sagan, Carl, 138
Saint-Simon, Henri de, 167, 176

Sandoz, Ellis, 292
Sapientia Christiana, 265
Sayers, Dorothy, 15, 326, 328
Schaff, Adam, 115, 117
Schlesinger, Arthur, 182
Schlier, Heinrich, 177
Schnackenberg, Rudolf, 169, 176
Schumacher, E. F., 61, 99, 116, 209, 211, 293, 328, 330
Scully, Malcolm, 51, 63
Seabury, Paul, 265
Senior, John, 14, 174, 177, 211, 243, 264, 329
Serra, Luis de, 175
Servan-Schreiber, Jean, 275
Sibley, Mulford Q., 60, 64
Sigmund, Paul, 218, 220, 241
Simon, Yves, 93, 329
Smith, John T., 199
Sobran, Joseph, 117
Socrates, 38, 50, 48, 121
Solzhenitsyn, Alexander, 5, 10, 11, 41, 108, 171, 176, 273, 282, 292, 293, 307
Sophocles, 50
Sorge, B., 211
Steinfels, Peter, 197, 211
Steintrager, James, 242
Stephenson, Carl, 60
Strauss, Leo, 52, 63, 218, 219, 220, 221, 224, 227, 235, 240, 241, 242, 244, 245, 248, 249, 250, 251, 252, 253, 254, 257, 260, 263, 265, 266
Stromberg, Professor, 31, 32, 41
Suarez, Francisco, 286

(The) *Tablet,* 40, 209
Tacitus, 49, 58, 225, 241

Talmon, J. L., 14
Thomas Aquinas, 26, 48, 49, 60, 66, 135, 147, 217, 220, 233, 235, 252, 243, 259, 262, 288
Thorson, Thomas Landgon, 47, 62
Thucydides, 49, 59, 321
Tocqueville, Alexis de, 273
Trivière, Leon, 312
Turner, Denys, 29, 274, 293
Twain, Mark, 21, 40
Tyrmand, Leopold, 200, 211, 259, 266

Urbino, F., 176

Van Dyke, Vernon, 231, 232, 233, 242
Veatch, Henry, 235, 240, 242
Vesce, P., 175
Viereck, Peter, 197
Voegelin, Eric, 16, 246, 322, 324, 325
Von Hayek, F., 193
Von Nell-Bruening, Oswald, 289, 294
Vree, Dale, 1, 14, 40, 116, 326

Ward, Barbara, 188
Wattenberg, Ben, 148, 268
Weaver, Richard, 36, 41
Weber, Max, 46, 166, 175
White, Theodore, 204
Wilhelmsen, Frederick, 14, 16, 19, 93, 116, 219, 241, 242, 247, 255, 263, 264, 265, 330
Wills, Gary, 263, 266
Woznicki, Andrew, 212, 266, 329
Wright, John H., 148

Yoder, Edwin M., 43, 62, 246

Also Available:

Papal Documents, Messages and Talks

POPE LEO XIII

Condition of Working Classes *(Rerum novarum)* 25¢ — EP0240

POPE PIUS X

Social Reconstruction *(Quadragesimo anno)* 25¢ — EP1020

POPE PIUS XII

Function of the State in the Modern World 25¢ — EP0500

POPE JOHN XXIII

Christianity and Social Progress *(Mater et magistra)* 25¢ — EP0200

Peace on Earth *(Pacem in terris)* 25¢ — EP0950

POPE PAUL VI

Apostolic Letter to Cardinal Maurice Roy, President of the Council of the Laity and of the Pontifical Commission on Justice and Peace, on the occasion of the Eightieth Anniversary of the Encyclical *Rerum novarum* ("The Coming Eightieth") *(Octogesima adveniens)* 25¢ — EP0230

The Development of Peoples *(Populorum progressio)* 25¢ — EP0410

Appeal for Peace—Address given to the United Nations General Assembly in New York, October 4, 1965. 10¢ — PM0090

POPE JOHN PAUL II

Address to the General Assembly of the United Nations, October 2, 1979. 30¢ — EP0005

Other Items of Interest

Morality Today—The Bible in My Life
Daughters of St. Paul

A unique way to study the Ten Commandments!

In simple and clear language, but with a very personal approach, each commandment is explained in all its aspects, negative and positive. We are invited to ponder...adore...and speak to God so that through instruction, reflection and prayer we may understand and love His holy Law.

All will find this book both informative and inspirational. cloth $3.00; paper $1.95 — SC0088

The Social Message of Jesus
Igino Giordani

Rich with historical detail, this compact volume presents a systematic study of Jesus' social teachings, which have the power to transform our world.
cloth $4.50; paper $3.50 — RA0170

Design for a Just Society

A brief, clear treatment of Catholic Social teaching, including:

- —the reasons why the Church speaks out on social issues;
- —human solidarity and brotherhood;
- —the vital importance of the family;
- —the true role of the political community;
- —the means of attaining and maintaining healthy and progressive economic life;
- —guidelines for world development and peace.

Quotations from papal documents, Vatican II and Sacred Scripture give this volume a richness that may be increased still more by following up the abundant suggestions given for further reading. The discussion questions and project suggestions can lead to fruitful life applications. Text $5.00 (Discussion manual and teacher's manual also available.)

The Redeemer of Man
Pope John Paul II

The Encyclical Letter, *Redemptor hominis,* March 4, 1979, the first of His Holiness' pontificate.
50¢ — EP0978

Daughters of St. Paul

IN MASSACHUSETTS
 50 St. Paul's Ave. Jamaica Plain, Boston, MA 02130;
  617-522-8911; 617-522-0875;
 172 Tremont Street, Boston, MA 02111; **617-426-5464;**
  617-426-4230
IN NEW YORK
 78 Fort Place, Staten Island, NY 10301; **212-447-5071**
 59 East 43rd Street, New York, NY 10017; **212-986-7580**
 7 State Street, New York, NY 10004; **212-447-5071**
 625 East 187th Street, Bronx, NY 10458; **212-584-0440**
 525 Main Street, Buffalo, NY 14203; **716-847-6044**
IN NEW JERSEY
 Hudson Mall — Route 440 and Communipaw Ave.,
  Jersey City, NJ 07304; **201-433-7740**
IN CONNECTICUT
 202 Fairfield Ave., Bridgeport, CT 06604; **203-335-9913**
IN OHIO
 2105 Ontario St. (at Prospect Ave.), Cleveland, OH 44115; **216-621-9427**
 25 E. Eighth Street, Cincinnati, OH 45202; **513-721-4838**
IN PENNSYLVANIA
 1719 Chestnut Street, Philadelphia, PA 19103; **215-568-2638**
IN FLORIDA
 2700 Biscayne Blvd., Miami, FL 33137; **305-573-1618**
IN LOUISIANA
 4403 Veterans Memorial Blvd., Metairie, LA 70002; **504-887-7631;**
  504-887-0113
 1800 South Acadian Thruway, P.O. Box 2028, Baton Rouge, LA 70821
  504-343-4057; 504-343-3814
IN MISSOURI
 1001 Pine Street (at North 10th), St. Louis, MO 63101; **314-621-0346;**
  314-231-1034
IN ILLINOIS
 172 North Michigan Ave., Chicago, IL 60601; **312-346-4228;**
  312-346-3240
IN TEXAS
 114 Main Plaza, San Antonio, TX 78205; **512-224-8101**
IN CALIFORNIA
 1570 Fifth Avenue, San Diego, CA 92101; **714-232-1442**
 46 Geary Street, San Francisco, CA 94108; **415-781-5180**
IN HAWAII
 1143 Bishop Street, Honolulu, HI 96813; **808-521-2731**
IN ALASKA
 750 West 5th Avenue, Anchorage AK 99501; **907-272-8183**
IN CANADA
 3022 Dufferin Street, Toronto 395, Ontario, Canada
IN ENGLAND
 128, Notting Hill Gate, London W11 3QG, England
 133 Corporation Street, Birmingham B4 6PH, England
 5A-7 Royal Exchange Square, Glasgow G1 3AH, England
 82 Bold Street, Liverpool L1 4HR, England
IN AUSTRALIA
 58 Abbotsford Rd., Homebush, N.S.W., Sydney 2140, Australia